I0902367

VOICES OF AMERICA

WINTHROP UNIVERSITY

MEMORIES AND TRADITIONS

1886–1945

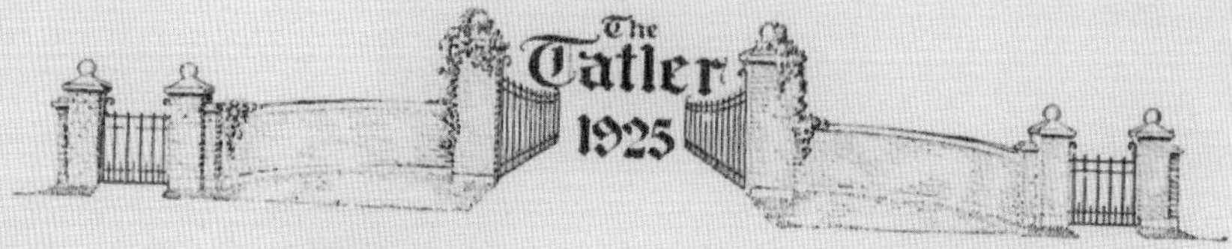

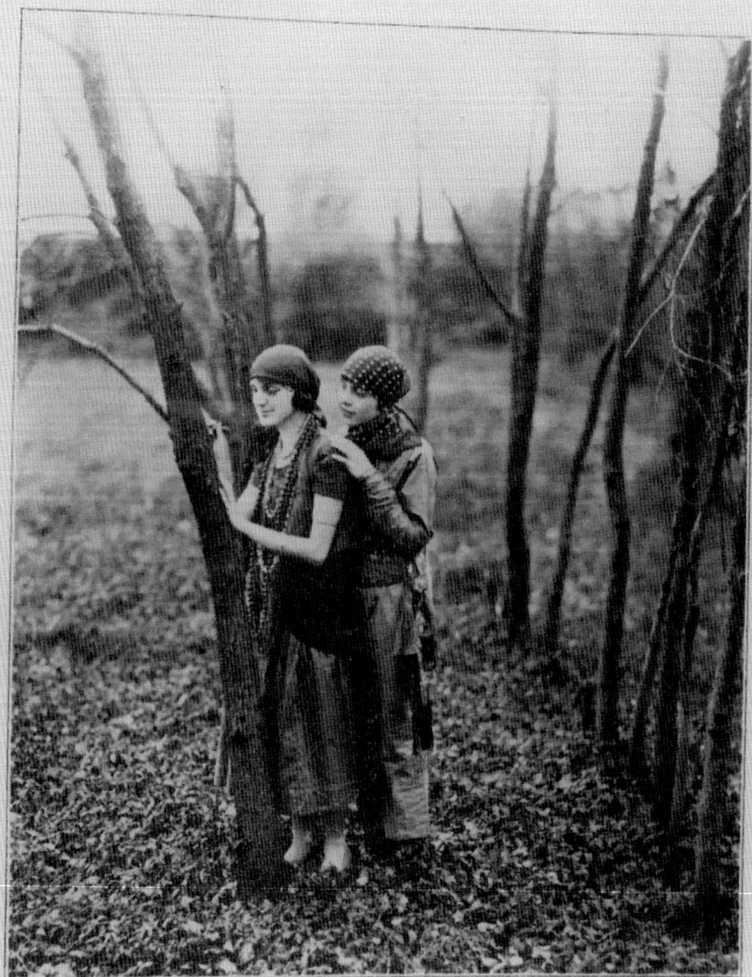

THE GYPSY TRAIL

"The heart of a man to the heart of a maid,
As it was in the days of old."

"The Gypsie Trail," from the 1925 Tatler

VOICES OF AMERICA

WINTHROP UNIVERSITY

MEMORIES AND TRADITIONS

1886–1945

Compiled by
Ron and Magdalena Chepesiuk

ARCADIA
PUBLISHING

ISBN 978-0-7385-0623-4

Published by Arcadia Publishing
Charleston SC, Chicago IL, Portsmouth NH, San Francisco CA

Printed in the United States of America

Library of Congress Catalog Card Number: 00-106089

For all general information contact Arcadia Publishing at:
Telephone 843-853-2070
Fax 843-853-0044
E-Mail sales@arcadiapublishing.com
For customer service and orders:
Toll-Free 1-888-313-2665

Visit us on the Internet at www.arcadiapublishing.com

For Gina Price White and Ann Evans, Winthrop archival assistantswho have played an important role in the growth and successof the department the past 28 years.

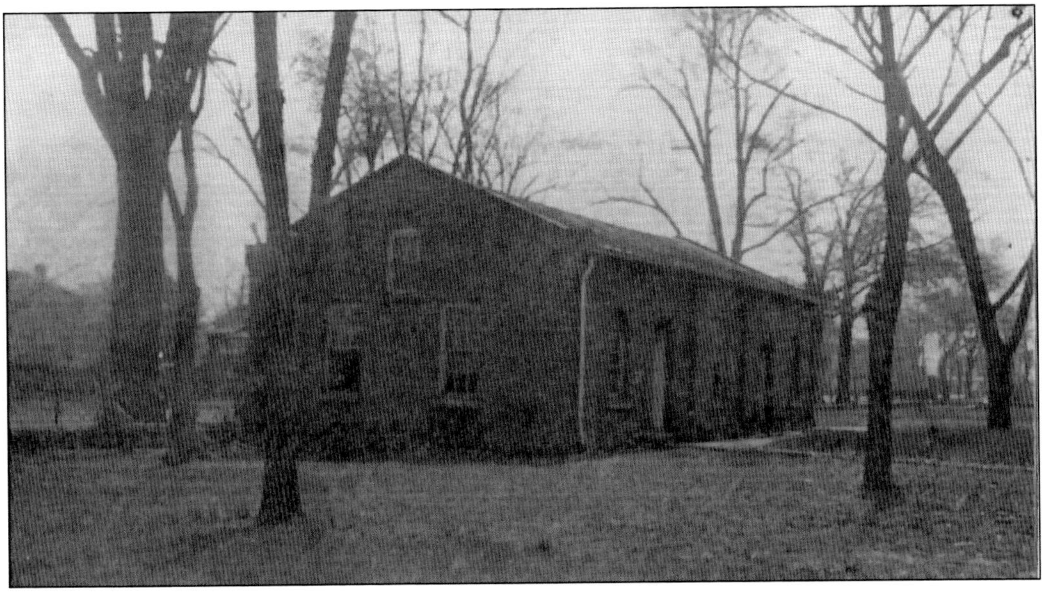

THE LITTLE CHAPEL, THE BIRTHPLACE OF WINTHROP

CONTENTS

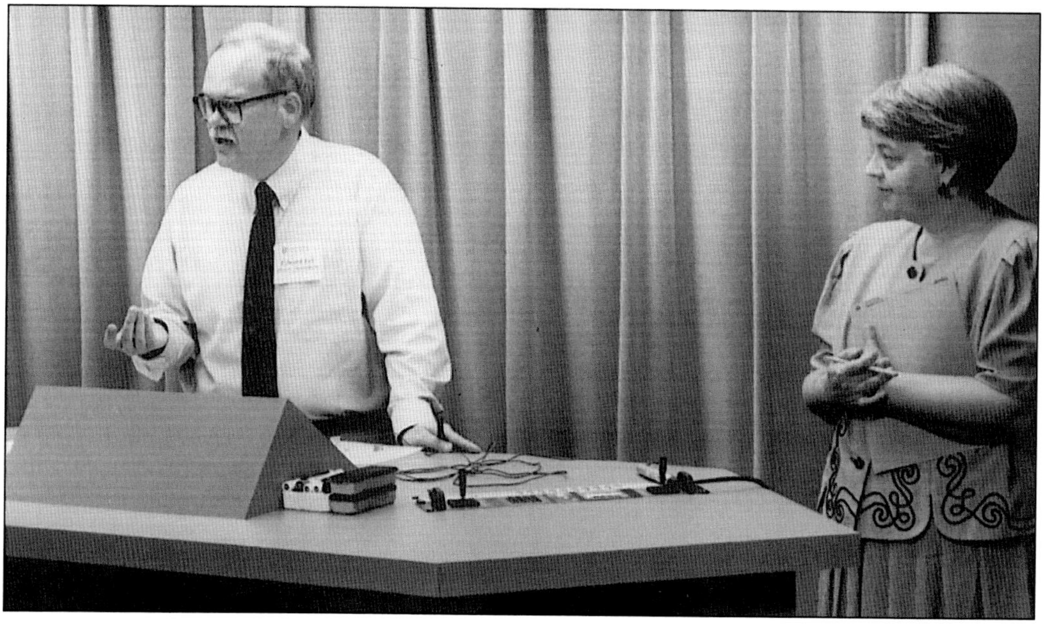

DR. J. EDWARD LEE (LEFT), ASSOCIATE PROFESSOR OF HISTORY, AND DR. BETSY BROWN, DEAN OF ARTS AND SCIENCES

ACKNOWLEDGMENTS

This is the fourth in a continuing series of books based on the valuable resources of the Winthrop University Archives. The series' last volume was a book of photos celebrating 112 years of illustrious Winthrop history. This book provides the insights of selected university administrators, faculty, alumni, and students into the great Winthrop tradition.

The authors would like to thank the people who made this volume possible. Dr. J. Edward Lee, Winthrop professor and historian, read the manuscript and provided valuable editorial suggestions. Dr. Lee's continued support of the Winthrop Archives during his tenure at Winthrop has been an important factor in its continued success and growth. Dr. Herring, dean of the Winthrop Library, provided support and encouragement throughout the project, which is greatly appreciated.

For several years, Gina Price White, assistant Winthrop archivist, has done excellent work and shares in the department's success. The late Dr. Arnold M. Shankman played a vital role in the Winthrop Archives' early growth, and we miss his support and friendship. We would also like to thank the many donors, many of whom have been Winthrop alumni, who have given material to the archives in an effort to preserve the university's memories and traditions. It is this kind of support that will confidently carry our beloved institution into the 21st century.

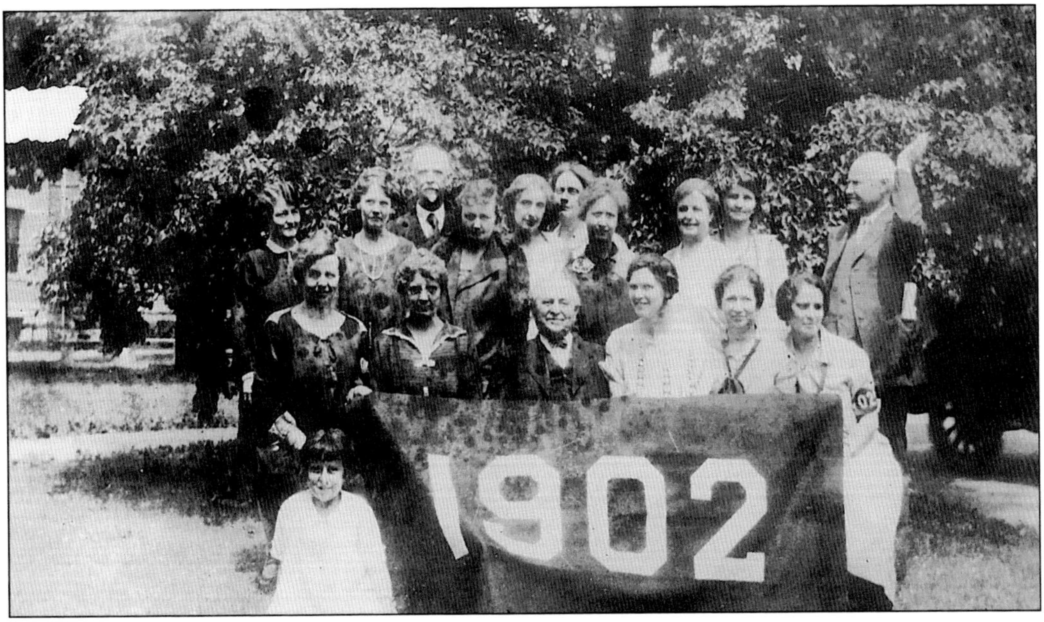

D.B. Johnson and faculty in 1902

Foreword

From the beginning there has been about Winthrop a missionary zeal. The college moved from Columbia to Rock Hill in 1895 because Governor Benjamin Ryan Tillman and President David Bancroft Johnson shared a commitment to offer rural South Carolinian women an opportunity to train as teachers and home economist. And no one could stand in the way of the mission.

In my own family, my grandmother, Victoria Sanders, left her York County family farm in 1896 to sharpen the intellectual tools necessary to educate the children of Guthriesville. A photograph of her as a newly minted teacher sitting in front of a modest one-room schoolhouse with students of all ages occupies a place of honor in my office. She was a crusader, on a mission, and this mission was replicated hundreds of times across the state over the years.

My mother, Ola Bankhead, continued the tradition, arriving at Winthrop just in time for the Great Depression to crash down upon South Carolina. Still, she clung to the educational opportunity offered by Winthrop, mastering the challenges confronting our state's citizens in the early 1930s. She would teach, and served for decades thereafter.

Winthrop University, throughout its history, has prepared women like Victoria Sanders and Ola Bankhead. And men like myself (Class of 1983) have benefited from the magic of Winthrop's classrooms. For over a century, the composition of the student body, the curriculum, and the campus has evolved but the mission remains unchanged: prepare in the best way possible the next generation. That is Winthrop's legacy.

—J. Edward Lee, Ph.D

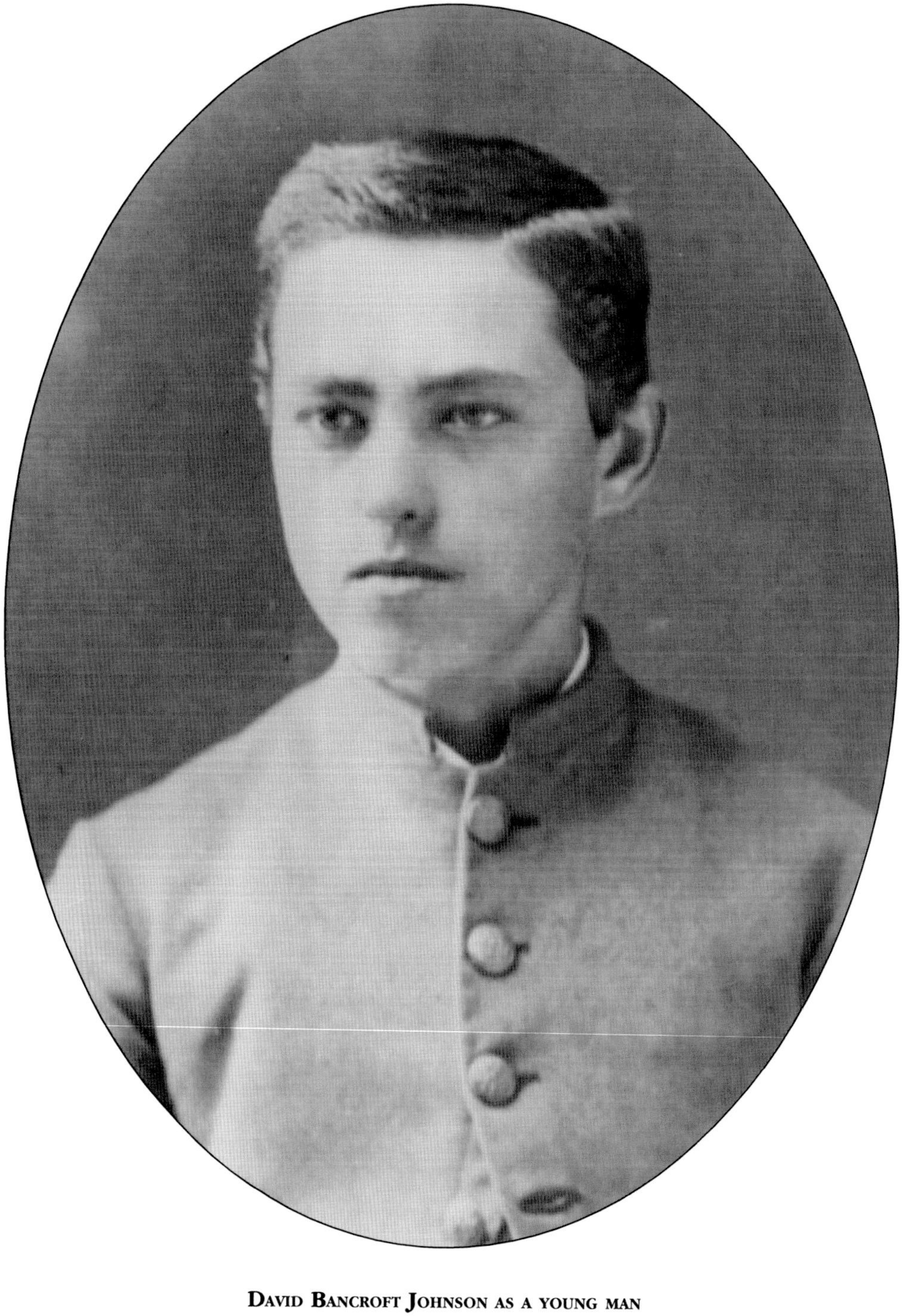

DAVID BANCROFT JOHNSON AS A YOUNG MAN

INTRODUCTION

Today, Winthrop University is a firmly established institution of more than 5,000 students on a 400-acre campus in the bustling city of Rock Hill. It has not always been this way, however. At its founding, Winthrop was a modest institution, with a small grant as its only source of funding. Its student body numbered just 21, and the campus consisted of a borrowed one-room building located in Columbia, not Rock Hill.

Winthrop's start, its struggle to establish roots, and its steady growth into the magnificent institution it is today constitute one of the truly remarkable success stories in South Carolina and, indeed, American education.

The prime mover in Winthrop University's establishment was a young educator named David Bancroft Johnson. Born in La Grange, TN, in 1856 and educated at the University of Tennessee, Johnson became Columbia's first superintendent of schools in 1883. Although hired as the schools' chief administrator, Johnson often had to go into the classroom to teach classes himself. One warm day in May 1884, he came home from lunch after a frustrating morning at work. He is reported to have said to his mother, "I wonder if there are young women in this city who would like to be trained as public schoolteachers. I have had three grades without teachers today. I taught one myself, but the others I had to dismiss for a lack of a teacher."

Women, Johnson decided, would provide the professionally trained teachers for an efficient public school system. He had no difficulty convincing the Columbia city school system to accept his recommendation that a training school for teachers be established in connection with the city's high school. Johnson became chairman of a committee responsible for requesting a grant from the Peabody Fund, a Northern-based philanthropic organization committed to putting Southern education back on its feet after the Civil War's devastation. He journeyed to Boston and met with the venerable Robert C. Winthrop, the board chairman.

Winthrop liked Johnson's idea; in fact, he was so impressed that he wrote a personal note a few days after Johnson's return to Columbia in which he said, "I'm entirely ready to accept your proposal." Soon after, the Peabody Board granted $1,500 to start what was to be Winthrop College.

Tradition has it that Winthrop gave Johnson $50 out of his own pocket. In gratitude, the fledgling institution was named in Winthrop's honor. Johnson now had money, but he still needed faculty. He searched Columbia for the right kind of building. Finally, he learned of the closing of the Columbia Theological Seminary because of a controversy over the teaching of Darwin's theory of evolution. Seminary officials agreed to allow Johnson to use the building for one year. The seminary's little chapel—a former stable designed by famed architect Robert Mills and the site of young Woodrow Wilson's first profession of his Christian faith—housed the school's first classes. Classes began on November 15, 1886.

The first year, 27 students applied, but Johnson, believing the number too large for the school to handle adequately, denied admission to 6. The one-year course of study utilized practice teaching and gave the students the opportunity to observe the operation and management of the Columbia city schools.

Some important changes occurred during that first year. In December the school hired more teachers: Miss Annie Bonham, who served as advisor of practice teaching, and Mrs. T.C. Robertson, who came in twice a week for an hour to teach drawing. To complete a practice room, including desks, maps, and charts, the school spent $125.

When the Winthrop Training School held its first commencement exercises on June 16, 1887, in the Columbia Opera House, only 14 of the 21 students who started the year graduated. Twelve graduates were Columbia natives, while one came from Summerville and another from Meador in Union County.

By the end of its second year of operation, the school had good reason to be optimistic about its future. When the Peabody Board met in 1887 to review the work of the training school, it indicated its pleasure with the school's programs by increasing its yearly appropriation by $500 to $2,000. In a letter to Johnson, the board commended him on the school's work, stating that "no institution of its kind is doing more thorough work or filling a greater want in the community. . . . Its example is conspicuous and far reaching."

The state was also beginning to take an interest in the school's welfare. In 1887 it granted a charter and began to provide financial assistance for the first time in the form of $150 per annum scholarships to one student from each county in the state. "Thus was the Winthrop Training School conceived and born, in old humanity, but with a rich fund of faith and devoted faith," wrote Dr. Edward Southey Joynes in 1887. No better words could have described Winthrop University during its Columbia years.

By 1890, Winthrop had outgrown its facilities in Columbia, forcing the college's board of trustees to consider finding a new home for the school. In July of that year, Dr. Joynes made a speech in Florence in which he advocated that the Winthrop Training School be offered to the state for support. Gov. Benjamin Ryan Tillman was enthusiastic about the idea, and at Joynes's suggestion, he appointed a committee to investigate costs and locations. In November 1891, the committee "endorsed the union of industrial and normal training and recommended that an act be passed providing for the foundation of a State Industrial and Normal College for Women."

On December 23, 1891, the state ratified the act establishing the South Carolina Industrial and Winthrop Normal College. On the same day, the legislature elected a board of trustees for the college and stipulated that the governor serve as the board's chairman. The legislature also authorized the use of 100 convicts to work as laborers for the construction of the college's buildings. Interestingly, one stock still remains in the basement of Tillman Hall, Winthrop's main administration building.

One of the first acts of the newly elected board of trustees was to open bids to South

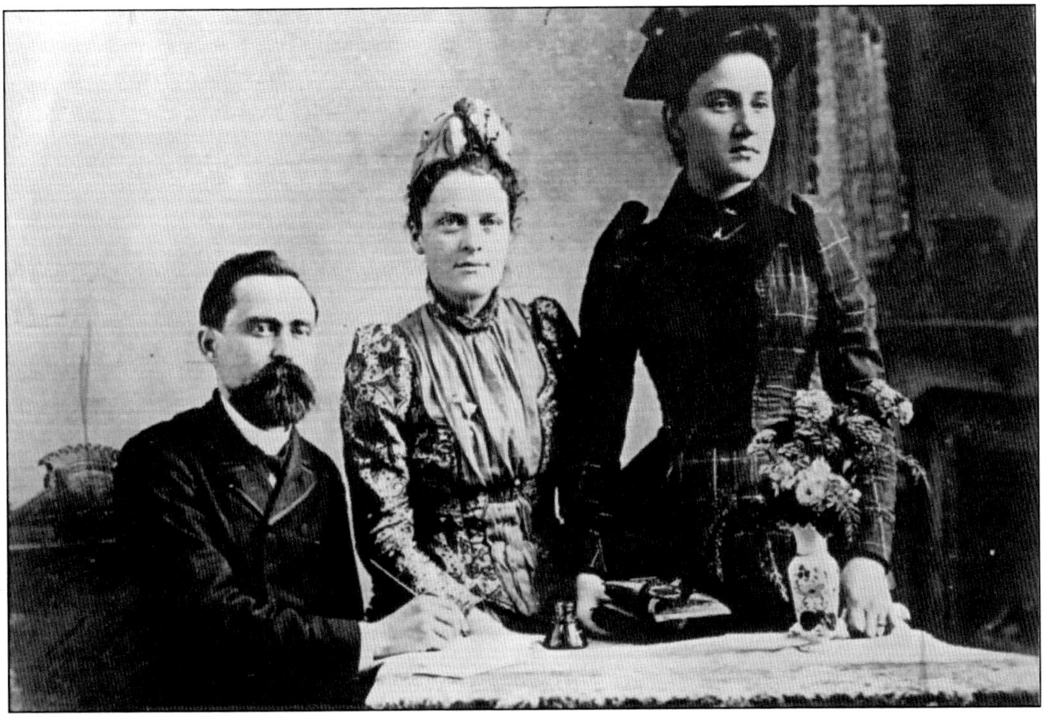

D.B. Johnson and teachers Mary Yeargin and Hannah Hemphill *They were members of the committee that the state legislature appointed in 1891 to visit potential sites in South Carolina and consider the offers from towns competing to give Winthrop a permanent home.*

Carolina cities that wanted to serve as the college's location. Advertisements were placed in state newspapers for 30 days. When the board met in March 1892, the only cites to make offers were Anderson and Columbia. At first, Anderson's bid seemed the most attractive of the two—an offer of $75,000 plus land to build on—but a court ruled the city's bonds invalid. After bids were reopened, Rock Hill and Spartanburg became the leading contenders.

Since the board had difficulty choosing between the two, it decided to visit each city in order to make the proper decision. Unfortunately for Spartanburg, the board visit coincided with the laying of Converse College's cornerstone, an event that undoubtedly influenced its decision.

Rock Hill's bid showed strong community support for the new college. In a referendum, an overwhelming 273 of the 297 ballots favored a bond issue of $60,000. Eager to attract the college, Rock Hill also offered a choice of two sites. When the 10 members of the Winthrop Board of Trustees met on April 2, 1893, their sentiments were clear—eight votes for Rock Hill and two for Spartanburg. Triumphant in its efforts to attract Winthrop College, the town celebrated jubilantly. As bells rang and factory whistles blew, a band led more than a thousand townsfolk in a victory march through the city.

A delegation from Winthrop's board of trustees visited Rock Hill on June 1, 1893, to settle details abut the bonds and the site for the college. Sixty bonds each were deposited in the Rock Hill First National Bank, and the Oakland site, about 1 mile north of town, was chosen as the college's future home. Two Rock Hill businessmen, Dr T.A. Crawford and W.J. Roddey, were elected trustees.

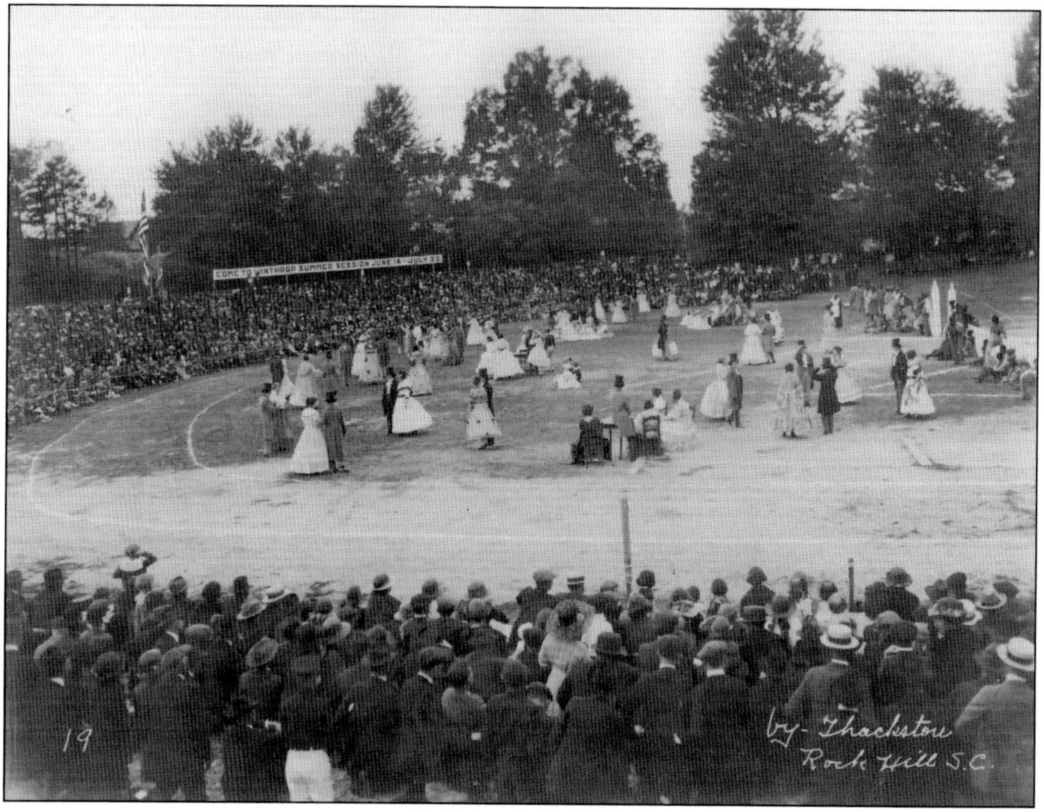

A SCENE FROM "THE MAKING OF SOUTH CAROLINA" PAGEANT, WHICH WAS SPONSORED BY WINTHROP AND ATTRACTED PEOPLE FROM ALL OVER THE STATE

With the site chosen, the Winthrop Board of Trustees moved quickly to build a campus. The board selected the Atlanta firm of Burne and Morgan, which had designed the Clemson campus in 1891, to design the first building.

On May 12, 1894, the birthday of Robert C. Winthrop, festivities for the laying of the cornerstone of Winthrop's impressive new Main Building took place. Robert C. Winthrop, unable to attend because of poor health and advancing years, wished the new college well, saying, "May it continue to be, for centuries to come, an ornament and a support to the state which has so wisely and liberally funded it." (Throughout the first years of the school, Robert C. Winthrop had sent gifts of money and books, many from his own collection, for the library. After his death in 1894, his family continued to send books for several more years.)

At 9 a.m. marshalls started to assemble in the streets. An estimated 10,000 spectators came from all corners of the state. Trains brought the entire Clemson student body of 500. At noon the official ceremony began in front of Main Building. Ira D. Jones, speaker of the South Carolina House of Representatives, praised the educational progress of the state as mirrored in Winthrop's rapid development. Governor Tillman then observed the historic date: "We have met to celebrate with fitting ceremonies the laying of the cornerstone of this state institution of learning."

At 1 p.m. a hushed silence fell as workmen lowered the cornerstone at the east front of the new building. As the stone nestled into place, a crescendo of cheers rose. For many of the dignitaries in attendance, years of hard work had finally come to fruition.

There was a feeling throughout the state that this was an important day in South Carolina history. *The State*, an editorial typical of South Carolina newspapers, wrote the following: "It is an era of which all may be proud, and may join the celebration of its inauguration. Heretofore, the state has devoted its money to the education of its men. But now . . . it says that women of South Carolina must no longer grow up in ignorance because they are poor."

To house the large student body, a dormitory was built in 1895, but no sooner had it gone up than the foundations for a second were being laid to accommodate a growing enrollment. In its 1896 report to the South Carolina General Assembly, the board of trustees reported more than 400 applied for admission, but only 310 could be admitted. By 1900 a new curriculum had taken shape in which students could work toward a four-year degree. Winthrop was giving its students the practical skills and sound educational background they needed to lead useful lives, to be good citizens, and to help others.

Change was also evident in the clothes students wore. Beginning in 1895, all students without exception, had to wear uniforms. The reason for the regulations were practical and egalitarian: to promote economy and to do away with class distinctions that might exist so that 'the richest girl in the school cannot distinguished from the poorest."

With uniforms came the introduction of the "Blue Line." On the first Sunday of each school year, the uniformed Winthrop students assembled before the Administration Building on the front campus, lining up two-by-two in denominational groups and then marching in a body from the campus to the Rock Hill churches. The college president and his wife, followed by leading student body officers, customarily headed the line.

With the ushering in of the 20th century, a tremendous building program began, making Winthrop one of the largest women's colleges in the country. President D.B. Johnson's energy, drive, and political skills were largely responsible for this boom period. To raise funds, he boldly approached some of the greatest philanthropists of the era, including Andrew Carnegie and J.P. Morgan, and persuaded them to give Winthrop money. During this growth period, enrollment at Winthrop skyrocketed. In 1900 it stood at 350; by 1918, more than a thousand. As Winthrop entered the Roaring Twenties, there was no doubt that the college was making a significant impact on South Carolina and the country.

The Roaring Twenties was not a prosperous period for South Carolina and its agricultural-based economy, but for Winthrop, the progress and growth of the century's first decades continued. To the college's faculty, students, and frequent visitors, the campus must have seemed like a place under perpetual construction. Enrollment kept rising, making it difficult for the college to house adequately its students. So serious was the space problem that three students often found themselves in a room designed for two. The construction of Roddey Hall in 1920 and Breazeale Hall in 1924 improved the situation considerably.

As the decade drew to a close, D.B. Johnson, the driving force behind Winthrop's growth, found his health fading. On December 26, the founder, and for 42 years president of Winthrop College, passed away. The campus and the entire state went into mourning.

Johnson had laid a firm foundation on which those who followed could build with confidence. In 1929 the trustees were able to report to the South Carolina General Assembly that Winthrop had 2,601 graduates certified to teach in South Carolina; the next highest number for any college in the state was 396. "This gives some idea of the important service rendered by the college to the teachers, boys and girls, and schools of the state," the board boasted.

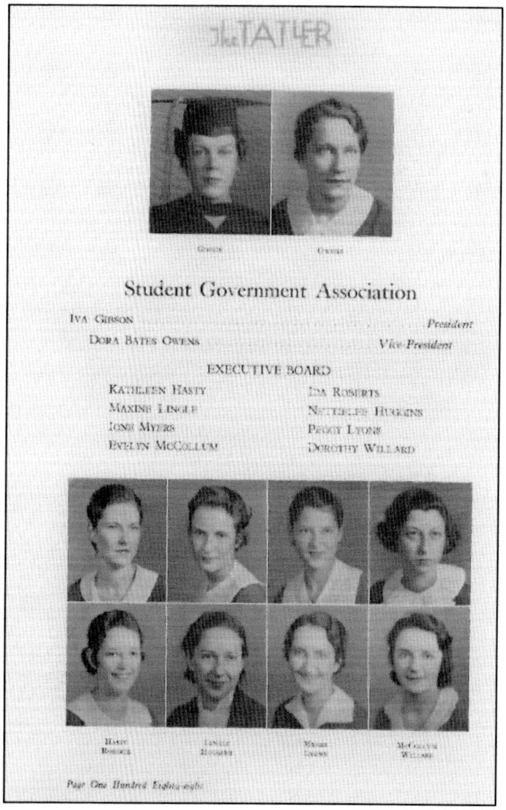

STUDENT GOVERNMENT ASSOCIATION OFFICERS FOR THE 1933–34 SCHOOL YEAR *President Iva Gibson went on to have a distinguished career as Dean of Students at Winthrop.*

Johnson's successor, James Pinckney Kinard, served Winthrop ably for 12 years as dean of the college and was very familiar with the school's operation. He filled the role of president capably from 1929 to 1934, bringing the college strong academic leadership. His accomplishments included the expansion of the Carnegie Library (now the Rutledge Building), the planning of the Amphitheater, the securing of accredited membership in the South Association of Colleges and Secondary Schools, and the construction of Kinard Building in 1929 to accommodate most of Winthrop's classes.

Kinard also had the task of leading the college through one of the worst economic periods in American history. Hard hit by the Depression, Winthrop was fortunate in one way: all the buildings started in the 1920s were completed before the budget cuts came in 1931. In that year, the state legislature chopped more than $74,000 from Winthrop's appropriation, forcing the administration to lay off teachers and make contingency plans to reduce salaries by 10 to 15 percent. By 1933 the situation had worsened to such an extent that Winthrop personnel had to wait several months to get paid. School officials even had to change the uniform regulations to cope with the crisis, decreasing the number of required dresses to two, simplifying the wardrobe, and cutting the cost of the uniform from $72.50 in 1931 to $43.55 in 1932 to $30.30 in 1933.

By 1934, however, the college had experienced the worst of the Depression. A slow recovery was on the way. Winthrop now began to seek funds from the Works Progress Administration (WPA), a newly created federal program designed to stimulate the economy, and an increase in appropriation even allowed the college to spend money on the purchase of boilers and the paving of College and Charlotte Avenues.

In 1934 Winthrop installed its third president. Kinard had accepted the presidency in 1929 on the stipulation that the college look for a younger man to fill the position. Five years later, Winthrop found him: 50-year-old Shelton S. Phelps, formerly dean of the Graduate School of George Peabody College for Teachers. Under Phelps's leadership, Winthrop gradually started to recover from its economic woes and once again became a college on the move. He worked hard to strengthen the curriculum and encouraged the faculty to obtain advanced training and degrees. Toward the late 1930s, building construction was once again a familiar sight on the Winthrop campus, as the school took advantage of the generous grants made possible by President Franklin Delano Roosevelt's "New Deal." Thurmond

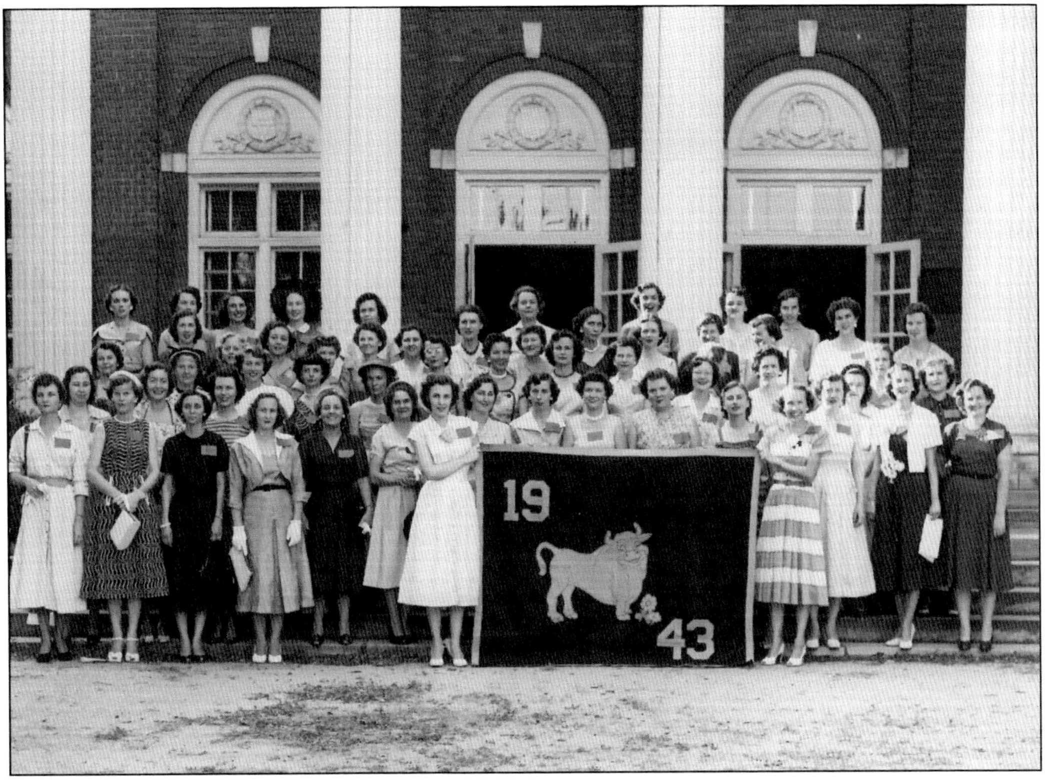

THE CLASS OF 1943 AT WINTHROP DURING THEIR 10TH REUNION IN 1953

Building and the Conservatory of Music were both completed during this time.

The Winthrop community, as did all segments of American society, played its part in the war effort. Students volunteered for anything and everything: helping to send out ration books, serving coffee and coca to the troops on the trains that stopped for a while on the back campus, and working with the Red Cross. Winthrop received a special honor in January 1944, when Mrs. D.B. Johnson christened the liberty ship S.S. *David B. Johnson*, in Brunswick, GA.

In 1942 the the federal government asked Winthrop College to house, feed, and teach young men involved in the Army Air Corps Civilian Pilot Training Program. Although Winthrop was a women's college, the administration believed that it could handle the cadets in such a way that the program would not interfere with campus life. Winthrop received $80,000 annually for cadet instruction and accommodation. Bancroft Hall became "Fort Bancroft," the home of the cadets who stayed for five months and received instruction in history, English, physics, and math. The government hoped that, by the end of their stay, cadets would be pressed physically and mentally for pre-flight and flight schools in other parts of the country.

When not in the classroom, the cadets engaged in a wide variety of activities to keep their leisure hours interesting; a 25-piece marching band played under the direction of Winthrop students. Softball tournaments were popular. The cadets even wrote and produced two plays: "Kiss Me Fool" and "Wild Blue Yonder."

During the war, Winthrop once again had a new president, Henry Radcliffe Sims, a lawyer by training who had served as ambassador of

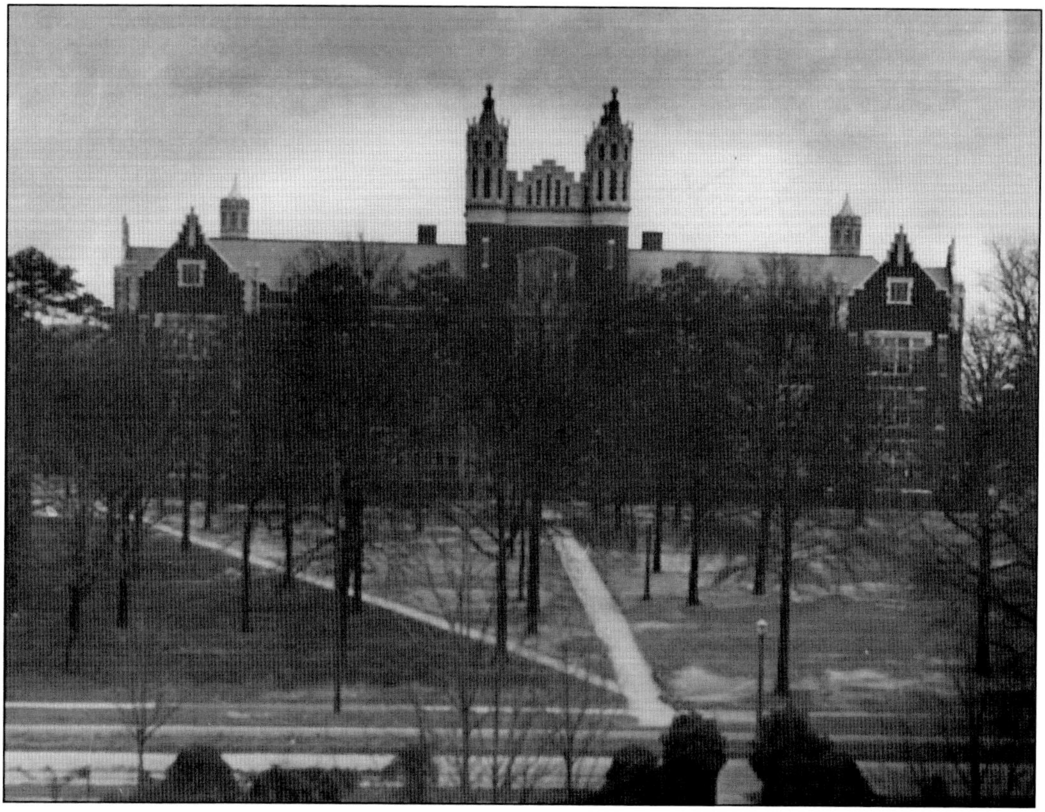

THE WITHERS BUILDING AS IT LOOKED IN THE MID-1940S

the South Carolina House of Representatives from 1923 to 1924 and then in the state senate from 1930 until his appointment as president. Before coming to Winthrop in 1944, Sims had served as an ex-officio member of the Winthrop Board of Trustees and already showed that he had a deep commitment to education and the college. As a senator, he wrote a bill that provided free school lunches for public school students and another that added the 12th grades to the school system.

Sims, contributing excellent business judgement and familiarity with state government, would build upon the good work of presidents Johnson, Kinard, and Phelps. As Winthrop approached the mid-20th century, it was no longer a young college in the midst of growing pains, but rather a mature established institution that looked to the future with confidence.

Chapter One

Winthrop's Beginnings

Dr. D.B. Johnson's Letter to Dr. Edward Southey Joynes. *This letter was written three years before the founding of Winthrop and gives keen insight into D.B. Johnson's views on education and his plans and dreams for his yet-to-be-built school. Edward Southey Joynes (1834–1917), the recipient of Dr. Johnson's epistle, helped bring D.B. Johnson to Columbia as the superintendent of schools. Joynes later helped Johnson to lobby for Winthrop College's transfer to state care.*

Martha's Vineyard, Mass.

July 20, 1883
Dr. E.S. Joynes,
Dear Sir,
Your letter was received yesterday and I hasten to reply.

My object in giving the notice as I did was to lead the teachers to think and to study about their duties from a different standpoint from that to which they had been accustomed and to open up new fields for investigation. I purposely refrained from mentioning text-books, inasmuch as the examination will be conducted without any recourse to any particular text-books. I should dislike to pledge myself to the use of any particular text-book by naming it in my notice of examination and besides I do not wish to cause the teachers to go to any extra expense when buying a book when they have one that covers the ground. Those who aspire to be teachers are certainly expected to be familiar with the common school branches and it would seem odd to me to prescribe certain text books for their use in the study of those branches that they ought to know already.

Physiology and hygiene will be taught in the State Normal School I am glad to see and will therefore prelude the necessity of mentioning a text book, I think. Any good elementary book like Hooker's, would give all that will be required. Phonics can be studied in any good Dictionary and is so

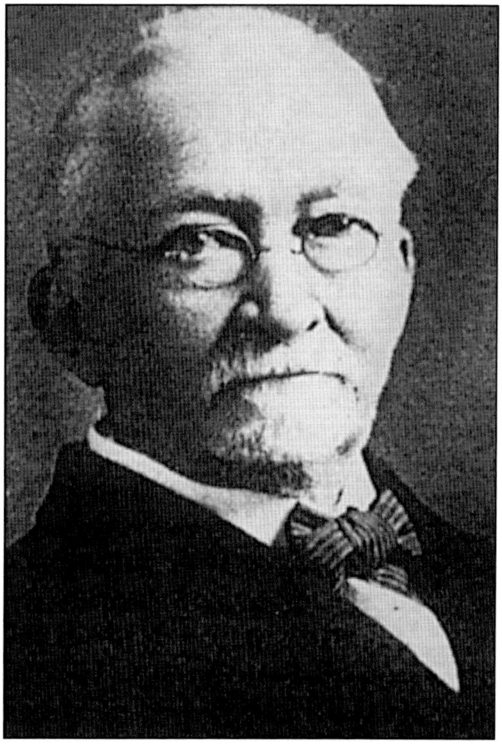

Dr. Edward Southey Joynes *Dr. Joynes was instrumental in the founding of the Columbia City School System and in bringing David Bancroft Johnson to South Carolina in 1883. He later helped Johnson lobby to have Winthrop transferred to state care.*

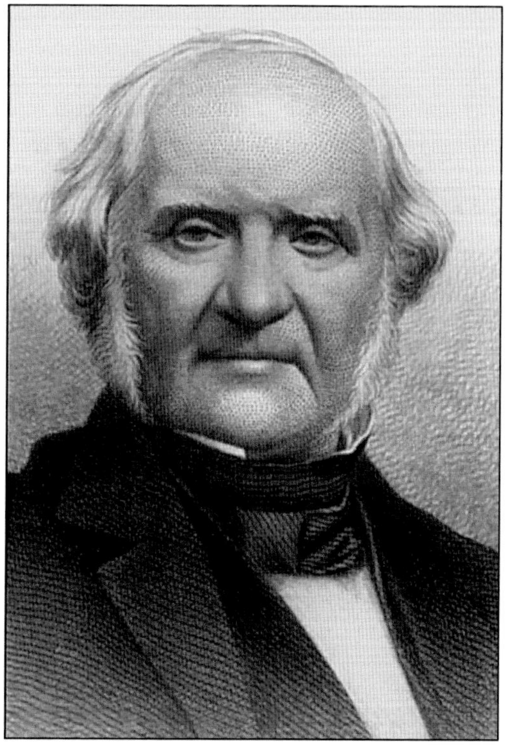

George Peabody (1794–1869) *Mr. Peabody started the Peabody Fund during Reconstruction to help Southern education get back on its feet after the Civil War. An initial grant of $1,500 from the fund started Winthrop College.*

simple that a thorough knowledge of it can be acquired from the analysis of the simple words of our individual vocabulary. As you have not printed the notice you can strike out the word "phonic." As for a text-book on Didactics I should not like to commit myself to any one man's theories where everything is in such an unsettled condition by recommending one book to the exclusion of others. There are a number of good progressive books of which I have no doubt the teachers have heard and which they can procure and study if they desire and are enthused with the proper spirit of progress. The best book for solid, deep reading and study on educational matters that I know of is that of Joseph Payne on the "Science and Art of Teaching" published by Willard Small Boston. It is too deep for the women to master in a short time however.

Col. Parker has gotten out a very recent and a very good book entitled "Notes of Talks on Teaching" published be E.I. Kellogg & Co. New York. I do not know but that it may be the best thing for our purpose. It is small, cheap and practical. I do not wish to place myself in any attitude of championship for any man however. I believe that the science of teaching is yet in its infancy and in the next fifteen years will change and develop into something

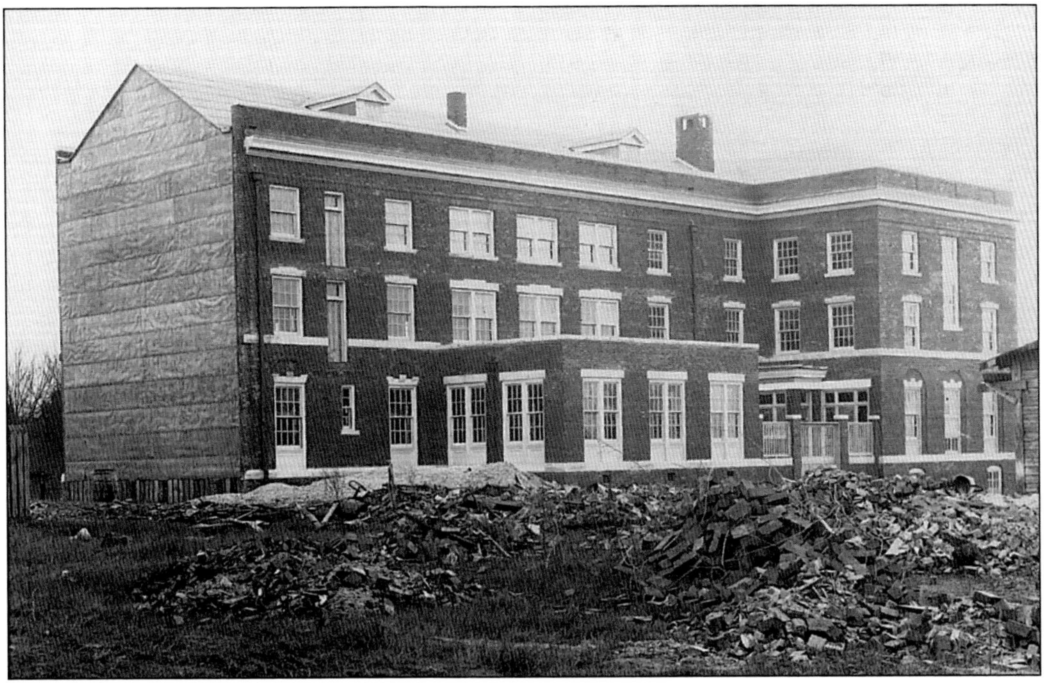

JOYNES HALL, NAMED AFTER EDWARD SOUTHEY JOYNES, SHORTLY BEFORE ITS COMPLETION IN 1926

different in many respects from what it is made out to be by the educational authors of the day.

You see that Parker is very much criticized all over the country and, if I should lend the country to believe that Parker is my model and all that, I should have Parker's battles to fight besides my own. Col. Parker is here and is giving some grand lectures which are being enjoyed by me very much, I came here especially to meet Parker and talk with him and hear him. You know he made Quincy what it was but not what it is, for Col. Parker had been working in other fields sometime and Quincy has dropped back form its former position.

The names of some of the other books that I have read and found very good are "Lectures on Teaching" by J.G. Fitch; "Early and Infant Education" by Currie; "Methods of Teaching" by John Sweet, etc. Perhaps the best way to do if the teachers have no books on education is to print the notice without naming any text-book and then make the suggestion as to text-book (Col. Parker's) individually and privately or these books that I have mentioned might all be published as a list from which to choose. Do as you think best. You are there and know the ground.

I am thinking and planning and working about everything connected with our school in Columbia and feel confident that we will have a grand success provided the Board carries out in thought, word and deed the spirit of the announcement of my election and I can see no possible reason why they will not and should not. I shall have everything ready at the proper time.

I will send you by this mail some resolutions adopted and sent to me unsolicited and unexpected. It might be well to have the Register copy. Confidence is a great factor in the success of any enterprise and whatever is done to establish confidence forwards materially the undertaking. The Board and people of New Berne brought grant pressure to bear upon me to keep me from going to Columbia at first and afterward to reconsider my action and remain in New Berne and because I remained firm I was afraid the Board and people were all angry with me. They were at first, but from these resolutions I am glad to see that they have come to look at the matter from a standpoint of reason.

Remember me kindly to your family.
Yours truly,
D.B. Johnson

P.S.: Calderwood "On Teaching—Its end and aim" is a good book and so is "Education" by Spencer—I wish that I could remain here with the Institute until Aug. 10, but I suppose I will have to be in Columbia by Aug. 7 for the Normal. Yours,
D.B.J.

(Written on side of front page) Please keep the written resolutions for me until I come to Columbia—D.B.J.

Rock Hill's Gift to Winthrop. *This is the title to the real estate given by the Rock Hill Town and Site Company to the Winthrop Board on Trustees. It was recorded on September 8, 1993, in the* Book of Transfers of York County *by W.J. Waters.*

State of South Carolina
County of York

Know all men by these presents, that The Rock Hill Land and Town Site Company, a corporation duly created and organized under the laws of the State of South Carolina, in consideration of the location of the South Carolina Industrial and Winthrop Normal College upon the property herein below described, and in further consideration of the sum of Five Dollars, to the said company in hand paid by The Trustees of the South Carolina Industrial and Winthrop Normal College–the receipt whereof is hereby acknowledged–has granted, bargained, sold and released, and by these presents does grant, bargain, sell and release unto The Trustees of the South Carolina Industrial and Winthrop Normal College:

All those blocks, lots or tracts of land lying in that part of the City of Rock Hill known as Oakland, in the County and State aforesaid, beginning at a stake on Oakland and Columbia Avenues, northeast corner of Block 16, and running thence down Oakland Avenue S $24^{1/2}$ E 955 feet to stake, corner of W.H. Stewart's lot: thence S $65^{1/2}$ W 190 feet with Stewart's line to stake: thence S $24^{1/2}$ E 200 feet with Stewart's rear line to stake on side of street to be opened: thence with said street S $65^{1/2}$ W 897 feet to stake on street to be laid off along and parallel with the right of way of the Charleston, Cincinnati and Chicago Railroad Company: thence along said street N $33^{1/2}$ W 1167 feet to stake: thence N $65^{1/2}$ E 1281 feet to the beginning, and containing thirty and one-half ($30^{1/2}$) acres, more or less.

Together with all and singular the rights, members, hereditaments and appurtenances to the said premises belonging or in any wise incident or appertaining.

To have and to hold all and singular the said premises unto The Trustees of the South Carolina Industrial and Winthrop Normal College, their successors and assigns forever. And the said Rock Hill Land and Town Site Company hereby binds itself, its successors and assigns, to warrant and forever defend all and singular the premises aforesaid unto the said The Trustees of the South Carolina Industrial and Winthrop Normal College, their successors and assigns against it and its successors and assigns against it and its successors and assigns, and all other persons whomsoever lawfully claiming or to claim, the same, or any fact thereof. In witness whereof, the said Rock Hill Land and Town Site Company has caused these presents to be signed by its President and its Corporate Seal to be herewith attached and attested by its Secretary this 2nd day of June, A.D. 1893.

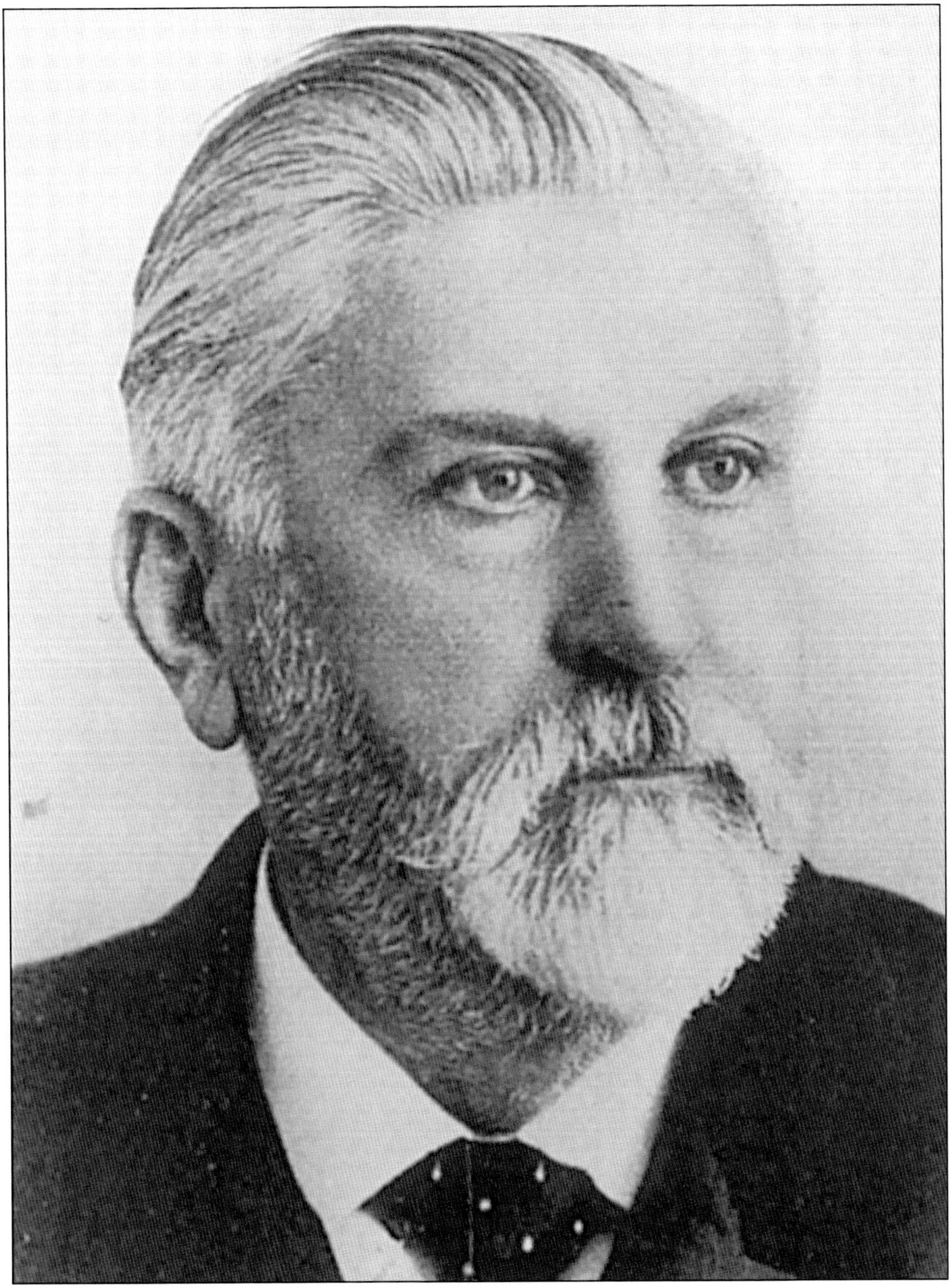

J.L.M. CURRY *Mr. Curry, the agent of the trustees of the Peabody Education Fund, played a big role in securing support for Winthrop during its early years. The early college catalogues described Curry as being "an earnest and able friend of the Winthrop School from its beginning, and much of its success and development is due to his support."*

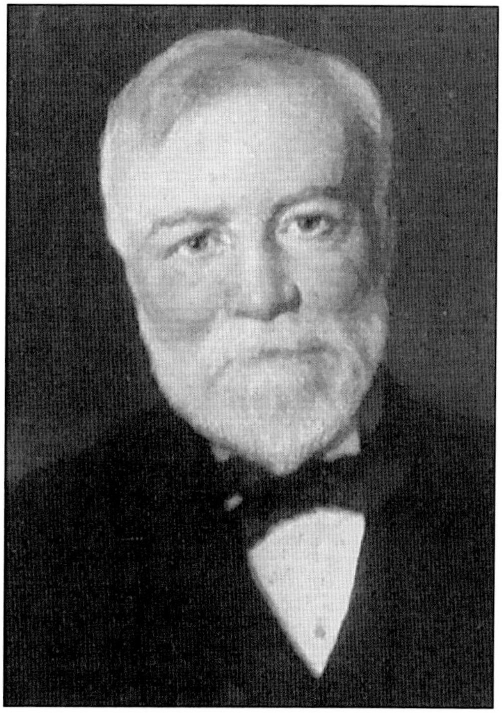

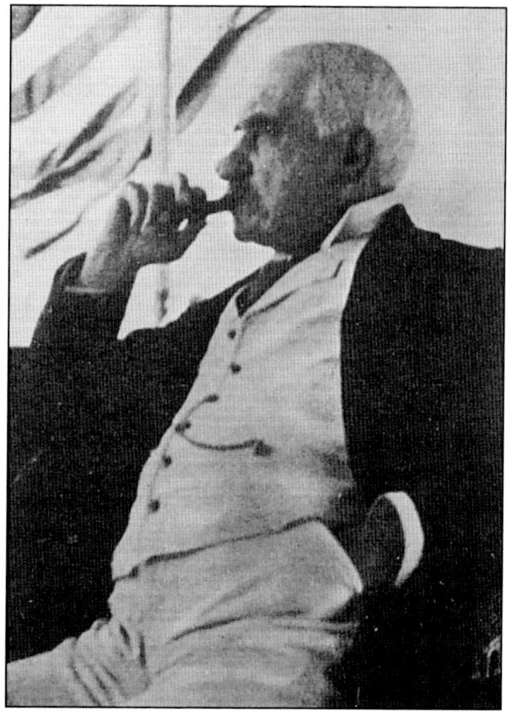

J.P. Morgan (left) and Andrew Carnegie (right) *The efforts of D.B. Johnson to build Winthrop did not stop with Rock Hill's gift. He approached the major philanthropists of his day, including the two pictured here.*

Signed, Sealed and delivered in presence of
Attest, J.M. Cherry, Sectry.
W.B. Wilson, Jr., President
W. H. Stewart
J.R. Boulware

State of South Carolina
County of York

Personally appeared W.H. Stewart and upon oath, states that he saw W. Blackmon Wilson, Jr., President, sign the within written deed, and the Corporate Seal of the said Rock Hill Land and Town Site Company affixed, and attested by J.M. Cherry, Secretary, and as the act and deed of the said Rock Hill Land and Town Site Company, deliver the same; and that he with J.R. Boulware witnessed the one execution thereof.

W.H. Stewart

Sworn to before me this 2nd day of June, 1893
J.H. Miller

Laying the Cornerstone—Governor Tillman's Address, 1894. *Benjamin Ryan Tillman, South Carolina governor and Winthrop Board of Trustees chairman, delivered the following address at the laying of Winthrop's cornerstone in Rock Hill on May 12, 1894. "Pitchfork" Ben Tillman (1847–1918), one of South Carolina's most colorful and controversial politicians, promoted the establishment of Winthrop College as a state institution even before he held public office. He was named "Pitchfork" for his fiery style as a South Carolina governor from 1891 to 1894.*

Tillman secured state funds for Winthrop College and was a member of the Winthrop Board of Trustees from 1891 to 1918.

Ladies and Gentlemen:
This is a great and glorious day for South Carolina. It is a day of promise and bright hope for York County; but the men and women whose breasts should swell and throb with deepest emotions of gratulation and pride are the men and women of Rock Hill—those whose pluck, self-reliance, far-sighted business instincts and patriotism made them enter the race for the prize and come out the winners. If, as is already clearly apparent, the prize is a greater, more valuable one than they themselves ever dreamed, then I know every one of you who comes to celebrate the public installation of this grand institution will join me in congratulations to the people of this ambitious, progressive little city, and your hearty sympathy is shown by this outpouring of people to witness her triumph.

We have met to celebrate with fitting ceremonies the laying of the corner stone of this noble State institution of learning. It is, as it were, the public and official birth of the Woman's College. As Chairman of the Board of Trustees, the task has fallen to me—and I perform it willingly—to make a few introductory remarks. And first let me say that in casting about in my mind for something fitting the occasion, I thought it would interest you to know something about the ceremony itself, and I went to work to look up the subject. I soon found that I had gotten into very deep water—so deep in fact that I have never touched bottom—for although I have ransacked encyclopedias and Masonic dictionaries, I can find nothing very clear on the subject, and absolutely nothing as to its origin. We read every day of the laying of the corner stone of this monument or that edifice or church, and it is always done by the Free Masons; but the Masons themselves, while they employ a most posing ritual and use symbols that are very impressive, are equally in the dark with ourselves as to when, where, or by whom the ceremony was instituted. In tracing the matter up, I got as far back as the Book of Job, one of the oldest books in the world. Job lived more than fifteen hundred years before Christ, according to the accepted chronology, and in that remarkable poem occurs this awe-inspiring query, promised by God himself to the Man of Many Sorrows:

Where was thou when I laid the foundations of the earth? declare if thou hast understanding.

Who hath laid the measure thereof, if thou knowest? or hath stretched the line upon it?

Whereupon are the foundations thereof fastened? or who laid the corner-stone thereof;

When the morning stars sang together and all the sons of God shouted for joy?"

Here we find mention of the corner stone of the earth, as though it were an edifice built by God himself; also of the "line" which Masons use for their measuring. Of course the Book of Job was written by a man, and necessarily his similes had reference to pre-existing conditions and customs, and the beautiful ceremonial which you will shortly witness will excite in your hearts and minds sentiments and thoughts of the most solemn and inspiring nature. The mind will dwell upon the idea of a great First Cause; a sure foundation; and a wise adaption of means to ends; while the heart will be lifted in gratitude for the blessings we enjoy in this world and the hope for a brighter life in the next; and, then, the imagination will picture brightest dreams and anticipations for the future of the institution which we propose to erect here, and the boundless benefits that are to accrue therefrom to our State and people.

Victor Hugo, in speaking of the pyramids, describes them as "so old that they have forgotten the names of their founders" and while, as we have seen, there is nothing in history touching the origin of the ceremony of laying the corner-stone, the first beginnings of Masonry and the origin of the order are

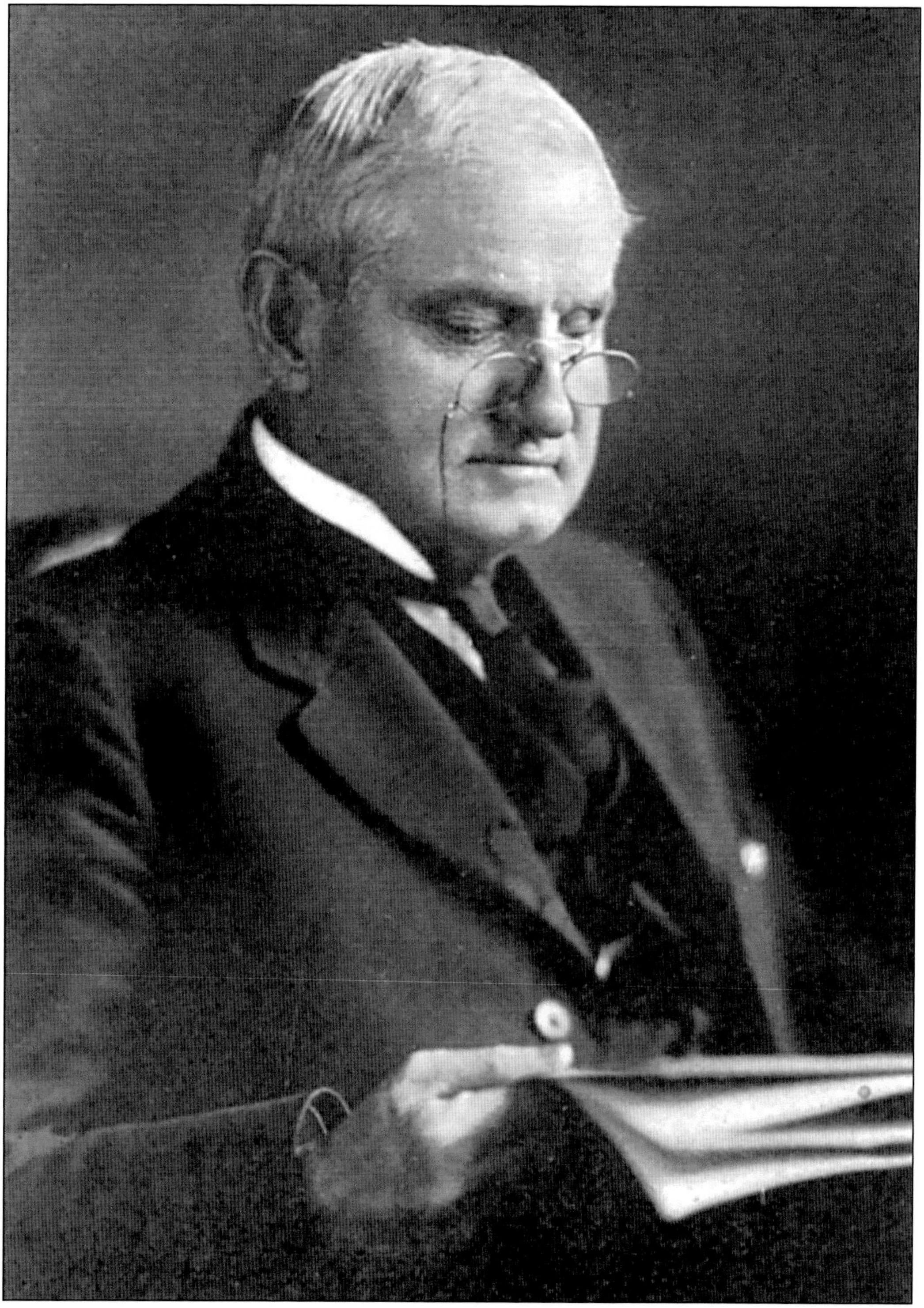

BENJAMIN RYAN TILLMAN

equally a mystery. It is claimed by some that the Masonic fraternity first became an organized or corporate body at the building of Solomon's Temple, which was dedicated nearly 2,900 years ago. Whether this be true of false, there is absolute proof that the Masons are the most ancient guild or order in the world; and, while Hugo's apothegm is applicable to the fraternity, it is certain that a ceremony similar possibly to the one which you will witness today, was performed at the beginning of the erection of that magnificent edifice which David's son builded [*sic*] to the Most High.

In the days of old it is true that the Mason was the man who hewed the stone, fitted it to its place, tried it with his level, and measured it with his square, fixed it perpendicular by his plummet, and placed it in position as the basis and starting point of the edifice. But while the stone-cutter of today may be a Free Mason, the Free Mason is no longer necessarily a worker with the hammer to chisel. The history of the transition from the active, practical workman to the speculative, mysterious philanthropist and doer of charitable works might interest you; but I must hasten on, and you will doubtless be more than willing to have your minds brought back from this excursion into the dim past, with its unknowable mysteries and its aspirations, to the present with its duties and high purposes.

The history of higher education in South Carolina for men is one of which our people may well be proud. The South Carolina College at Columbia was founded in 1801, ninety-three years ago, and it has always deserved and received handsome support from the State. The Citadel, another school for boys, was established fifty-one years ago. Until within the last eight years these two colleges, which were promptly reopened as soon as the white people regained possession of the government in South Carolina in 1876, were considered ample by those who had control, to supply all the needs of our people for higher education by the State.

But the wheels of progress were moving, even in South Carolina, and, after a somewhat protracted and bitter struggle, another school for boys—Clemson College—was established in 1889, by Act of the General Assembly, and opened its doors to students last July. This school is a new departure. The three fundamental ideas which have actuated those who pled for it, and who have opened it so successfully, are: (1) cheapness, (2) dignity of labor, and (3) the application of science to practical affairs. It is a "bread and butter" school in every sense of the word, seeking to fit men for occupations they intend to follow, while giving a good practical drill in the English branches. It was contended by those who opposed its being founded, that the men should be educated first and then left to acquire technical or special training afterwards. The fundamental idea of the Clemson curriculum is that the two shall go together; that, while, the mind is being drilled to reason correctly and brain cultivated by the acquisition of knowledge, the hand and eye shall also be trained, and that, instead of devoting time to physical culture in the gymnasium, on the baseball ground, or on the tennis court, the boy shall receive all necessary muscular development by performing labor which is educational on the farm, in the work-shop and from military drill.

That this college has met a long felt want and that our people have faith and hope for the new system of education, you have ocular demonstration in the splendid corps of cadets, numbering over 500, who have paid their way across the State to give an earnest of the pleasure they feel in adding eclat to the occasion which has brought us together. Consider that ten months ago every one of these erect, manly looking youngsters was a gawky, slouchy country lout or a city dude, while half of them have been at Clemson only since February, and you will give due credit to those in charge of it for the transformation going on in their minds is equally marked. These youths are the seed corn of our country. They are being taught

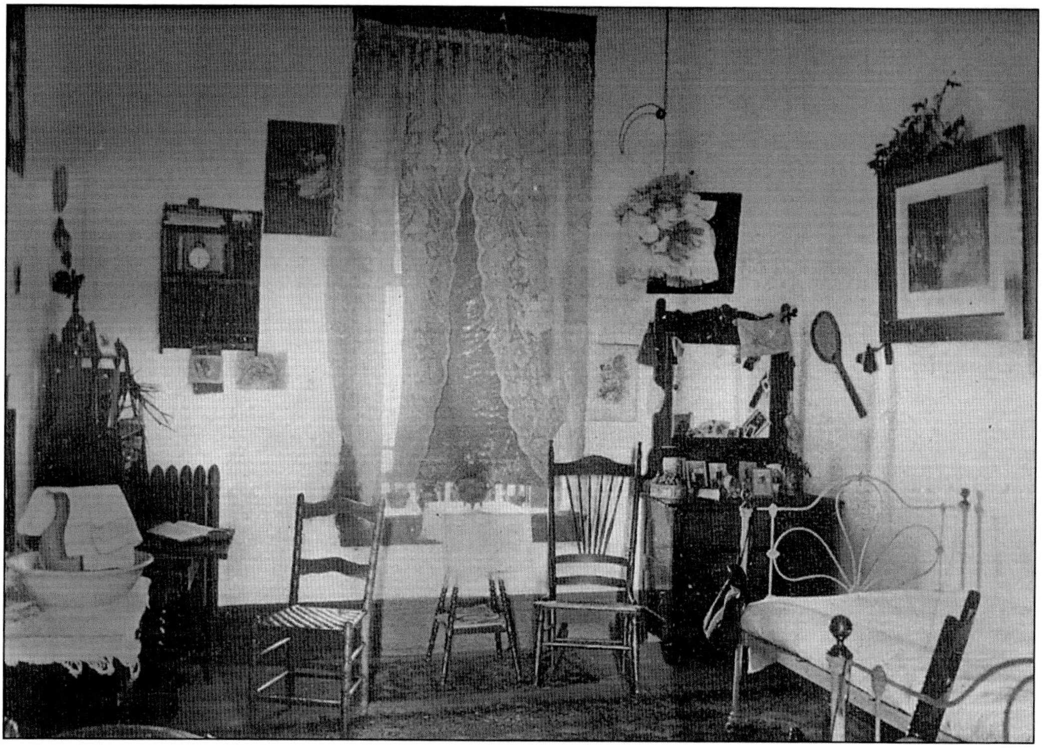

COLLEGE DORMITORY ROOM, *c.* 1895.

that God helps those that help themselves; that success in life requires self-reliance and labor; that work is honorable; that work is necessary, and that South Carolina will never achieve greatness except through the efforts of her own children; that knowledge of things is better; and that skill, energy and perseverance, with diversified pursuits, will alone make South Carolina great and prosperous.

We find that when we come to recapitulate, that the South Carolina College, hoary with age and rendered illustrious by the famous men it has educated, stands strong among its clustering elms, in our Capital City. The Citadel, equally honored by its alumni, is doing its special work in Charleston. Clemson, which is spanned by such a bright rainbow of promise, is fanned by the mountain breezes of Oconee. All for boys.

What have we done for our women? Where does the State educate its future mothers? The answer to the one question is nothing; the answer to the other is alas! too often "nowhere." But, thank God, this great wrong will soon be righted. This reproach on our justice and our statesmanship will no longer cause us to blush. We have waited too long—too long—but tardy justice will be done to the sisters of the boys for whose education the State has spent millions of dollars, while the girls have received nothing.

Grander in design than any or all of them, larger and more elaborate in architecture, more beautiful and ornamental, as is fitting the Winthrop Normal and Industrial College of South Carolina will ere long pierce the heavens with its stately spires, and the sky of York will be spanned by another bright rainbow of promise, that will attract the gaze of the people not only of this State, but of many States. The building, whose corner-stone we lay today, is one of the

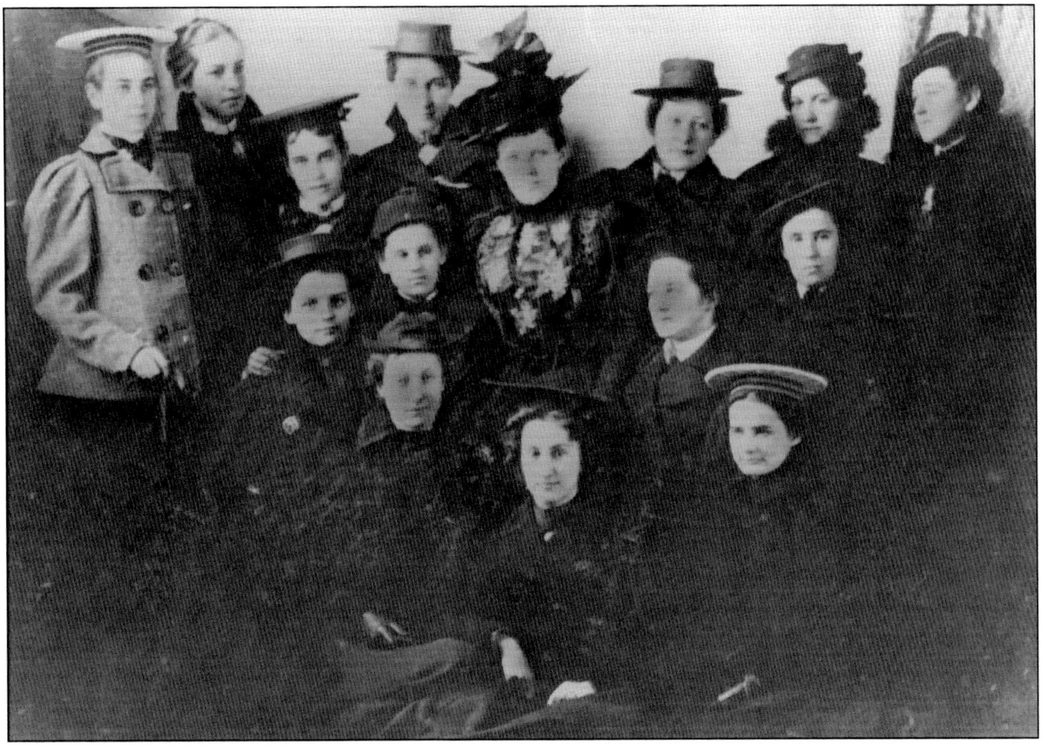

CLASS OF 1894

largest single school edifices in the South, and, when the two dormitories, which are required to complete the plan, are erected, it will be the largest woman's college of its kind in the Union.

Be it said to the credit of the men of the State that, whether from shame of their long neglect, or from a sturdy realization of the necessity and importance of the system of training which we propose to inaugurate here, there has not been one dissenting voice thus far raised against the building and the equipment of this college, since the idea first took shape three years ago.

Before I proceed to give a brief outline of the scope and plan of the institution as it has been mapped out by the Board of Trustees, I would go back a little to speak of Clemson. As you all know, that college is located at Fort Hill, the old home of Carolina's greatest statesman, John C. Calhoun. The history of its endowment by Mr. Clemson, whose name it bears, it is not necessary to give, as you are all familiar with it. It is of the connection of the school with Calhoun's memory and spirit, for he is its presiding genius, that I wish to speak. In 1850, Daniel Webster, Calhoun's greatest compeer in the Senate, was made Secretary of State in Filmore's Cabinet, and his place was filled by appointment by the Governor of Massachusetts. In March of that year, Calhoun passed the land of shadows, and this successor of Webster, a man of noted ancestry, of ripe scholarship, the highest integrity of character, the broadest statesmanship, eloquent and every way fitted to do the subject justice, pronounced a eulogy upon the dead Carolinian in the House of Representatives, of which he had been a member for ten years previously, which was eminently worthy of both. This is the bond of union between the two men. Disgusted with the trend of political affairs, for he was a friend of the South, this man retired from public life and devoted himself to other pursuits and such good works as have made his name a household word in America; so that, when George Peabody, the celebrated philanthropist who has done so much for education in the South, died, this gentleman was appointed Chairman of the Board of Trustees to carry out his will. This was more than twenty-five years ago, and you can readily see that he must be very old. At his home in Boston, he is calmly waiting the call of the Master. It was our hopes and purpose, and we used every effort, to have him grace this occasion with his presence, but his physical condition did not permit. In his absence it is my privilege to read to you the following letter: [*Governor Tillman here read the letter from the Honorable Robert C. Winthrop, which is printed hereafter. The reading of Mr. Winthrop's name evoked great applause.*]

I will say here, by way of parentheses, that it was through Mr. Winthrop's fostering care as Trustees of the Peabody fund, that the Training School for teachers, started in Columbia in 1886, began the work which laid the foundation of the institution which we are now erecting.

I know I voice the sentiment of every man, woman and child in this audience and in South Carolina, that it is altogether fit and right that we have honored Calhoun's friend and eulogist by giving his name to Clemson's twin sister. And I know that you all will unite with me in the prayer that this grand, good old man may be spared at least to see the fruition of our hopes in the assembling within these walls of the 600 South Carolina girls for whom we are preparing. Neither of these men can receive any honor from the association of their names with the two colleges. Let us hope that the youths of our State, from this association, will emulate their illustrious example.

This school is to be known as the Winthrop Normal and Industrial College. These two words, "normal" and "industrial" are the two lodestars which must guide our people out of the bog of poverty, ignorance and stagnation which surrounds us. Within their meaning lies our only hop—the one says educate, the other says work. I would not be understood as claiming or intending that the women of our State do not work, or that they are ignorant. In fact, some years ago, in discussing the cause of our depressed financial condition, I made the assertion and I stick to it yet, that only two classes on our population did their share of work. No observant or fair-minded person will deny that our wives and daughters have met the changed conditions wrought by the emancipation of the slaves with much greater success and fortitude than the men, and that they do a much larger proportion of the work than we do. On the other hand, it is equally patent that the bulk of the labor among the colored people is performed by men.

But to return to the scope and purposes of the two lines of teaching which we expect to pursue here. We desire to say that we fully realize and understand the great need of better teachers—teachers trained specifically for that vocation. There are hundreds and thousands of fairly well educated women in our State, many of whom are following the noble avocation of teaching. But the mere possession of knowledge does not carry with it the power of imparting it, of exciting emulation, of making study interesting, of training children how to think and to exercise their reasoning powers. I have often thought that teachers are born, not made; and we occasionally meet with those who have a genius for imparting knowledge without any normal training. But the improved systems which have been adopted in the Winthrop School, and the facility with which all the graduates of the Winthrop School, and the faculty with whom all the graduates of that school obtain positions at more remunerative wages than others of equal education who have not had its advantages, are proofs that normal training is an absolute necessity and invaluable. Without reflecting in the slightest upon

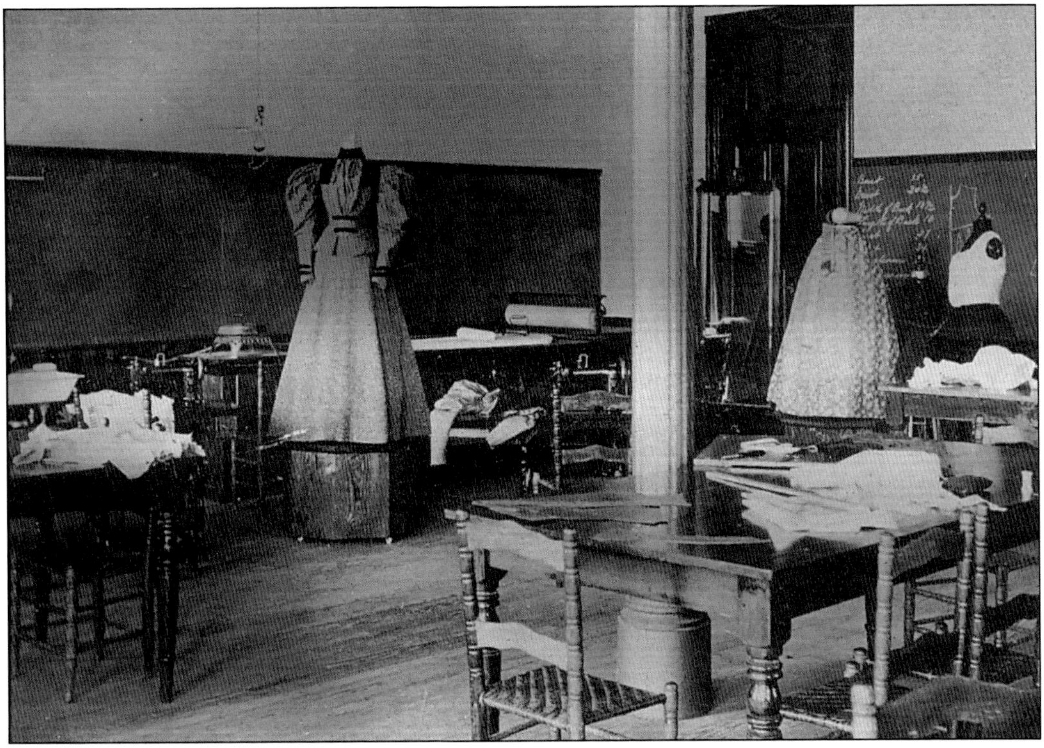

SCHOOL OF DRESSMAKING, *C.* 1895

the work which has hitherto been done in this line, it is our purpose to enlarge and improve on that work, and it will be our ambition to have such professors, and inaugurate such a curriculum, as shall not only furnish facilities for persons already educated to get this normal training, but shall take the young girl fresh from her home and carry her through all the classes up to the highest proficiency in the normal department, conferring degrees for the varying degrees of proficiency. There will never be any restrictions as to the number of normal students, but will take all who apply for this specific training, from whatever part of the country.

But along with the normal, co-ordinated and of equal importance, will be the industrial feature of the school. Somebody long ago said, "knowledge is power." In these latter days, we have come to learn that knowledge is also money independence. And knowledge coupled with skill, backed by industry, will always insure any woman, however fragile, absolute exemption from want and poverty. Every father who thinks aright would have his daughter, if thrown on her own resources, able to earn her own support. The effects of slavery upon our habits and customs are, however, still plainly visible. We are disinclined as a people to have our women leave home to seek their fortunes or enter into industrial life. The consequence is, that with the system of education which has hitherto prevailed, preparing women solely to adorn the drawing-room and shine in society, our women have been altogether helpless and our system of education has been a fatal blunder. How many thousands of our women, tenderly nurtured, carefully trained at expensive boarding-schools, have been themselves by the death of father, brother or husband thrown on their own resources, left to battle with the cold, hard world, by the loss of their protectors? Every day we come across some of these, and while an increasing number have found positions of late years as clerks in stores, the vast arm have had no other venues open to them except work as seamstresses or in common factories. In these latter, owing to the fact that manufacturing industries of our State have developed only in the coarser fabrics, their labor has not been remunerative, and it is sought only as the *dernier recort*. Any one who has visited the Northern cities and factories is struck with the painful contrast in the dress, demeanor, intelligence and evident prosperity of the female labor, compared with that which we see here in the South. We can and must change this.

In the industrial department of this college it is our intention to teach everything, and have the students practice every industrial art, that will lead to independence. Music will be taught, but only as an industrial art—in other words, with only such proficiency in singing and playing that will insure livelihood. As an ornament it will not be taught at all, and those lacking in special talents will not receive tuition in it. But don't understand me as meaning that we intend only to fit those who enter the industrial departments for making their own support. We shall have a laundry, where the girls will do their own washing and ironing. The chemistry and practice of cookery will be taught, and everything connected with house-keeping. The dining-room and dress-making departments will receive attention, and all that goes to make up those thousand and one things which a woman has to do to make a pleasant home, will be taught in the manner possible. They will be taught by having them done by the students themselves, for we will have no servants except for the drudgery work. All the distinctions of wealth will be done away with. Every pupil in the school will be required to wear uniform, and a girl's whole clothing outfit for the year will cost not exceeding $20. I am getting into deep water here, for I am not altogether skilled in this department; but I know every father and husband will sympathize with our aspirations along this line. I will simply say, as a corollary, that I have a daughter off at boarding school, who has been gone nearly a year. She carried off a big Saratoga trunk full, and her mother sent her so many dresses since she left that she will have to buy another trunk to get back home with—and we are determined that no girl shall ever leave the Winthrop College with, or bring to it, a Saratoga trunk.

There will be no conflict between the Normal and Industrial departments. In fact, the normal students will be required to take industrial training in order that we may be able to have a manual training taught by the Winthrop graduates in our common schools, when this feature shall be grafted upon our school system, as we hope to see done ere long.

Now, I am going to do some very plain talking. While our inspirations and ambitions are all in the direction for fitting women for self support, both as teachers and as followers of industrial avocations, I want it understood that I, at least, am irrevocably opposed to anything being done or taught that shall tend in the slightest degree to rub the bloom off the peach. God forbid that this school shall ever send forth a woman who has been unsexed. We would have the clinging, helpless creature able to stand erect and walk; we would have the trembling bird given wings to fly from home—seek avenues of independence—until she can find a mate and build a nest for herself; but never, never have any of the daughters in South Carolina, who shall be trained in those walls, by reason of the strength and self reliance which we hope to impart here, become other than helpful wives and happy self-respecting mothers. Woman's special province in life is that of the home-maker. Her greatest glory, her proudest distinction, the object of her creation in fact, is that of motherhood. "Woman, God's last, best gift to man," is associated with all that is

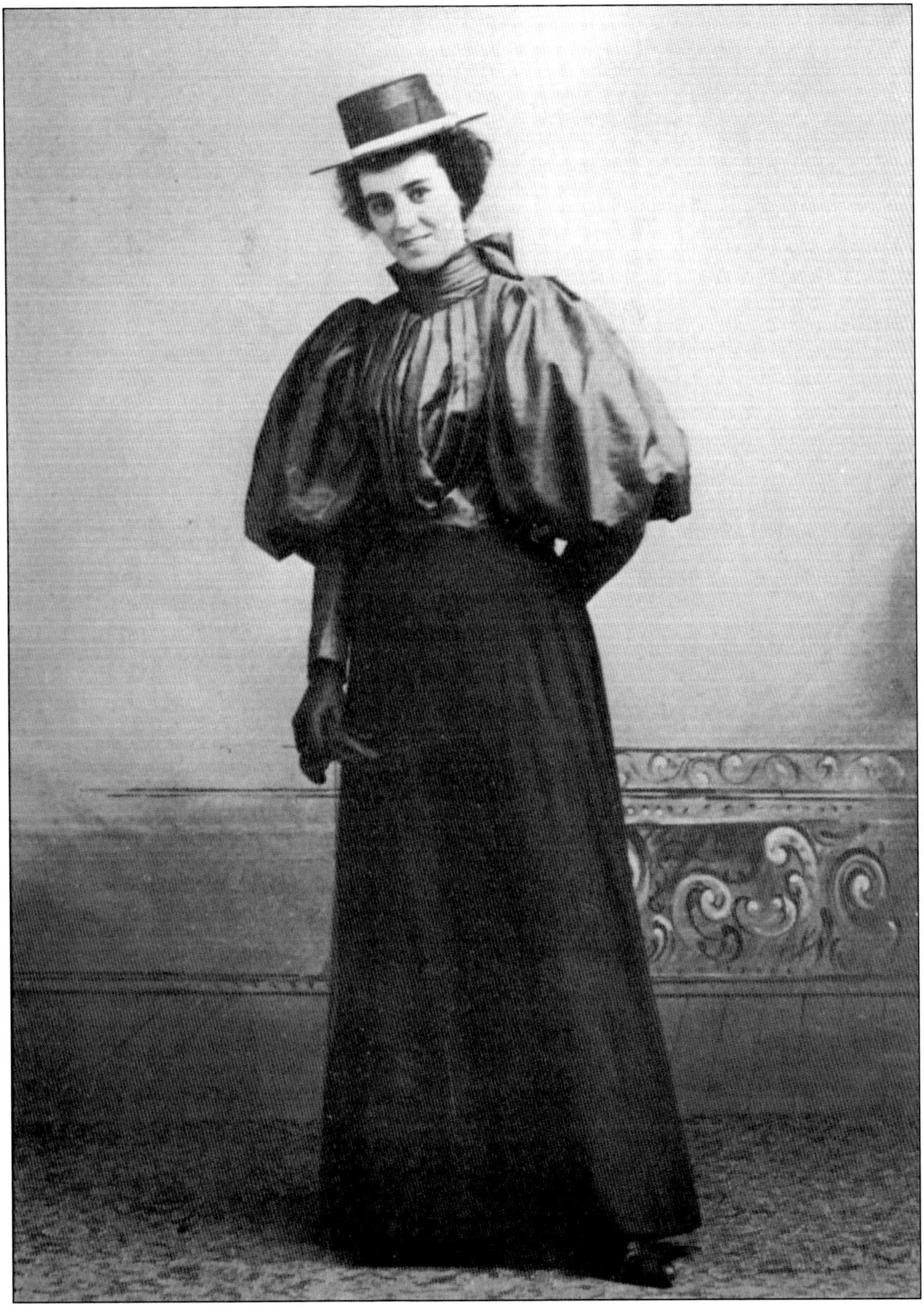

Spring uniform, 1895–96

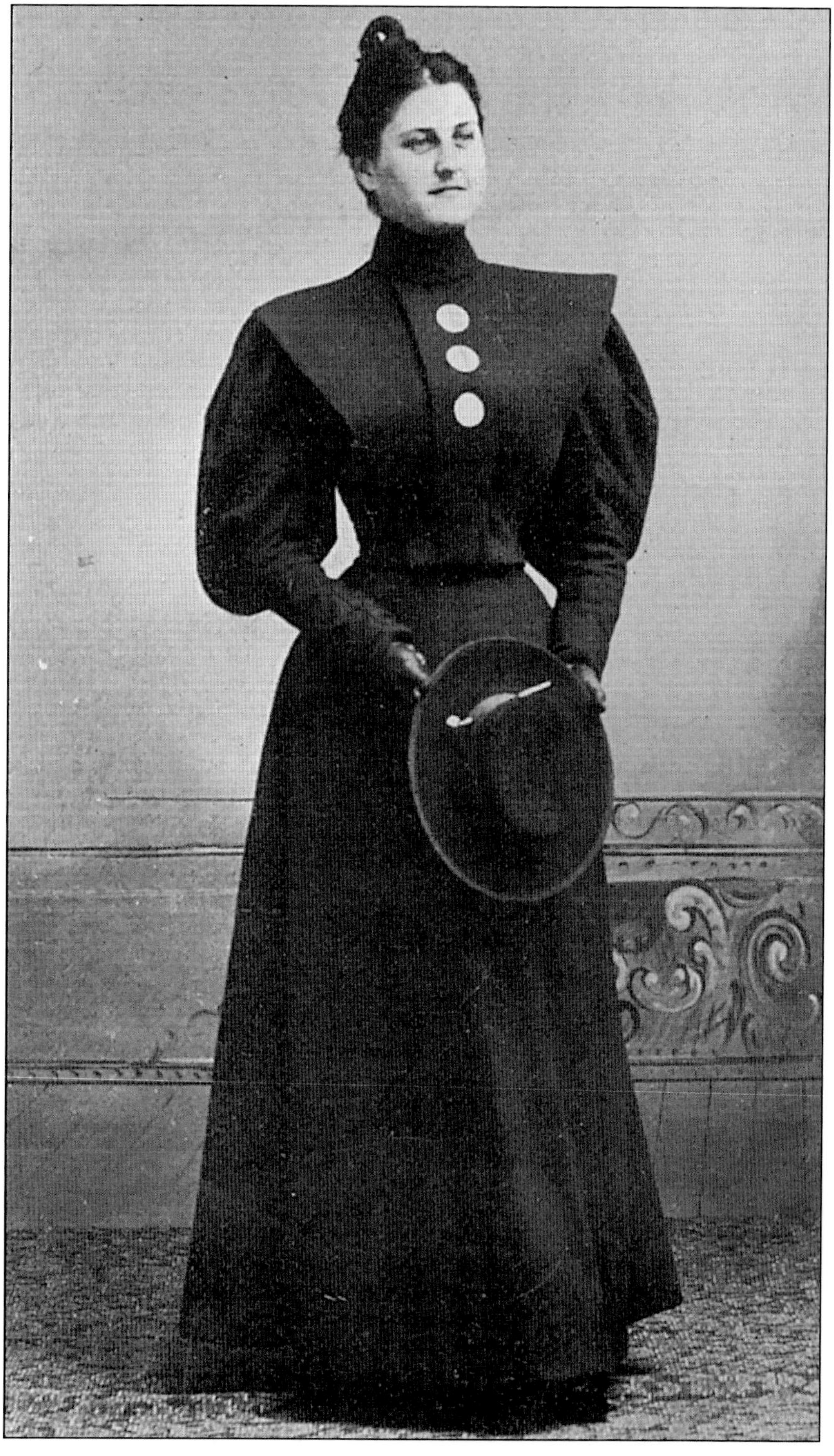

THE FATIGUE UNIFORM FOR FALL AND WINTER

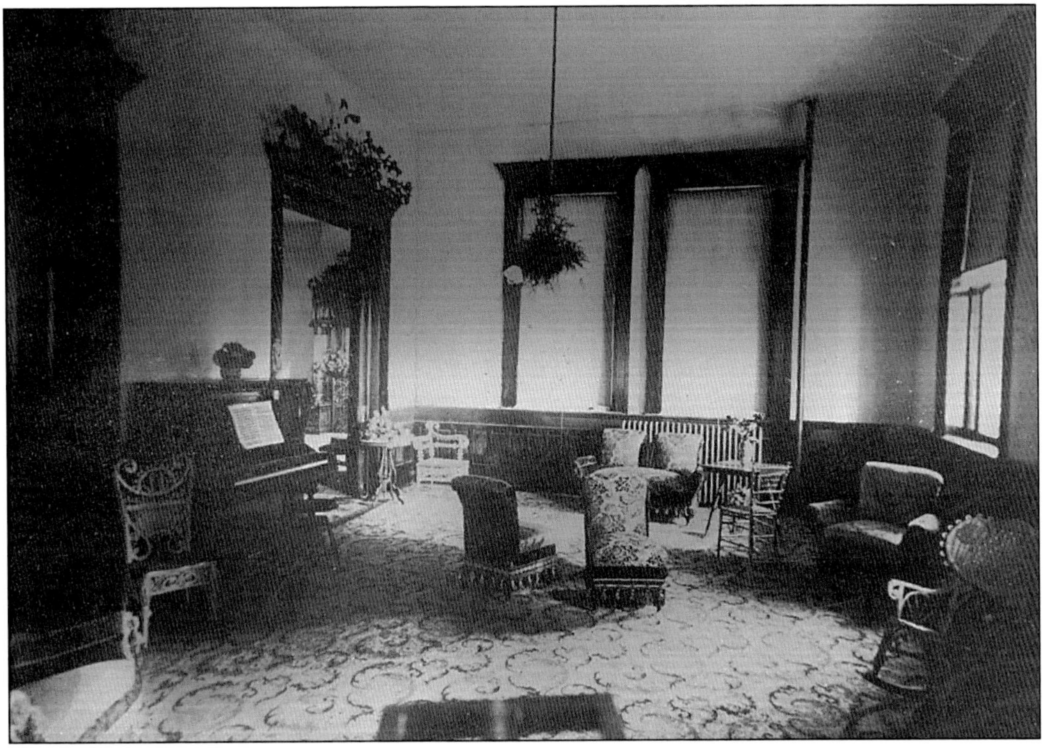

Reception parlor in Tillman, *c.* 1895

brightest and best and noblest in men's lives. As daughter, sister, wife, sweetheart, mother, she is an inspiration and a solace. As a wife, she doubles man's joys, and she halves his sorrows, simply by sharing them; but the highest, purest, most self-sacrificing love in the world is that of mother. It is to fit women to be mothers—high, noble, properly trained mothers, the natural and proper guardian of children, that this school is founded. We will start it in that path, give it the bias and the direction to which it should be held, and thus best discharged the high duty imposed which it should be held, and thus best discharged the high duty imposed upon it by those who have place us in control.

Contrast the picture I have drawn, of a woman trained in all the domestic arts and economics, and some bread winning occupation; self-reliant and strong, yet withal modest, self-respecting and lady-like, with what we sometimes see, oftener read about—a strong minded, bold, brazen, pert, self-asserting female, prating of "woman's rights," "man's selfishness and tyranny," the "degradation of nursing children," and so on, ad nauseam. The first, a picture to illustrate Wordsworth's noble lines:

She was a phantom of delight,
When first she gleamed upon my sight,
A lovely apparition, sent
To be a moment's ornament;
Her eyes as stars of twilight fair,
Like twilight, too, her dusky hair.
But all things else about her drawn
From May-time and the cheerful morn.

This is the picture of his sweetheart when the beautiful vision first crossed his path; now read the poet's tribute to his wife in the next verse:

A creature not to bright or good
For human nature's daily food.
For transient sorrows, simple wiles,
Praise, blame, love, kisses, tears and smiles;
The reason firm, the temperate will,
Endurance, foresight, strength and skill;
A perfect nobly woman planned,
To warm, to comfort, to command.

Of the other I have no fit description, for the poets have never sung her praises; but her position in the estimation of all right thinking men and women can be pretty well set forth in the last line of a piece of doggerel from school the other day by my six-year-old daughter, who took great delight in repeating it:

I know a little girl
With a little curl
Hanging right down her forehead;
When she is good
She is very, very good
But when she is bad she is horrid.

These composite, unnatural, unsexed women, striving to be like men and to do like men, not essentially "bad," perhaps, only so out of place and out of time from wrong ideas of rearing they have lost all the finer graces and charms which have always made men the slaves of the sex, and have gained nothing in exchange except their own morbid self-esteem. Such women are simply horrid, and it will be the ambition and care of all friends of this college that it shall never send forth or harbor one of these horrid creatures. Every true man acknowledges the existence of and pays due respect to "woman's rights." Wordsworth gives her the right to command, and all men, since Adam set us the example in obedience, even to do evil, have obeyed when the behest was given by a true woman in a womanly way.

The young men who will be trained at Clemson, in the manner I have indicated, will naturally look hither and seek among the students who will flock to Rock Hill, for their future helpmates. They are even here now, reconnoitering the ground. And after Winthrop gets fully under way, I think it ought to be the fixed policy of the management of the two colleges to have frequent migrations to and fro; for it will inspire and help the boys to come here, and the girls will be equally benefitted by an occasional excursion to Clemson, the alliance is a natural one, and the two schools run into each other and are just as much bone of one bone, flesh of one flesh, as though already married.

But I must hasten to a conclusion and leave to the distinguished orator of the day a fuller and more eloquent discussion of these themes.

Before closing I want to give emphasis to one thought. I have already pointed out the unanimity with which men of all classes, conditions and ideas have joined hands in adding to erect this school. It is the one thing and the only thing upon which the men of South Carolina are at present united. Only alluding, in passing, to the bitterness and the division which exist among our people, allow me to express the hope that this point of union may grow and spread; that the inspiration of this day may prove a harbinger and help to hasten the restoration of that harmony and friendly feeling which once existed, and which must necessarily return before we can have any great degree of prosperity. Our interests are one, our ancestry is the same, let us yield to the rule of justice and reason and the government of the majority; for we are brethren. Why not dwell together as brethren?

As in the days of old the ancient Sabines were brought to peace with the Romans by the women who had been seized and borne off captives to become the wives of the latter; so may the women of South Carolina become our peacemakers. Let them take hold of the work in earnest—go to all the campaign meetings in full force to make their fathers, husbands and brothers behave

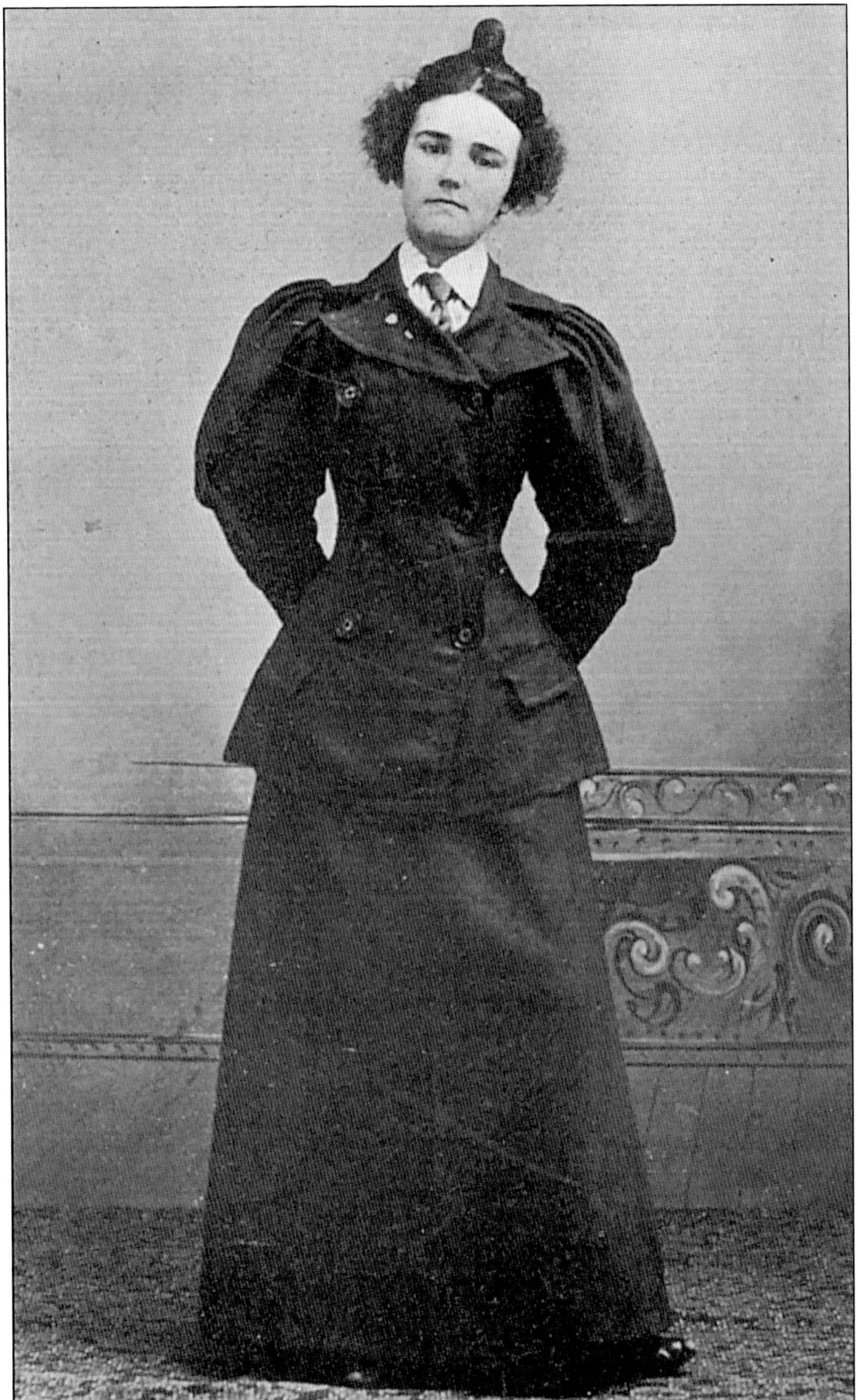

THE DRESS UNIFORM FOR FALL AND WINTER

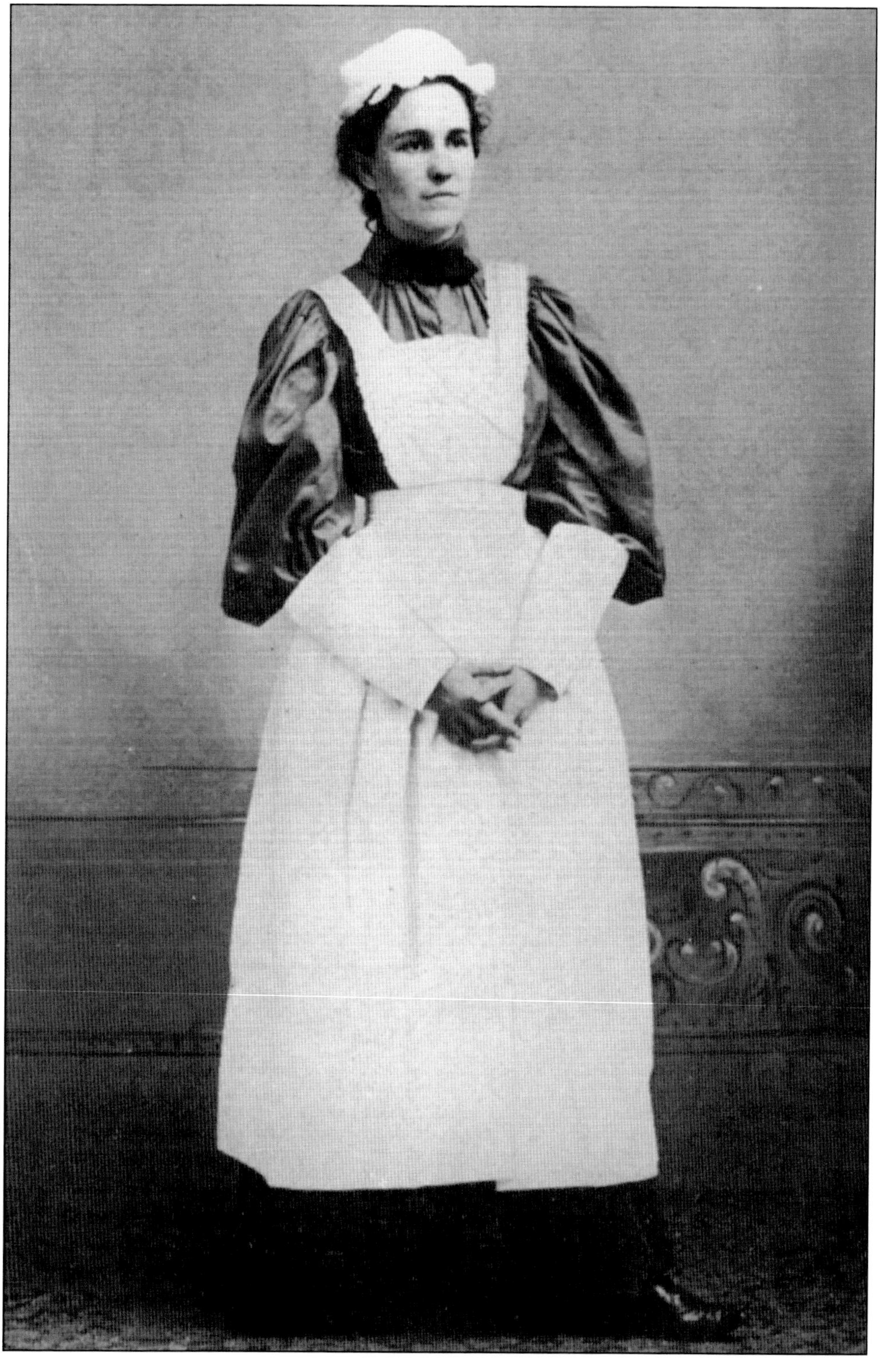

COOKING SCHOOL SUIT, 1895–96

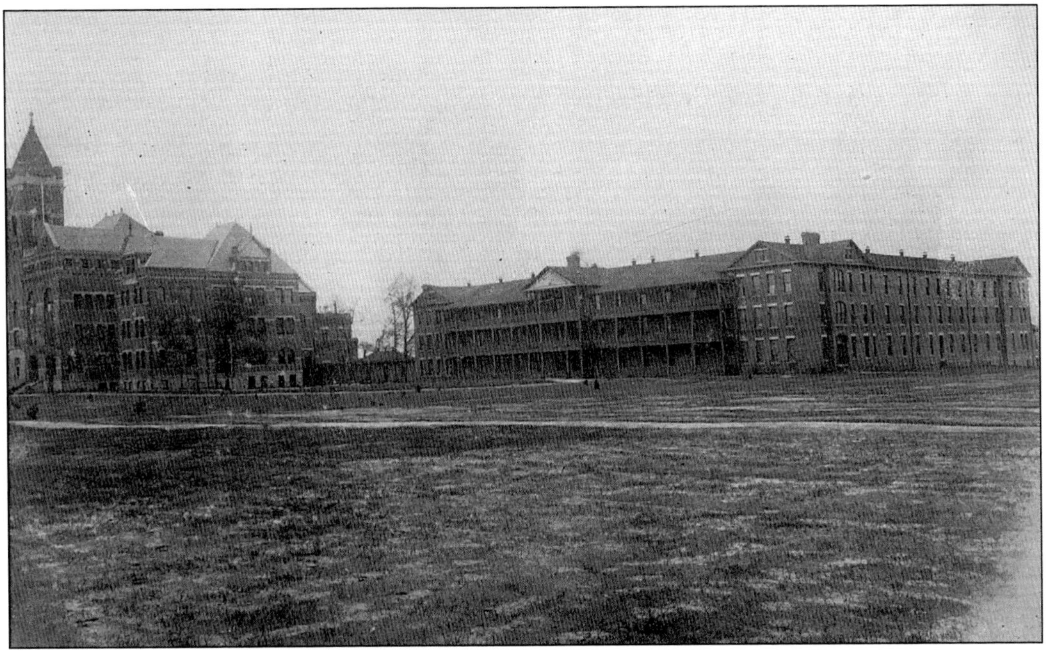

College and dormitory, *c.* 1895

themselves; and at the end of the summer we shall have something better than prohibition or the subtreasury, "Peace in all our hearts, Peace in all our homes."

Opening Day, October 15, 1895 (Leila Russell). *Leila A. Russell (1971–1963), Class of 1989, was instrumental in Winthrop's early development, serving as organizer and first president of the YWCA, the first county supervisor of education in South Carolina, and alumnae executive secretary from 1895 to 1945.*

When the state of South Carolina created Winthrop College, the South Carolina College for Women, she wrote an act that will stand out in large letters on the pages of time and eternity. There has been great interest in the institution from the time of the passage of this act by the General Assembly in 1893 to this day.

Where the college was to be located was a focal point of interest and deep concern. Numerous cities in the state wished to secure it and offered attractive sites plus goodly sums of money. A committee of three—President Johnson, Miss Hanna Hemphill of Abbeville, and Miss Mary Yeargin of Laurens—were appointed to visit these places making bids and select the best location. Rock Hill was chosen as a result.

For more than a year after the bill was passed plans moved forward and the corner stone was laid on May 12, 1894. From that time to the momentous occasion which took place on October 15, 1895, when the college threw open her doors to enroll 300 young women, interest was centered on the buildings being erected. Much of the construction of these was done by prisoners from the state penitentiary.

At last all was in readiness and the long-looked-for date October 15, 1985, was at hand. The Winthrop that had been in Columbia for nine years merged with the one to open in Rock Hill, known at first as Winthrop Normal and Industrial College, now Winthrop College, the South Carolina

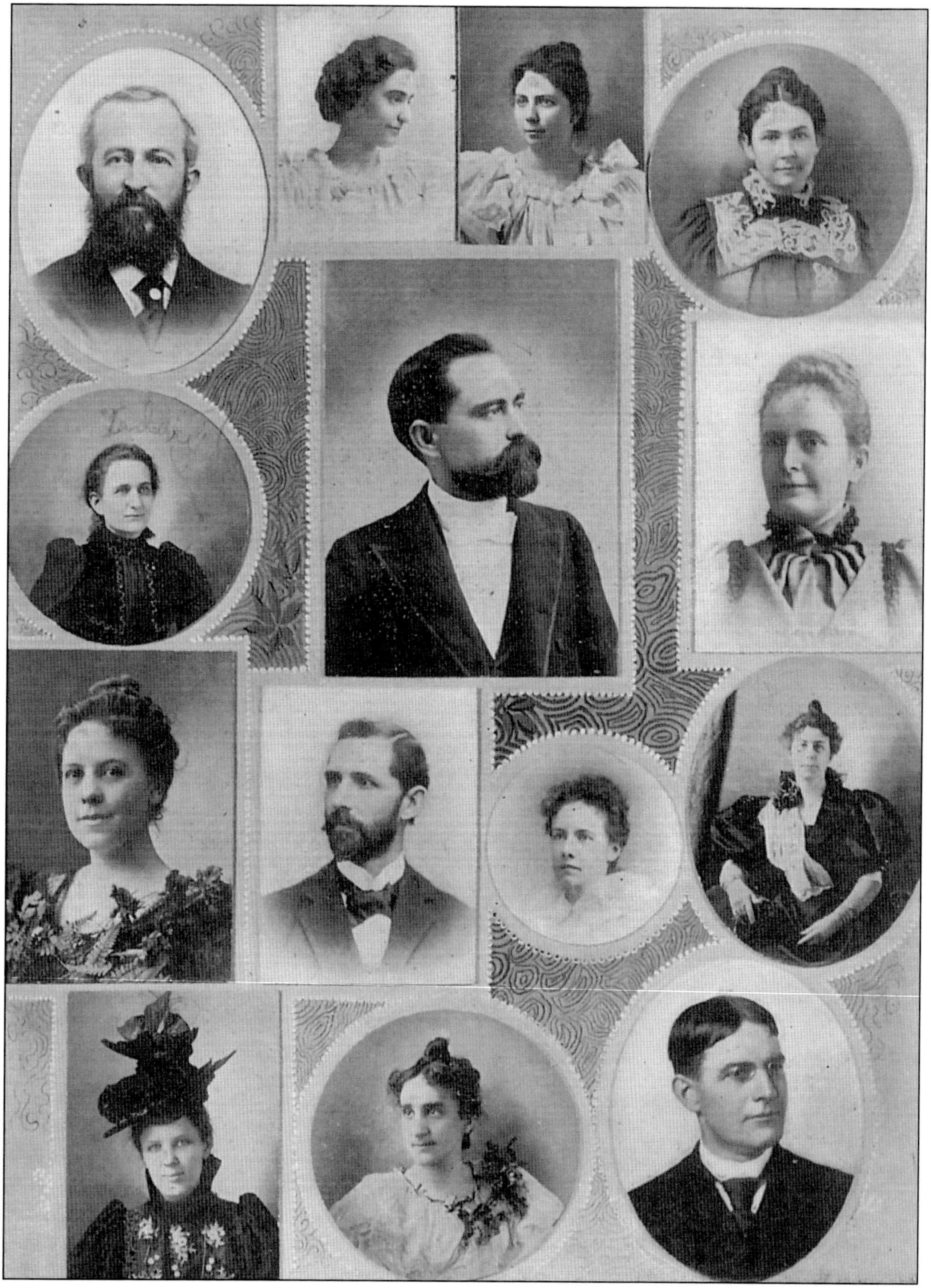

Members of the 1897–98 faculty, with President Johnson in the center

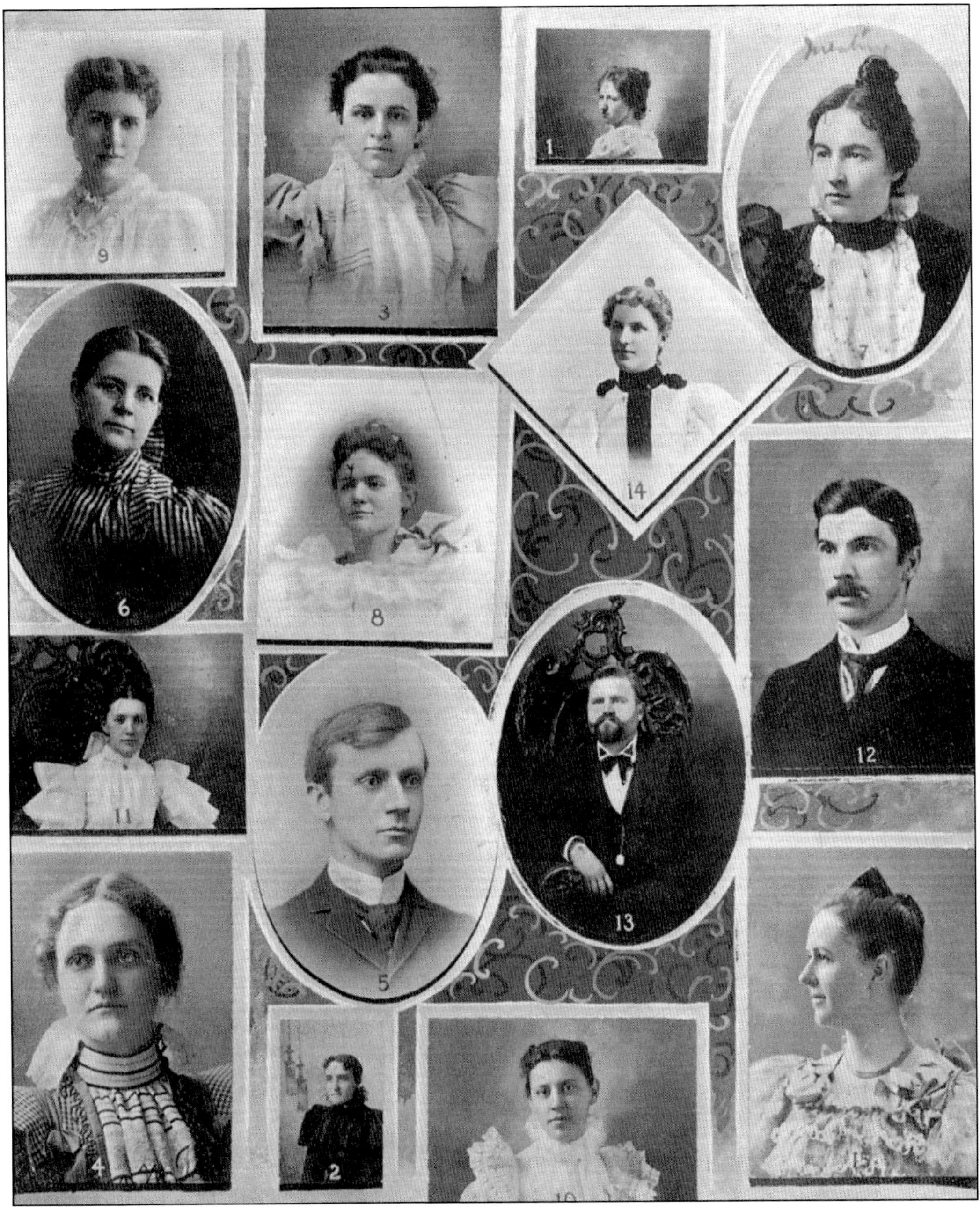

MEMBERS OF THE 1897–98 FACULTY

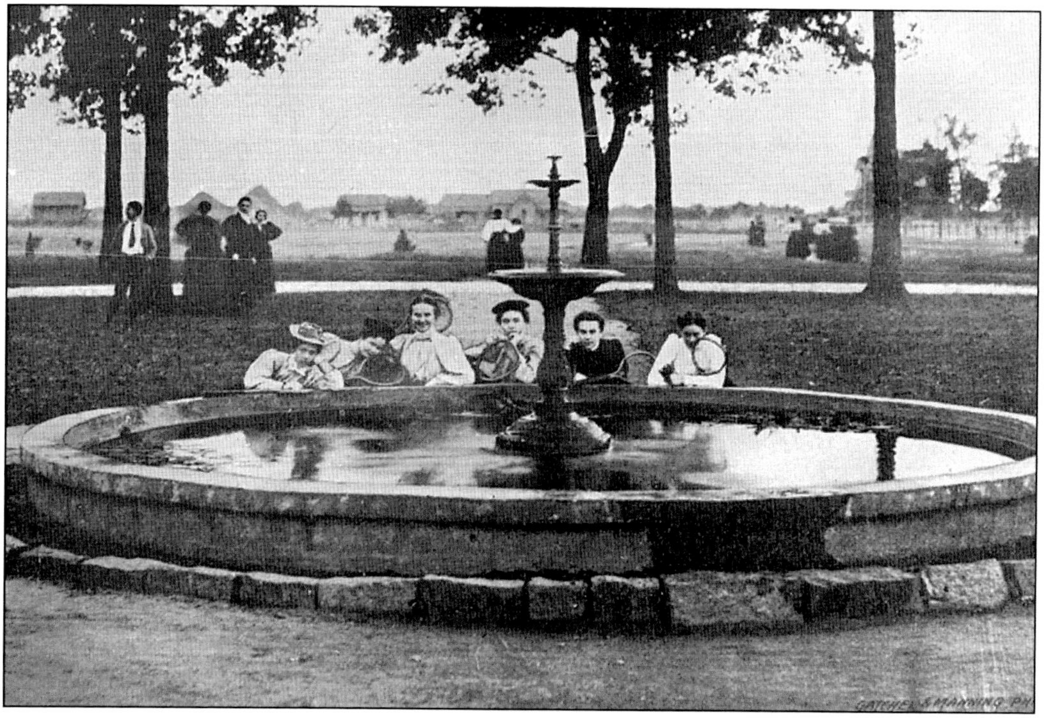

STUDENTS IN FRONT OF THE COLLEGE FOUNTAIN SOON AFTER WINTHROP'S MOVE TO ROCK HILL *Notice the area in the background where Dinkins now stands.*

College for Women. The corner stone bears the first name.

On the afternoon of October 14, the long train from Columbia pulled out crowded with young women both from the upper part of the state and the lower as well as those from the central part. There were the juniors and seniors who had been attending the Winthrop that had been in Columbia. There were freshman from high schools, and sophomores from colleges elsewhere—a merry, expectant throng. New experiences in a new college with a new faculty awaited them. The governor of the state and several members of the Board of Trustees, together with notables, were aboard that train. It was a gala occasion for which we were bound.

There was the singing of popular songs. There were groups, each with a leader, giving college yells as onward we sped during that beautiful October afternoon. At last we heard the conductor announce "Rock Hill." There was quite a crowd of interested citizens at the station. Always ready to serve the college, many of them were there in their carriages and buggies to aid in getting students, faculty, and friends out to the college. There, too, was the street car, drawn by Lec and Tric (two mules) driven by that well-remembered Calvin. The train pulled out to the back campus, however to aid in getting everyone who was Winthrop bound to her destination. The changing were still camped there. Mr. R.B. Cunningham, the business manager, who served the institution so efficiently for many years, was at the back gate with Dr. Kinard to aid everyone in getting up to the one dormitory, now known as Margaret Nance Hall, named for President Johnson's mother. There were only three buildings there in 1895—the Main, or Administration Building, this one residence hall, and the power house and laundry combined.

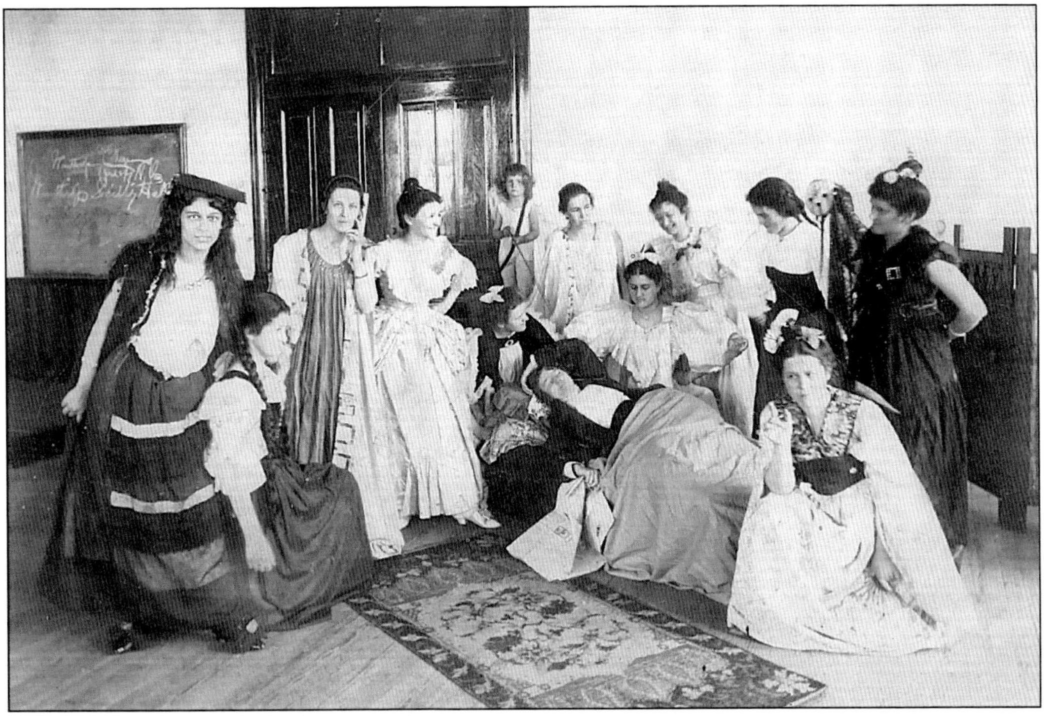

Students from the Class of 1899 *This photo was titled "Reveries of a Bachelorette Winthrop."*

The dining room and kitchen were in the basement of the Main Building.

There was no such thing as an infirmary there then. That fall we had an outbreak of measles, there was a light epidemic of small-pox in the state and numbers of our students were vaccinated and quite sick because of this, so certain rooms on the first floor of the west wing of the dormitory were set aside for students who were sick.

That first night, shortly after we arrived and were greeted by the kindly gray-haired hostess, Mrs. Simpson, a sister of Hon. B.R. Tillman, an electric storm arose, the lights went out and there was confusion confounded for a short while. The electrician soon had the lights on and everything quieted down, and we all went down for supper in the dining room presided over by the most capable, lovable person, Mrs. Ada B. O'Bryan.

The tables in the dining room each seated twenty persons. A teacher was at an early date assigned to each table, and students took turns in waiting on these tables.

The opening day, October 15, was bright and clear, the program was very interesting, and the auditorium was well-filled with the townspeople and friends. The students marched in as did the faculty. When this program was over the classifying of students took place and college classes began.

The students each evening observed study hours, and there was a teacher on duty each week to make sure this study period was worthwhile. In those days students had to be chaperoned. If they wished to do down town, a teacher must go with them, so teachers and students had their lives regimented to a certain extent.

The first Sunday we were in Rock Hill President Johnson and Miss Russell led the line to church—not a "blue line," however,

APPLICATION FOR ADMISSION TO THE WINTHROP NORMAL AND INDUSTRIAL COLLEGE.

Date ....

Name in full ....

Post Office ....

County in which you live ....

Date of birth ....

Name of parent or guardian ....

Do you intend to become a teacher ....

If not, what is your main purpose in desiring to attend this institution? ....

....

What school did you last attend? ....

What did you study during your last term at school, and what grade or class were you in? ....

Do you wish to enter as a tuition paying student? If not a certificate of inability to pay tuition must accompany this application. A blank form for this certificate will be furnished by the President when desired ....

If admitted to this College, do you promise to be an earnest, diligent and obedient student, and conform to its regulations and usages while here? ....

Are you in sound health? ....

How long do you expect to remain a student in the institution? ....

.... *Name.*

Please fill in the foregoing blank.

All must pay tuition who are able to do so. In order to secure free tuition the parent or guardian must file with PRESIDENT JOHNSON a statement of inability to pay, certified to as correct by he County Auditor. A blank form for this statement will be furnished by the President when desired. Only residents of the State are given free tuition.

There are places in the dormitory for 450 students. These will be assigned in the order of the applications; first, to former students; second, to new scholarship students; and third, to other new students. Up to thirty days before the opening of school preference will be given to applicants from South Carolina in the dormitory rooms; afterwards those applying will be accommodated according to the dates of their applications and the facilities on hand, without reference to their place of residence.

The expenses of the non-tuition-paying students in the dormitory will be \$95.00; the expenses of non-tuition-paying students boarding in private families will vary from \$105 to \$120. By adding \$40, which is the tuition for the year, to the above amounts, the expenses of any one who pays tuition can be readily ascertained. When places are assigned in the dormitory they are for the full nine months, and not for a portion of the year. Students will not be allowed to board out of the dormitory except with close relatives, and then only by special permission of the President.

Even if you have already made application in some other way, or attended Winthrop College last session, the President would like for you to fill out this blank application, in order that there may be no misunderstanding or confusion.

There is no place at the College for the idle or frivolous. Only those are wanted, or will be allowed to remain, who are willing to do earnest, conscientious, hard work, and will comply faithfully and cheerfully with the rules of the College. There are so many good students who want the places here that we do not wish them to be crowded out by those who regard their opportunities lightly.

The Winthrop Normal and Industrial College is open to girls who are not less than fifteen years of age, of good moral character and sound physical health. No pupil will be admitted who has not already a good knowledge of the ordinary branches of an English education, viz., Arithmetic, Grammar, Geography and History.

☞ If you have never attended this institution, write President Johnson a letter stating your advancement in your studies and where you have been educated. Send him also a statement from your last teacher as to your deportment, scholarship and habits of study.

The President will be glad to have letters from former students concerning their work next session. Send this application in a sealed envelope to

D. B. JOHNSON, President,
Rock Hill, S. C.

APPLICATION FORM USED BY WINTHROP IN THE LATE 1890S

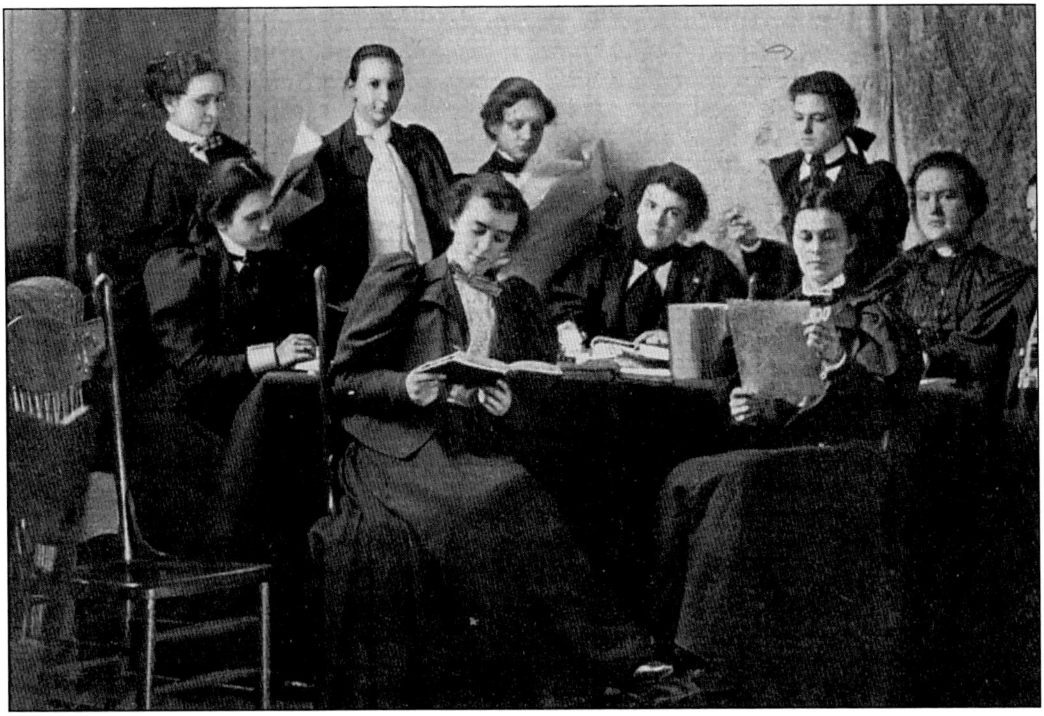

THE EDITORIAL STAFF OF THE FIRST ANNUAL *TATLER*

for the students had not received their uniforms; in fact, did not receive them until almost Christmas, if memory serves right. At last they arrived—very stylish, navy blue broad cloth suits, leg o'mutton sleeves, tight basques, long skirts, with brush braid, sweeping the streets. Each student had a blue sailor hat. And thus Winthrop College opened and began her marvelous service to the state of South Carolina.

HISTORY OF THE CLASS OF 1898. *This poignant essay was written by students of Winthrop's senior class of 1898. It appeared in the very first issue of* The Tattler, *the student yearbook.*

On the 15th day of October, 1895, the doors of Winthrop were thrown wide open to receive the fair daughters of South Carolina.

Fifty enthusiastic girls were enrolled in the Sophomore class. Some of these who still brighten the halls are pursuing special studies; others have chosen their field of labor. Out of this large number only five have been fortunate enough to be a part of the class of '98.

It is not an unusual spectacle to see this almost inseparable group in the various parts of the building.

However it is not my purpose to dwell upon the characteristics of my classmates, but to recall some of the happy events which we have enjoyed together during our college life.

The first year at Winthrop will ever be held by this class as a peculiarly pleasant one. In the month of November we had a delightful trip to Atlanta. To say we enjoyed the visit would not fully express it, for who would not have been overwhelmed with the pleasures provided by our wise President, and the sight of all our brothers and cousins from the different colleges of the State.

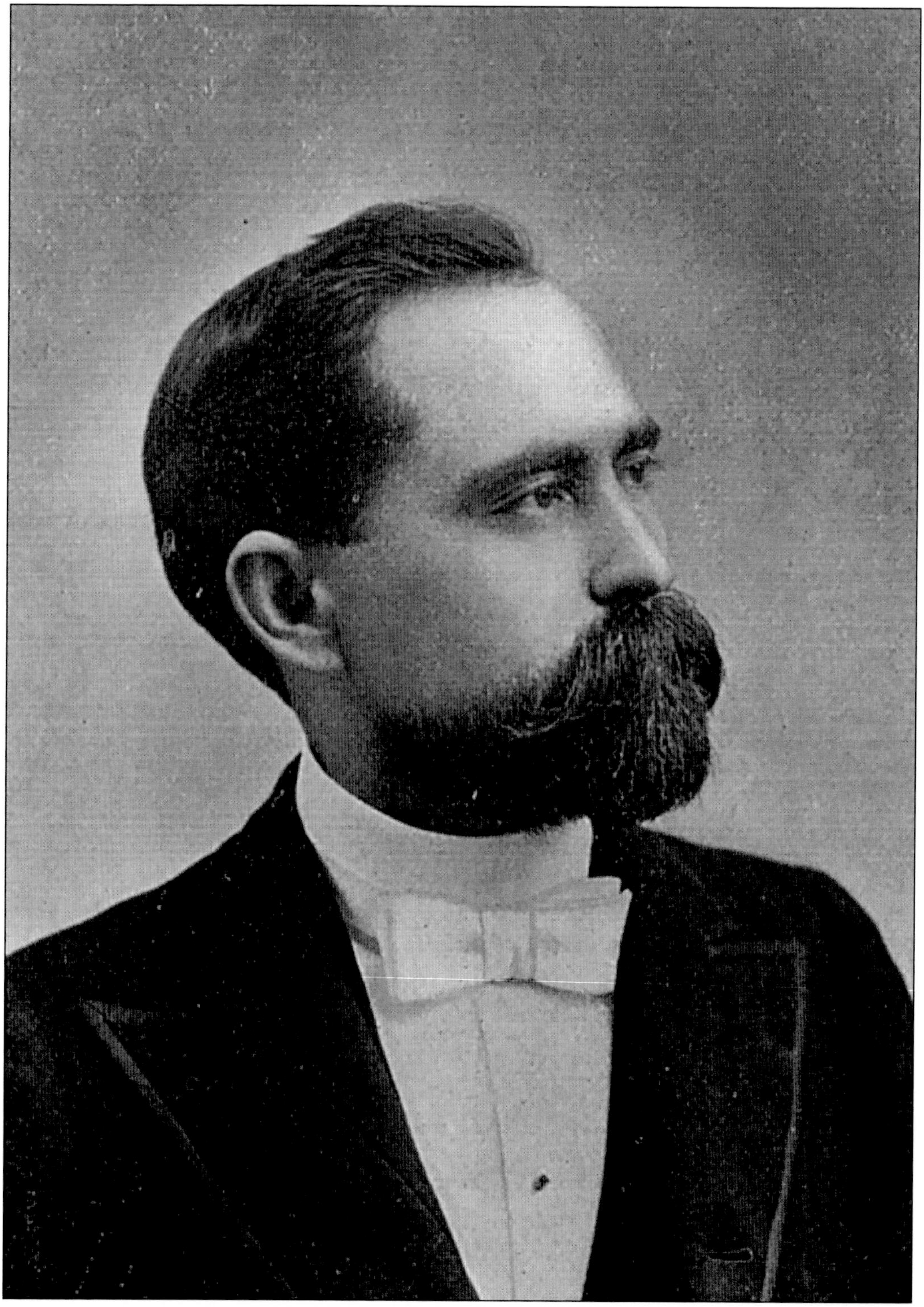

PRESIDENT JOHNSON

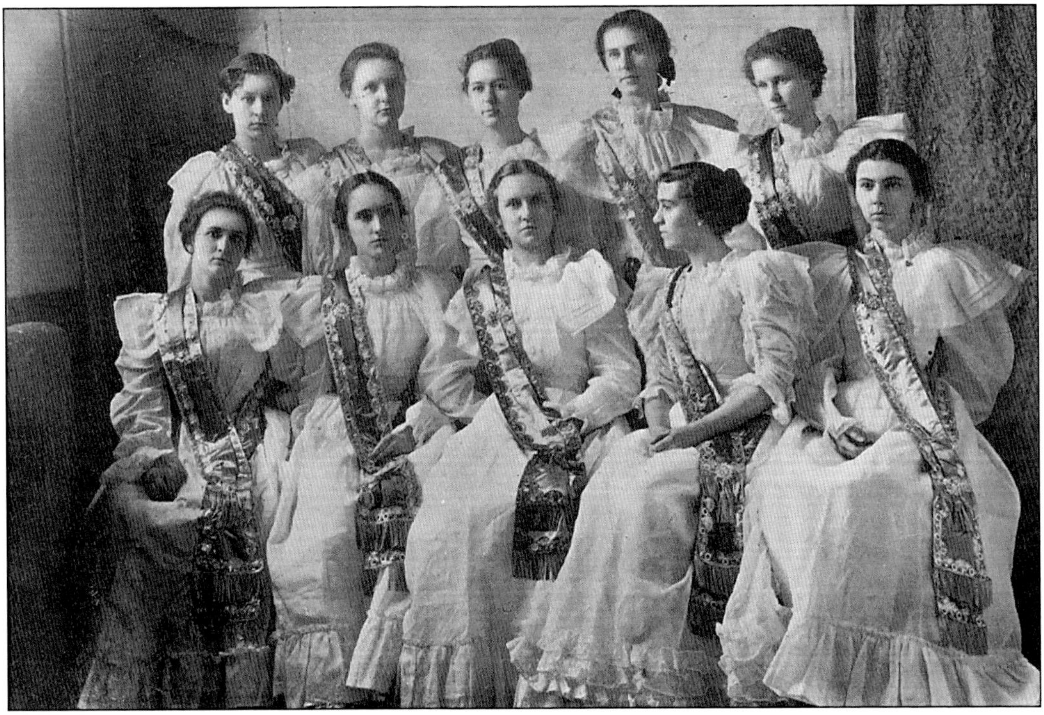

College marshals, 1898

The first of April was a memorable day. The members of the faculty can never forget their experiences, nor can the dedicated expressions of faces fade from the memory of the girls. Who could forget the forlorn appearance of Dr. —-, dreamily looking out his window, his door roped by the Seniors, who had just deserted. But, girls, we had to give up when we attacked another professor. Oh! How he did pour the water through the transom upon some who thought they would escape a problem in Math. Just one day.

We were refreshed during our spring term by a day in the balmy air of the lofty mountains of North Carolina. The mountaineers, although expecting a body of girls, were greatly astonished when the train stopped and about four hundred girls in blue were let down in their midst.

The first commencement was attended by a large concourse of people from all parts of the State. Rock Hill put on her holiday attire, and, with the jingling of the street car bells, her quiet suburb was in a bustle and stir for several days.

The opening of the second session brought to our ranks many recruits, who were heartily welcomed, and made to feel at home in our class.

If a casual visitor should happen to see a Junior ascending the stairs with checked apron and note book, he would almost probably think she belonged to the cookery department. But no, she is winding her way to the laboratory to make chemical experiments. Never shall we forget those implicit directions. At first we saw no immediate danger in such simple tests, but we were soon convinced that we could no longer risk our lives in experimenting alone, so had to leave that to our wise teacher.

The most interesting feature of the year was the "Star Course," a series of entertainments. They were looked forward to with great pleasure, especially when we

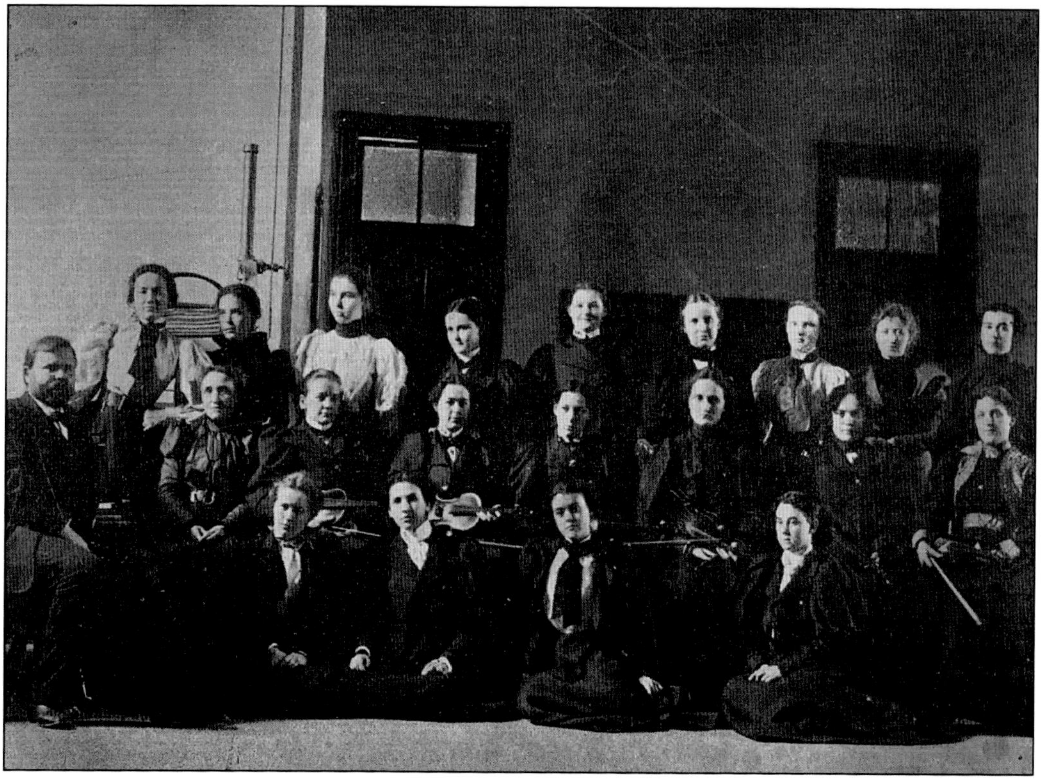

The College Choir, 1897–1898

were permitted to receive our friends.

One delightful night, a few weeks before the close of school, if you had peeped in you might have seen an interesting crowd of about seventy-five young ladies. Why such an assembly? The Juniors were receiving the Seniors, Post-Graduates and our President in honor of the Seniors. We had looked forward with pleasure to this happy event for several weeks, for we felt highly honored to have with us such distinguished guests.

When the bell announced to the students that the third year of Winthrop was about to open, there were thirteen Seniors found in their allotted places. Before the first term had ended we were saddened by the departure of one from our small number on account of sickness.

Can you realize, my dear classmates, the swiftness with which this year has passed? It seems only yesterday that it was announced we should go to Astronomy "Thursday morning at nine-forty-five." How we enjoyed those recitations, especially when Prof. B. showed us plates illustrating the different heavenly bodies. Every one felt, when she finished the course, that she was a mere speck in this great universe. Still we gained much in the knowledge of the order and system of God's works.

We appreciate the honor bestowed upon us by the Junior class in the delightful reception given to us. And we wish that their brightest anticipations may be realized in their Senior year.

The Night We Turkey Trotted in Old North. *Christine South Gee (Class of 1903) presents a witty account of a student escapade at the turn of the century. Mrs. Gee later served as a Winthrop Board of*

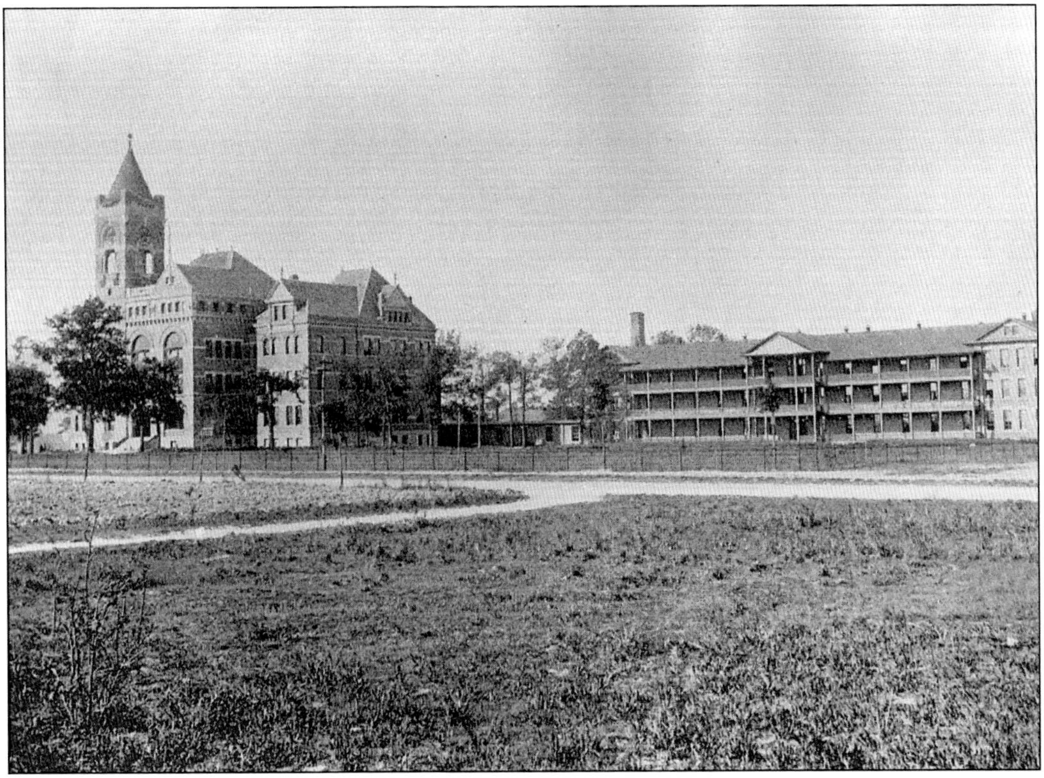

OLD NORTH (LATER MARGARET NANCE HALL) TO THE RIGHT OF TILLMAN IN THE LATE 1900s

Trustees member from 1944 to 1962 and received Winthrop's first honorary degree in 1966.

The campus was surely deserted during those last days of the Christmas holidays. Oh, no—Debe [nickname for President D.B. Johnson] couldn't bear to be separated from his children at Christmas time. The State Legislature—along about 1901-1902—prodded by impatient parents decided to return the Winthrop girl to her home at Christmas.

It was the last day of the year—the very last day of the nineteenth century. Young blood pinned up all the week on the Winthrop campus had to have an outlet. To those young things the coming of the new century meant the fulfillment of all their dreams. It must be celebrated by an adventure. An adventure to us was doing anything forbidden—our lives were so hedged about by rules and regulations. These rules were not resented. In the bottoms of our hearts we loved them—they were security and protection. But the new century was coming—there must be some fun.

In the brain of a senior on senior hall (back corridor of second floor of Margaret Nance) was born the idea of a "turkey trot" at midnight. It was a serious offense to be out of our rooms after 10 o'clock. But then we would never live to see another century come in—we must live while there was time.

Three minutes before midnight the two seniors living nearest the corner Assembly Hall, each completely draped in a sheet, quietly left their room, were joined by the two across the hall, then by the ones living next door, and the next, and the next.

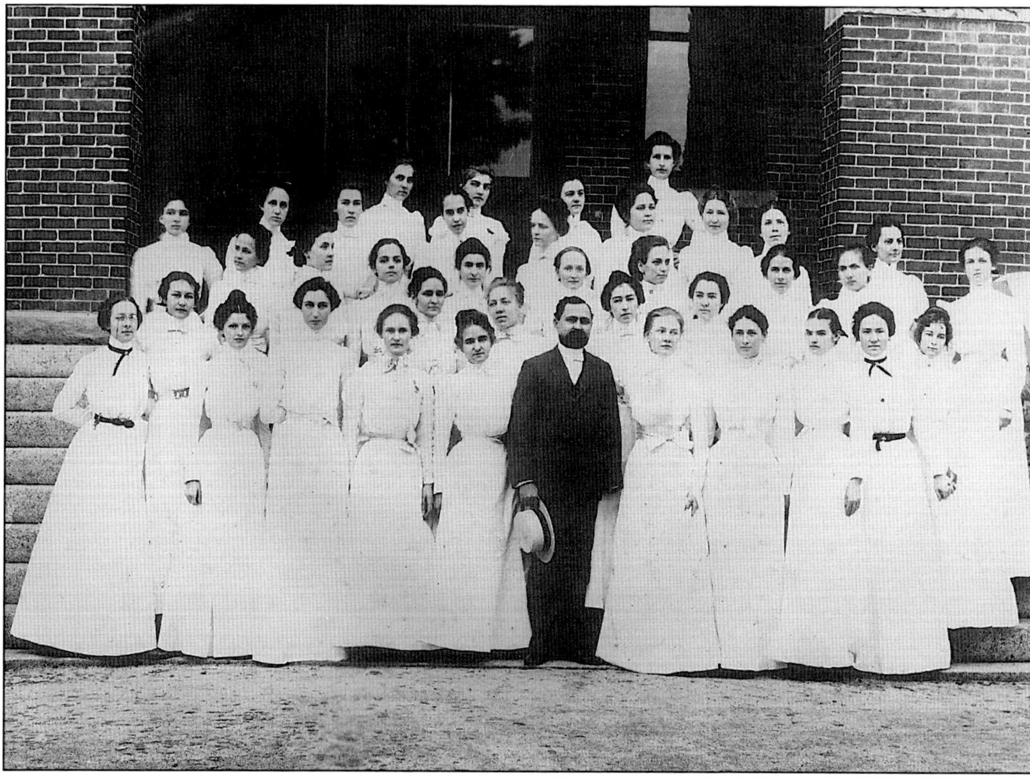

The graduating class of 1900

They trotted on tiptoes, turkey fashion, toward the bathrooms, up the stairs to third floor, down the stairs to second floor front corridor—being joined as they progressed by other adventurous souls all draped in white until the party numbered about fifty. The group of white-sheeted figures avoided the first floor—Mrs. Cochran, the matron, lived there. In a few moments the clock in Assembly Hall struck twelve. On we trotted. Soon Mrs. Barron, the night matron, came in sight. We trotted a little faster. Mrs. Barron had a little rheumatism. We knew we could outtrot her—Mrs. Barron soon knew it, too. She was seen to knock on the door of the teacher on duty. Now the trotters knew it was time to cease trotting because two people could head us off. Word went down the line to run for cover. All of us got back to our respective rooms except two seniors.

New Year's Morning, 1900, dawned bright and clear. We went to breakfast. There was tension in the air. Already it seemed to be known that Mrs. Cochran was very much agitated over this dreadful thing that had happened. All discipline had broken down—a large group of girls draped sheets through the halls at midnight. If that could happen at Winthrop, anything could. Two seniors had been caught. There was consternation in the hearts of all the trotters. We knew we could not let the seniors suffer alone.

Chapel time—8:45—came. We went with heavy hearts. Our beloved "Debe" would scold and say we had betrayed his trust in us. But, no, he evidently did not know yet. For he was saying he was going to give us a holiday because it was the first day of a new century! But somehow there were about fifty girls in that group in Main Building auditorium who could not be very happy. We knew that as soon as Mrs. Cochran could

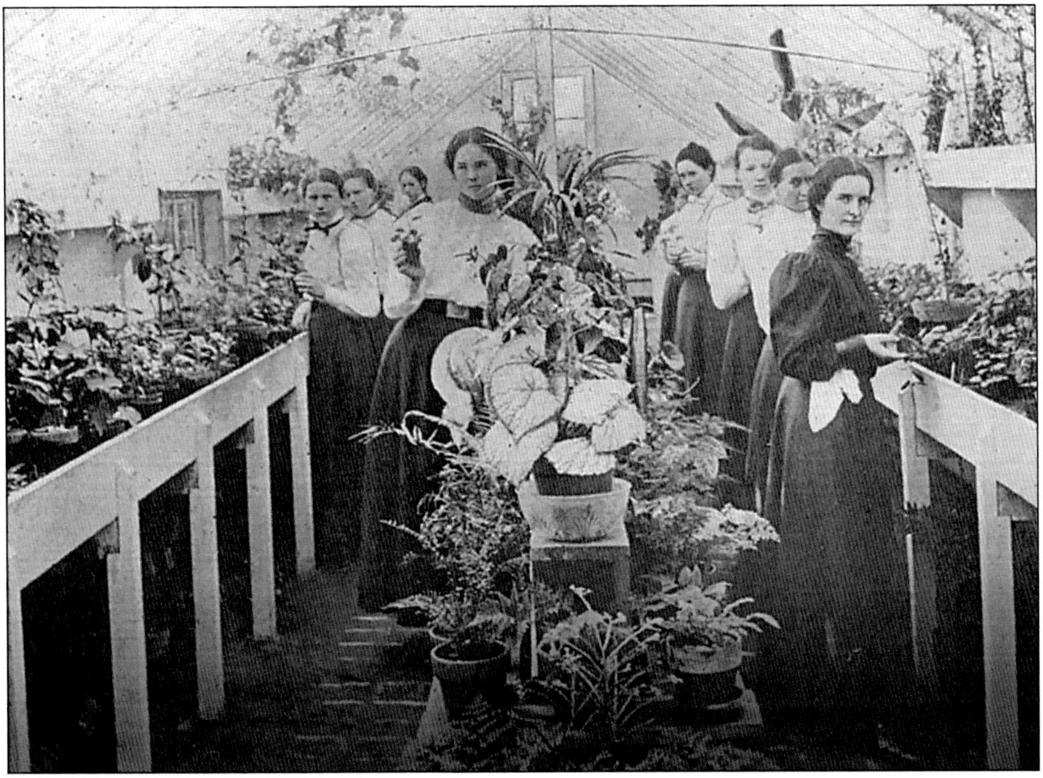

The Propagation House at the turn of the 20th century

get "Debe's" ear, he would have the names of those two seniors. What could we do?

We were not long in working out a solution. We would have a mock faculty meeting on the stage in the Main Building auditorium that night, disclose the names of all participants, sentence them to restrictions to this "forty-acre campus" for a period to be determined by "Debe" himself.

Invitations were issued to Dr. Johnson, all the faculty, and all the students to be present in the auditorium at 7 p.m. Each of the participants in the turkey trot was assigned a faculty member or officer to represent. She was to make herself look like that person, in most instances in borrowed clothes from the person we were impersonating. Ansie Holman, who represented "Debe," borrowed the big overcoat with a cape that he always wore. Mabel Moorer had herself look exactly like Mrs. Cochran and was therefore furnished with a list of all the turkey trotters. I represented Miss Wolf, the physical education teacher.

The faculty caught wind of what was going on and entered into the spirit of the occasion. Many of them borrowed uniforms from the college girls and came into the auditorium with their arms around each other, college girl fashion. It is said that Dr. Johnson went up into the unlighted gallery where he could watch what was going on without himself being seen.

"Debe" presided at the mock trial. "Mrs. Cochran" presented her charges of a breakdown in dormitory discipline and recommended that each participant be restricted to the campus for one month. The recommendation was accepted by the "faculty," passed on to "Dr. Johnson."

The meeting adjourned. Nothing more

56 WINTHROP NORMAL AND INDUSTRIAL COLLEGE.

Rock Hill.

Rock Hill is situated in the upper part of South Carolina, near the foot hills of the Blue Ridge Mountains; has fine water, a pure and bracing atmosphere and a healthful climate, and on account of its railroad connections is easy of access from all parts of the State. It is on the main line of the great through route of travel from New York to Florida, the Southern Railway, at the highest point between Charlotte and Augusta. It has Methodist, Presbyterian, Baptist and Episcopal churches, an excellent system of public schools and fine society.

The people are energetic and public-spirited, and are noted for the way in which they work together for the success of all their public enterprises. It already has a population of about 5,000, and with all of its natural advantages of climate, water and geographical position, and with the public spirit and sentiment of its citizens, and with this great educational institution for girls within its borders, secured by its pluck and faith in itself, it is destined speedily to become one of the most important cities of this commonwealth.

It is at the intersection of the Charlotte and Columbia branch of the Southern Railway and the Three C's Road, and may be easily reached from any part of the State by the many connections of these two roads.

A description of Rock Hill in 1895 from the college catalogue

was ever heard of the turkey trot.

The Reminiscences of Ida Jane Dacus. *Ida Jane Dacus (Class of 1898) was the first head librarian of the Winthrop University Library, serving from 1900 to 1945, and the first certified librarian in South Carolina. On October 16, 1969, the Dacus Library was dedicated in her honor. This reminiscence was written on October 14, 1962.*

I am thinking tonight of things that happened at the end of the last century. Just Reminiscing.

It was as the close of the century—to be perfectly exact, the fall of 1895, at the time when Dr. D.B. Johnson's dream and vision became a reality. Dr. Johnson had long felt the need and importance of educating young South Carolina women—Clemson College had been opened for the education of the boys of South Carolina. Mr. Robert C. Winthrop, president of the Peabody Educational Fund, lent a helping hand. He made small donations and the school, located in Columbia, was named for him.

After urgent appeals by Dr. Johnson, assisted by Governor Tillman, the college in 1891 became an institution of the State. In 1895 it was moved to Rock Hill and the State legislature appropriated money for the construction of two substantial buildings, the present Main Building and North dormitory. Both are still used.

About two hundred and fifty girls made up the first freshman class of the new college at Rock Hill, named Winthrop. To the honor and credit of the trustees, the name "Winthrop" has always clung to the college.

Governor Tillman's sister, a Mrs. Simpson, assisted President Johnson in the care of his two hundred and fifty young innocents. She had a room in the center of the dormitory. The President had a room just opposite hers. I can see Mrs. Simpson now in my imagination. Her hair fell in ringlets almost to her shoulders. She was as straight as a stretched string. She was a most commanding figure, in voice and manner. Her voice needed only to be heard to be obeyed.

She seemed to thrive on caring for the two hundred and fifty young innocents—not so our beloved young bachelor President. He became very nervous and had to go to a hospital for six weeks' treatment. He was not allowed to see a woman, speak to a woman, hear a woman speak, nor even to hear the rustle of a feminine skirt. He came back to us a wiser man. He realized that the ways of woman are hard to understand, and at times most trying on the nerves. He did not live in the dormitory any more.

I have dreamed entirely away from my first thought—early dormitory life at Winthrop.

The tale that I am thinking about happened one cold stormy night. It was a few months after the opening of the college. A storm had put out all lights, on the grounds and in the buildings. It was a black night everywhere. The midnight hour was approaching. The thunder roared. The lightning flashed. Above the noise of the storm a girl's voice was heard. She loudly screamed, "A man is in the house."

Footsteps were heard, racing up and down the halls, from one floor to another, and back again. Girls were frightened terribly. Pandemonium reigned. Just at this time dear Mrs. Simpson rushed out. Her voice calling loudly, "Come to me girls, " was heard above the howling of the wind, the screaming girls, and the patter of the feet of the supposed man, running up and down the halls. Just at this time our beloved President appeared on the scene in his long nightshirt—which although stylish at the time was not a pretty garment. Mrs. Simpson cast her eyes on him, and shrieked, "Man, get back to your room. You are enough to scare the devil to say nothing of these girls, already scared nearly to death." This is one time our dear bachelor President obeyed orders.

Footsteps continued to be heard—pitter-patter, pitter-patter—man or beast—as he,

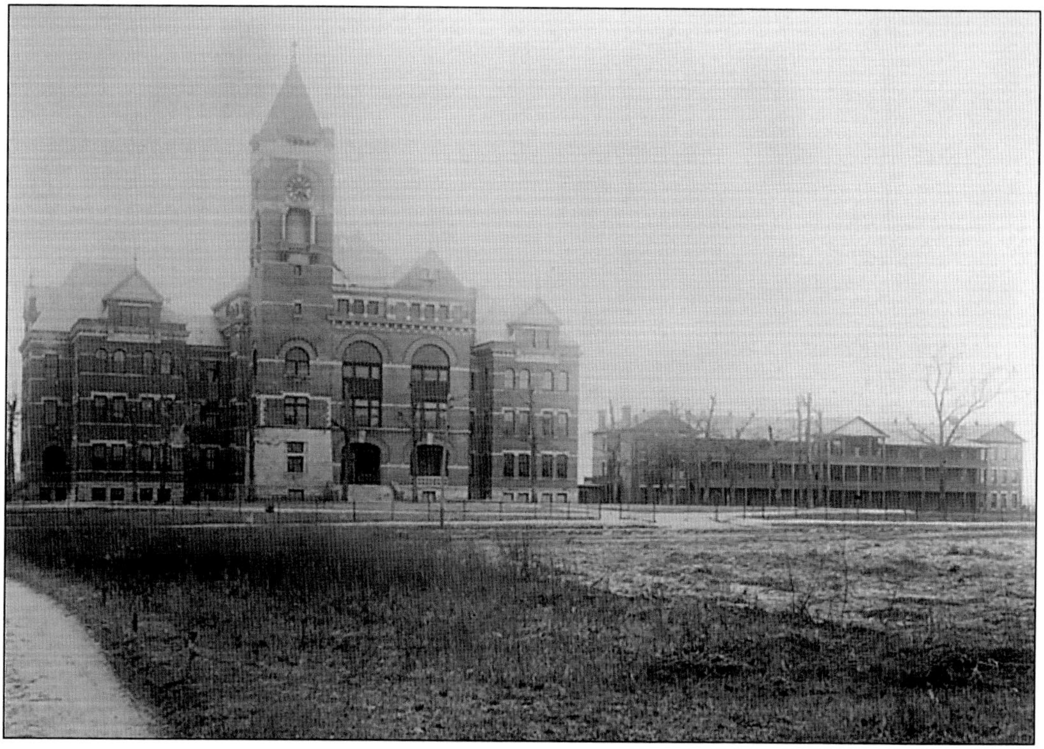

A FASCINATING VIEW OF ALL THAT WAS WINTHROP SOON AFTER ITS MOVE TO ROCK HILL

she or it raced up and down the halls, more frightened if possible than the scared to death girls. They gathered around Mrs. Simpson at her command.

Suddenly the storm was over. The lights came on. There was a lunge and a plunge through an open window; into the flower beds just underneath. Were there any tracks in the flower bed next morning? Yes, but the tracks were not a man's tracks.

It is now after nine o'clock. My big dog, Yum-Yum, is asleep at my feet. It is my sleeping time too—I will stop reminiscing and begin to sleep and dream.

I have had a good time. I will say good night with a prayer that our dear Heavenly Father will continue to bless Winthrop and all that love her.

Reminiscent, but factually true. Witnessed and told by a member of the first freshman class at Winthrop, who wished that you may live to be eighty-seven years old, and will be as well and as happy as she is tonight.

THE STORY OF WINTHROP. *"The Story of Winthrop" was first published in the 1907 edition of* The Tatler, *the Winthrop yearbook. The editor of the 1920* Tatler *thought it "too good a thing to be buried in the Archives of the past," and obtained Miss Minnie McFeat's permission to republish the article. Miss McFeat was instrumental in establishing the first preschool at Winthrop. Winthrop's first preschool was offered in 1900, the year the college's kindergarten opened under Miss Mcfeat's direction. The Mcfeat Nursery was later renamed in her honor.*

Brilliant midsummer sun was shining down upon a typical New England farmhouse which stood stiff and sternly erect as a Puritan should, to meet the darts of the Heavenly Archer. To one side stretched the

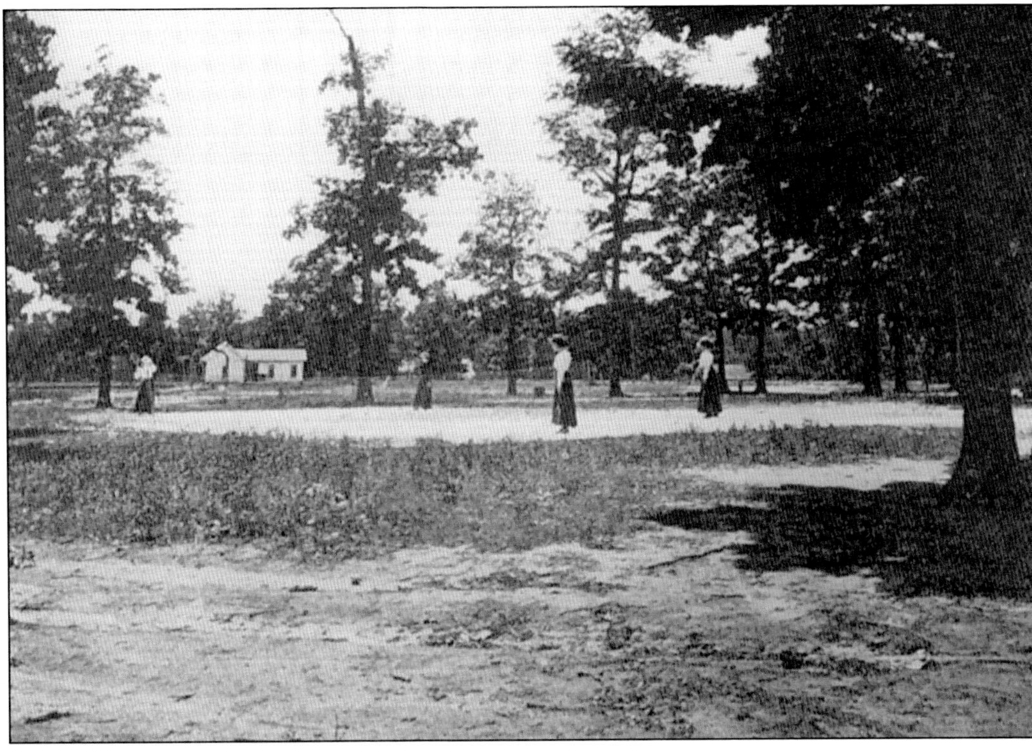

A rare view of Winthrop students playing tennis at the turn of the 20th century

cranberry patch. Up and down the rows, filling her pail with the tempting red fruit, a woman passed to and fro. The swish of her garments, the rustle of the bushes, the tinkle of the berries as they fell into the pail, were the only sounds that disturbed the noonday stillness. There was nothing to indicate that this day was to be unlike the days that had proceeded it—that it was to be the birthday of a new life that was to affect most powerfully the old life of a faraway Southern State.

The sun shone hotter and hotter, the berries fell faster and faster into the pail. The stillness was broken by another sound, the sound of horses' feet, as a carriage came swiftly into view and paused in front of the house. A stranger dismounted, walked with quick, determined steps to the door, lifted the knocker, and waited. He was a man with a mission. An idea had taken possession of him. You saw it in his eye. You read it in his walk. You felt its presence even though you did not know its name. In a few moments the door opened; he gave his card to the servant and was ushered into the dim, quiet parlor to wait. The servant walked swiftly to the cranberry patch and handed the card to the picker of the fruit, who read aloud in her surprise, "D.B. Johnson, Columbia, South Carolina." What can a gentleman from South Carolina want with me? Giving her pail to the servant, she hurried to the house. The gentleman from South Carolina arose to meet her as she entered the dimly lighted parlor. The dreamer of a dream that had scarcely yet been dreamed, the Superintendent of a school that was to be, the President of a college that was yet unborn, looked into the eyes of the woman who was to be the first teacher of the visionary school, the teacher who could help to make such a school as he dreamed of a reality. Mr. D.B. Johnson and Miss Mary H. Leonard

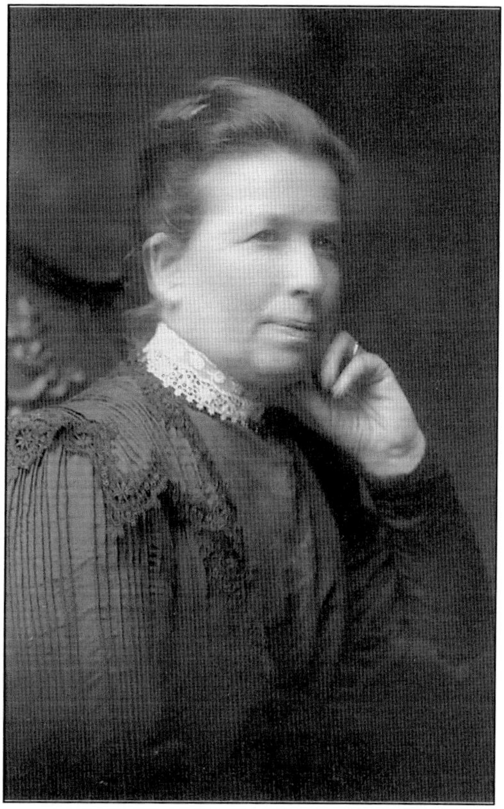

Mary Hall Leonard, Winthrop's first teacher

shook hands, and then he told her of his mission.

He had dreamed a dream, he had seen a vision, and he was seeking means to realize this vision, to make this dream come true. He had experienced a great need. As organizer and superintendent of a new system of schools in Columbia, S.C., the need had pressed heavily upon him—the need of trained teachers for his work. There was plenty of fine material going to waste in South Carolina. Some means for utilizing this material must be found. Filled with this idea, he had gone forth seeking aid. He had obtained a private interview with President Cleveland, a member of the Peabody Board. From Washington he had gone to Boston to see Robert C. Winthrop, the President of the Peabody Board. To him he unfolded all his plans and received immediately Mr. Winthrop's hearty endorsement and promise of assistance at the next meeting of the board. From Boston Mr. Johnson had gone to celebrated Bridgewater Normal to find a teacher for the new school. Miss Mary H. Leonard had been recommended and he had driven out to see her. After talking with Ms. Leonard, Mr. Johnson was convinced that he needed her services, and she on her part promised to give them should the visionary school materialize. It did and very rapidly. The following Fall saw some sixteen bright intelligent young women of Columbia in a modest little brick chapel belonging to the Theological seminary, reciting their first lesson to Miss Mary Hall Leonard, Mr. Johnson looking with proud delight, for his prophetic eye discerned clearly that this was the beginning of the end to which he looked forward.

Those sixteen young women were having a hard time of it. Blazing the way for others is never an easy task. So impressed were the Superintendent and the teacher that upon this pioneer work depended the realization of the vision, that they never let up for one minute in their requirements of those first raw recruits. For the next few years that training school became in very truth what one of its members had facetiously dubbed it, a "straining school"; it was pressing onward "toward its mark of higher calling," and it attained it. Witness its triumph in these very words, recorded in the Act of Legislature, which touched with its wand that little training school and turned it into the great Winthrop Normal and Industrial College.

"It being understood that this act is to effect an enlargement and continuation of the life of the Winthrop Training School for Teachers . . . and a recognition of the good work done by the school the past six years in training teachers of the common schools of the State."

O, ye sixteen of blessed memory, not in vain did you weep tears of anguish over "lesson-plans." Not in vain did you walk

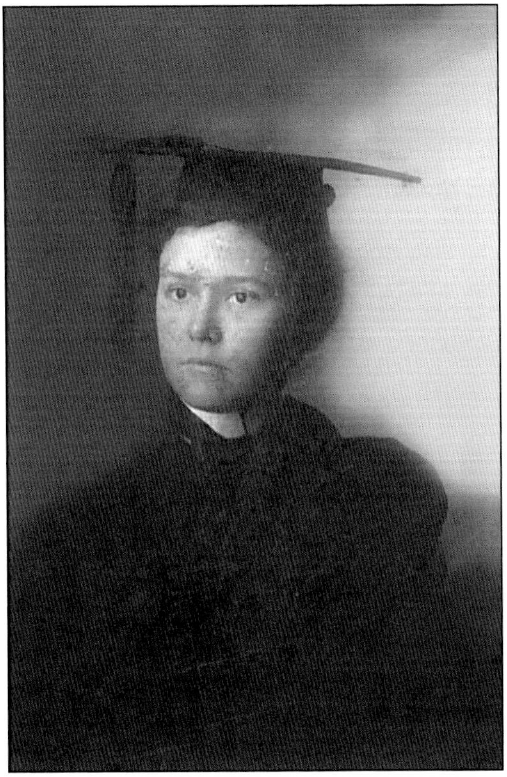

Tweedy Gardner as a senior at Winthrop in 1899 *She one of the thousands of graduates who went on to serve their state and country*

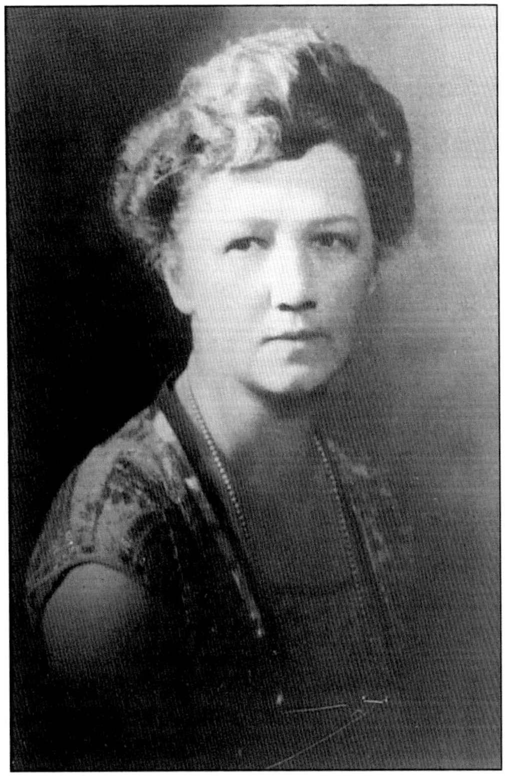

Mae Rutledge Smith, who later became Mrs. D.B. Johnson

the market-place seeking brains of sheep, or cow, or hog, you cared not which, for you dared not to go into the presence of Miss. Mary H. Leonard to give a lesson on brains without brains. Not in vain did you stand meekly in that presence to receive the criticism on that lesson given with or without brains. Not in vain were you torn to pieces so that there was not enough of you left to keep company with your sad thoughts. Your "lesson-plans" have lived in thousands and tens of thousands of "lesson-plans" wrung from reluctant students of the Winthrop of today. Your object-lessons, with or without brains, have been duplicated times without number in the institution which your good work has made possible. Never forget that the Winthrop Normal and Industrial College, wonderful as it is, great as it is and ever should be, is but the sequel for the story that you have helped to write, the story that was begun on the hot summer day when Mr. Johnson went forth in search of a teacher and found her in the cranberry patch. Students of the old Winthrop, and students of the new Winthrop as well, never forget that we owe a debt of gratitude to that splendid, magnetic, enthusiastic teacher, Miss Mary H. Leonard, who wrote so well her part of the story that neither time nor eternity can ever efface the writing.

There were other writers, too grand, inspiring teachers, such as Miss Annie E. Bonham and Miss Fanny C. McCants. And first, last, and all the time shall our hearts go out in dearest love and esteem to him whose

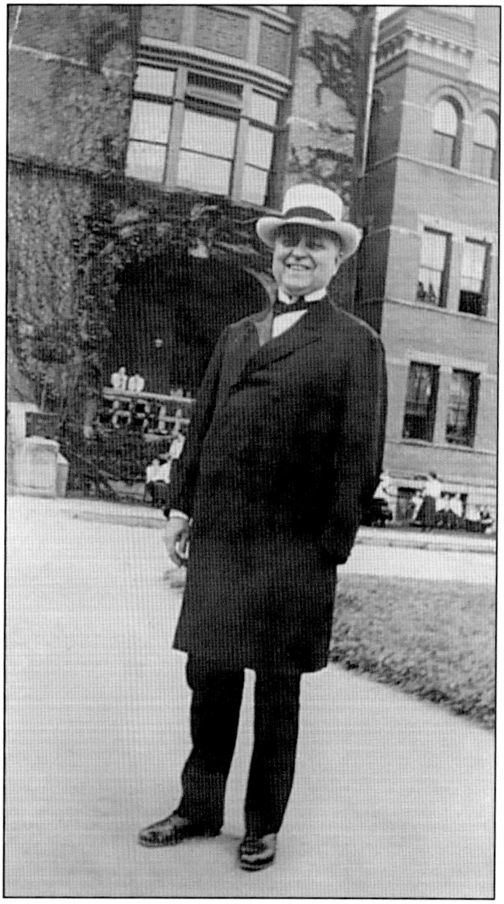

D.B. Johnson shortly before his death in 1928

hand penned the first lines, and who is still writing, for the story of Winthrop is not yet ended. "Great trees from little acorns grow." From the little acorn the Winthrop Training School, whose kernel contained so sweet and strong a life, has sprung a great tree like unto the great world-ash, Yggdrasill. Its roots have gone downward, reaching into the very hearty soil of South Carolina. Its head has pushed upward toward God's heaven. Its branches had pushed towards God's heaven. Its branches shall spread outward till they shadow with protecting love every home in South Carolina.

A Prayer for Dr. Johnson by Reverend Francis W. Gregg. *Winthrop founder and President David Bancroft Johnson died on December 26, 1928. Reverend Francis W. Gregg of the First Presbyterian Church in Rock Hill, along with the Reverend Alexander Martin of the Oakland Presbyterian Church, were in charge of Johnson's funeral service. Johnson was an elder in the Oakland Avenue Presbyterian Church.*

Almighty God, our heavenly Father, thy stately steppings have been our midst, and this great assembly gathered here from the utmost bounds of our state manifests the sense of loss which thy dispensation hath brought to the heart of our people.

We recognize thy sovereignty over all our lives. Our times are in thy hands. Thy love, and thy wisdom are behind all thy providences, and we bow in humble submission. With tear-dimmed eyes and sorrowing hearts we can look up to Thee and say, "Thy will, not ours, be done," for we know that thy will is best for all thy children.

We come to thank Thee for this great life thou hast given us. We thank Thee for the man he was possessing so many of the finest traits of noblest manhood: we thank Thee for his high ideals of service to his fellow men and to thy Kingdom: for his utter devotion to the task of living up to these ideals and of inculcating them in the hearts and lives of the people of our state through her young womanhood; and for that large measure of success which Thou didst grant him in this great endeavor which he had set for himself: we thank Thee for this institution with all its multiplied ministrations which stands here today as his monument.

Oh Lord, our God, we would remember before Thee today, for thy mercy and blessing, our state now bereft of his service and leadership: this institution that loses the touch of the hand that has guided since infancy to its present high place in our educational system: the Board of Trustees on whom will fall responsibilities

A Tribute

David Bancroft Johnson

David Bancroft Johnson was a friend on whose fidelity, justice, and kindness we could depend with securest faith. His life and his example have written in letters of gold the highest ideals of courage, of honesty, and of unselfish service. We whose lives he has touched throughout his long and useful years of earnest work have gained by that contact higher aims, nobler aspirations, and a more satisfying conception of the meaning of life. To have known him was a benediction. He was simple and sincere, straightforward and fearless, and above all, fair and sympathetic in all his dealings with us. We loved him and we trusted him.

There needs no monument of massive bronze, nor of Parian marble, to keep alive his memory. It is enshrined in the heart of hearts of every Winthrop daughter. Through all time we shall arise and bless his name. All that is mortal lies peacefully at rest on the Campus of our Alma Mater, the crowning work of a noble life; but his spirit will ever hover as a beneficient influence inspiring and guiding those who knew him and those who will carry on the work to which he gave his life.

THIS STUDENT TRIBUTE APPEARED IN THE 1928 *TATLER*

never had before: the faculty with its added responsibilities and new adjustments: the student body scattered for the holidays from seaboard to mountain crest, unable to be present; but whom mourn with us the passing of their beloved President who loved to speak of them as his "Daughters": that vast throng of his "Elder Daughters" who have passed out from these walls and encircles the globe serving God and man as he taught them to serve: his church in the loss of an officer who was exemplary in life and wise in council: this community to whose frequent calls for service and leadership he ever gladly and ably responded. For all these we pray that their grace may sustain in the hour of sorrow and loss and enable to carry on in the spirit of this noble life.

Most gracious Lord, we would commend to Thee that smaller circle of his dear loved ones to whom his going away means more than it can possibly mean to any others. Do thou bless them each one. Grant them thy help in every new problem they must face. Keep their feet in the way that leads to the Glory Land that for them all there may be in the meeting again in the Heavenly Home.

And now Lord, as we come to lay away from our sight his body—the tabernacle in which he dwelt while among us—worn out on the field of splendid service to which he utterly devoted it, not counting the cost; we thank thee for the sweet refreshing of thy Word to which we have just listened: for the assurance of life triumphant over death in Jesus Christ. We thank thee for the message that he lives today-more alive than ever before, and that in a new and more glorious body he shall live forevermore—we thank thee for the great and blessed hope of the meeting again.

Inspire us, we beseech thee with his visions and his ideals: fire us with his zeal and his courage: help us to emulate his life of unselfish service and to perpetuate its principles from generation to generation in the hearts of all our people: and for each of us may the dark shadows of this hour be lit up with the bright hope of the meeting again where shall be no more sickness, nor pain, nor parting; but only peace and joy and glorious fellowship forever.

And all this we ask in the name of Jesus Christ, our gracious Lord and Redeemer. Amen.

CHAPTER TWO

THE WINTHROP EXPERIENCE

YOUNG LADIES OF WINTHROP, BY D.B. JOHNSON. *This is the opening day address given by President D.B. Johnson in 1908. Johnson was fond of giving an opening address to students during his long tenure at Winthrop. Many of the speeches contained much of the same material, and they give insight the curriculum and student life at Winthrop.*

Young ladies: We meet together here this morning to formally begin the fourteenth session of Winthrop College at Rock Hill. I hope that you will help us to make it the best session in the history of the College. The results of the year's work will depend as much upon you as upon the Faculty. I earnestly trust that we are all here prepared in strength, and health and a spirit of determination to do all in our power to make the most of the opportunities that shall come to us during the coming school year.

If we would make Winthrop all it should be for the women of South Carolina, we must see to it that high ideals—that a high sense of honor obtains here. I am grateful to the Winthrop girls of previous sessions for the high standards of living and working set for the Winthrop student. I have often spoken of their loyalty and good behavior and fine spirit of earnestness and devotion to duty. I wish to be able to do this of you at the end of this session and confidently believe I shall be. I feel sure that you will maintain and advance, if possible, the standards set you. The way, however, to do right for the session is to begin right now—today. Come out and stand for the right from the beginning. It will give you strength to be right for the whole session. If you are a Christian, show your colors at once, so that no one may possibly think you otherwise. If you have not enjoyed a Christian life at home, I hope you may do so here through the influence of our Christian students organized as a

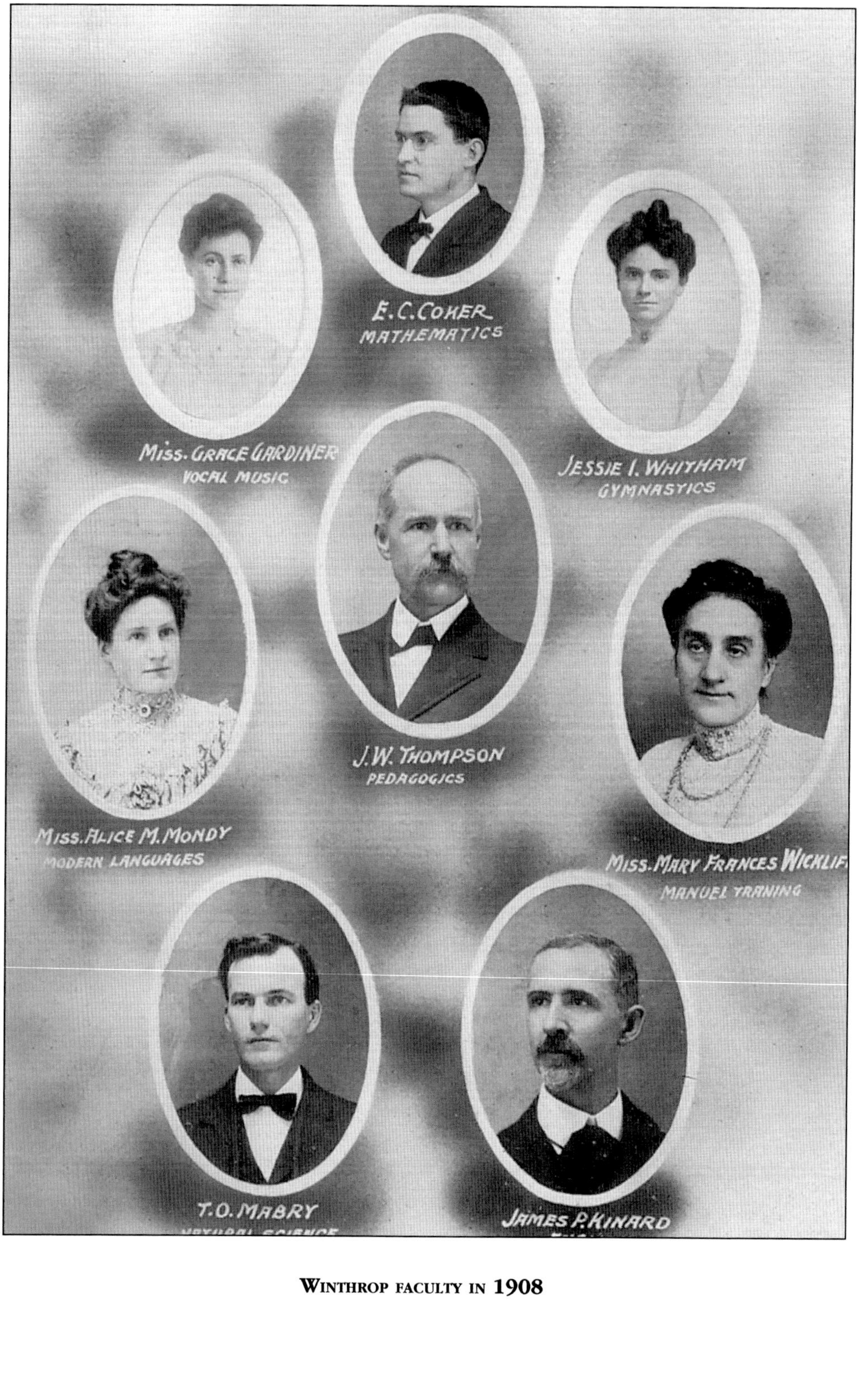

WINTHROP FACULTY IN 1908

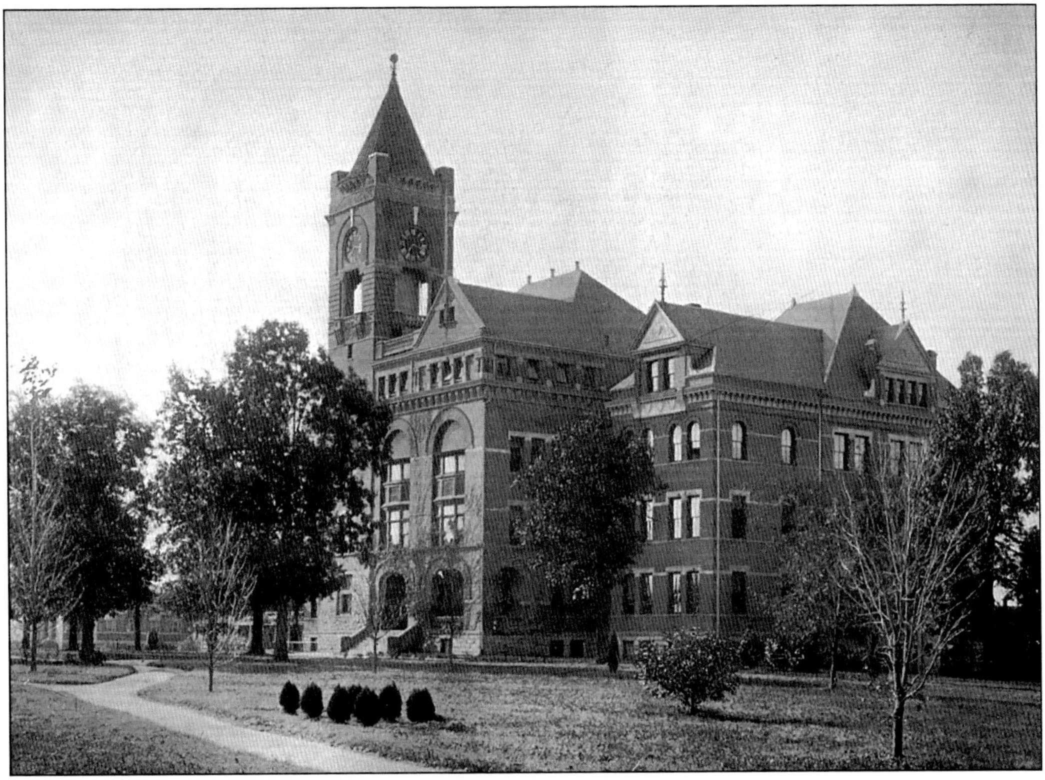

MAIN BUILDING, 1908

Y.W.C.A. for mutual help in Christian living and to extend the helping hand to others. Membership in the Association will be of great help to you in living up to the standards of a Christian home, and I hope you will cast your lot with the students of that organization without delay.

I hope that you will all find the College a pleasant, happy home for the coming nine months. Many of you—the old students—look upon Winthrop, I know, as a second home and the others will be made to feel at ease and at home speedily, I am sure, by the thoughtful kindness and considerate attention of us all, Faculty and old students.

I am sure that all of us are interested in seeing to it that Winthrop's reputation for the cordial reception of new students shall be maintained.

It will give me pleasure to serve you whenever I can. I shall expect you to come to me freely for advice and counsel and help. I want you to understand that I am deeply interested in each and every one of you personally as well as professionally, and am anxious that each one of you shall be happy here and shall do well in her studies and in every way.

Before taking up the detailed directions always given at this first meeting of the session, I am going to ask Dr. Alexander Martin, one of the pastors of the city, to say a few words to you.

You will find the rules of the school in the catalogue and on the cards tacked on your dormitory doors. You can read them in about twenty minutes, and it is your duty to do so. You cannot obey the rules without knowing what they are, and I take it that all earnest girls want to obey the rules of the school. I will not attempt to call attention to all of the rules here this morning. It may be helpful, however, to mention a few of our general requirements at this first meeting of our student body, in order that all may be able to begin right from the first day of school.

There must be quiet in the dormitories and main building during study hours. Pass quietly through halls and corridors.

Do not injure or deface school property of any kind: walls, books, desks, school furniture. Do not drive nails or tacks in the walls. I have had all the halls and rooms in the dormitories freshened up with whitewash and I hope you will keep them so. A student who will deliberately mark up the walls of a building ought not to be here. I expect much help in this matter from the Winthrop School Improvement Association.

The College grounds must not be left except by permission of the Matron in charge of the dormitory where you have your room, with whom you will file such requests.

Observe study hours carefully.

Be punctual at chapel, class, and meals. Prompt in reporting at opening of session—Rule 29. No one can come to college ahead of time and remain in town with friends without special permission.

Five minutes are given to pass from class to class.

You may study in one of two places during the day—the library or your dormitory room. Must be in one or other, however, no walking about or loitering in halls or on grounds.

We have tried to make a room on the Gymnasium floor comfortable as a study room for those living out in town.

All announcements for the bulletin board must be posted through Mrs. Davis, the President's Secretary.

Registration cards. Call attention to agreement.

You all come prepared, I am sure, to observe our requirements faithfully and cheerfully, according to voluntary pledges made by you before leaving home, and before admission here, and filed with me; and it will be a point of honor with you, I feel sure, to keep your pledges. I wish to depend upon your sense of honor and of right rather than anything else. It is impossible to provide a rule for every detail, and it is not desirable, even if it were possible.

Examinations for entrance for higher classes and to pass off conditions have all been held, according to the announcement in the catalogue and by postal card. There is nothing in the way now of immediate organization, and we hope that much time will be saved by our new arrangement for these examinations. It is taken for granted that those students who were not present for examination, to pass off conditions, at the time given for it, desired to go over the subjects again in class, and such students have been classified accordingly.

What are accredited schools. Read list in Catalogue.

Pupils are expecting to enter College on certificates from accredited schools. They must present a certificate, or statement from the head of the school, to the effect that the applicant has completed the course of nine grades and passed in subjects required for admission to our Freshman class.

Rules III & IV. p. 68 Catalogue.

Where the regular course of the accredited school has not been taken, admission to Freshman Class will be allowed only in those branches covered by certificates issued.

Students who were here last session and stood the county examination last July will be classified by the record here. This same rule applies to students from accredited schools.

Remember that you will be held responsible for all the work required in your course of

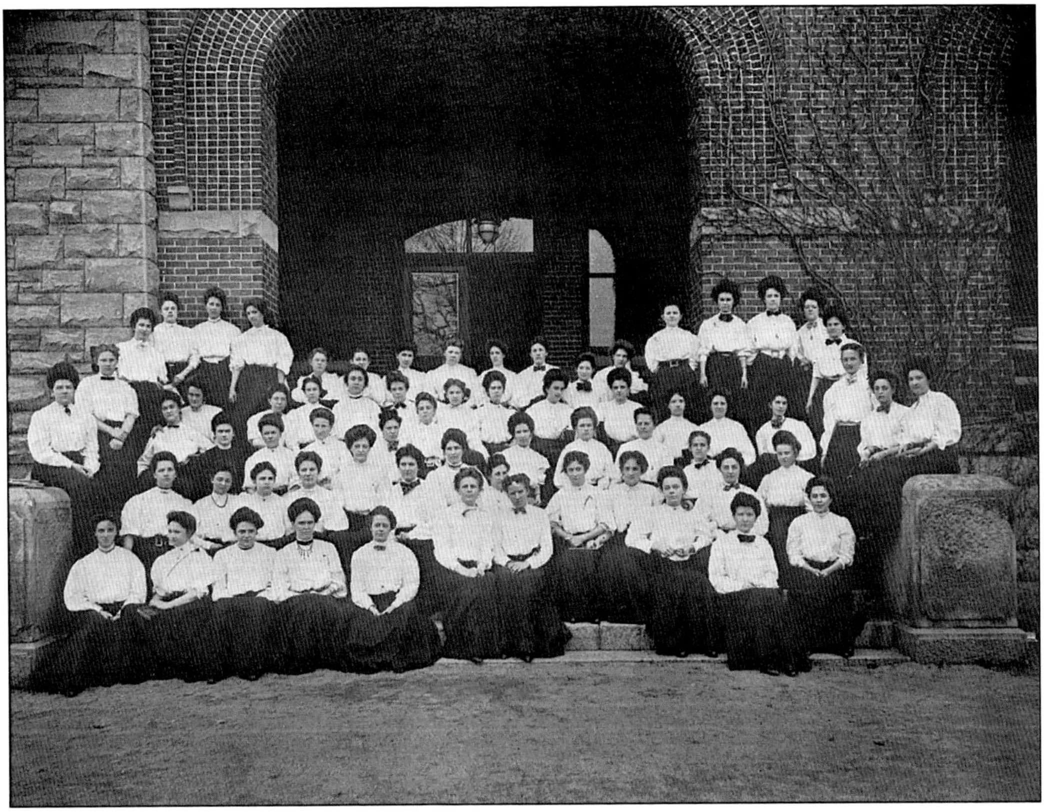

Senior Class, 1908

study. If, for any reason, you fail to take up a subject required, we will not accept an excuse that you were not reminded of it.

Before any one can be enrolled as a student, she must secure a receipt from Mr. Cunningham, the book-keeper, showing that she has paid all the College dues required.

I will be in my office this afternoon at 4 o'clock to confer with any one who may wish to see me about her course of study or any other matter. No one will change her course or any study without consulting me. The old pupils will please give way, for these first few days, to the new, as they have always so considerately done. The Committee on Entrance Examination and Classification will be in room 14 this afternoon to assist me in seeing students about their courses of study. A committee of Y.W.C.A. will be on hand in the main hall-way and at my office this afternoon, tomorrow, and probably Friday, and will be glad to give the new students any assistance or information in their power. They will be known by their badges, gold and white ribbon.

I am going to ask the new students who are full Freshmen to remain a few moments after the others are dismissed, and also all students, old or new, who expect to take the special stenography course, which requires an examination in English to enter the Sophomore class; the special dressmaking course, which requires the regular examination and also an examination in sewing; the special millinery course, the special book-keeping course, which requires an examination in mathematics to enter

Winthrop Normal
and
Industrial College
of South Carolina Rock Hill, S. C.

Pleasant and Healthful Location. ::: Pure Water

CAMPUS of forty-seven acres, unsurpassed Buildings and Equipment; Main Building (Offices and Class Rooms), Dormitory, Infirmary—all joined by covered ways. Excellent sanitary sewerage. Ventilation perfect. Hot and Cold Baths on every floor. Only two students placed in one room. Single beds.

Resident Woman Physician. Gymnasium, with trained Instructor. Library of New Books [additions over a thousand volumes yearly]. Able Faculty in all Departments. Religious life carefully guarded.

48 Officers, Teachers and Assistants

500 Students

Normal, Scientific and Literary Courses with Industrial Studies.

Graduates of the Normal Course will be granted, in addition to the degree, a Life License to teach in the Public Schools of the State.

Shorter Normal Courses are offered leading to Certificate [Life License to Teach] and to the Degree of L. I.

SPECIAL COURSES.—Stenography and Typewriting, Dressmaking, Millinery, Cooking, Bookkeeping. Either of these courses may be completed in one year, and is rewarded by a Certificate of Proficiency.

Thorough instruction given in Cooking, Floriculture, Free-Hand and Industrial Drawing, Designing, Photography, Reading and Physical Culture. Arrangements have been made to train Kindergartners.

A course for training in Library Methods is given.

MUSIC.—In this Department instruction given in Piano, Sight Singing and Chorus Singing.

SCHOLARSHIPS.—Each County is given as many Scholarships as it has Members in the House of Representatives. A Scholarship is worth $100.00, and Free Tuition, and must be won by competitive examination.

Expenses for session of nine months:

For Students Paying Tuition - - -	$144 00
For Students Having Free Tuition - -	104 00
For Scholarship Students - - - - -	4 00

For Catalogue or other information, address

D. B. JOHNSON, President,
Rock Hill, S. C.

AN AD FROM 1916 SHOWING HOW FAR WINTHROP HAD PROGRESSED IN A SHORT TIME the Sophomore class; the special course in Domestic Science, which requires that applicants must have completed the work of the Sophomore class and a course requiring physiology and science, with cooking and the industrial; the special music course, which requires the regular entrance examination to the Freshman class; and all who wish to take music; the special kindergarten course, special elocution, special art, or special vocal music.

Those who take any course other than the Normal and General Literary must choose one of the following industrial studies: Stenography, freehand drawing, designing, book-keeping, sewing, cooking, floriculture, millinery.

Elective periods are limited to work taken in one of the following departments: Pedagogics, English, Mathematics, Science, Latin, Modern Languages, and History.

At the close of last session, I asked that all students give me during the summer without fail their options and electives in order that I might arrange the schedules promptly. All the students did not do as directed in this matter, however, and the schedules arranged may not, therefore, suit all. They have been arranged with reference to those who did send in their options and electives. Others will now have to make their options and electives conform to the schedules arranged.

A Junior or Senior elective chosen in the Freshman class is counted 2/3 value or as near that as practicable.

Juniors and Seniors give options and electives.

Names of those who will take different industrial studies—sewing, cooking, floriculture, millinery, horticulture, stenography and typewriting, bookkeeping.

Explain "Condition." Average under 60. Two conditions go over whole subject again. If you have one condition, one opportunity is given to make it up. If you fail in that, you will have to go over whole subject again. The passing mark has been raised to 70% to go into effect for this term.

You should arrange your financial matters with the book-keeper at any spare time you may have to-day. The first payment called for in the catalogue must be made before a student can be regularly enrolled in any class.

A student living and boarding in town may have a locker assigned her by applying to Mrs. Davis. 25 cents must be deposited with Mrs. Davis for each key, to be refunded when the key is returned.

Uniform. All students, whether regular or special, are required to wear the uniform dress, and the dress requirements as laid down in the catalogue will be strictly enforced. All new pupils are required to deposit $17.00 with the book-keeper to insure the purchase of the articles mentioned on page 84 of the catalogue. All old students, except seniors, are required to deposit $10.75 to purchase articles mentioned on the same page. If an old student is reported by the uniform committee as being properly supplied with any of the articles which the $10.75 covers, the amount covering the cost of the articles will be remitted. Whatever is left of this deposit, if anything, after furnishing the student with a complete and satisfactory uniform, will be returned to the student.

No teachers will be on special duty during study hours in the dormitory. We shall continue the honor system inaugurated five years ago. The girls will be trusted to observe the rules under the general supervision of the matrons and teachers.

The same dormitory rules which were in force last year and which seemed to give such general satisfaction, will be in force this year. No visiting at night during study hours —7:00 to 9:20 o'clock. At the ringing of the

9:20 bell any one may visit quietly until the warning bell for retiring at 9:50 when all must go to their rooms and prepare to retire promptly when the 10 o'clock bell rings. All lights must be out at ten o'clock and there must be quiet after that hour.

Students may go on the campus at 12 o'clock for exercise, fresh air, and sunshine as they do now at 4:00 P. M. All remaining in the buildings must keep quiet.

The Seniors did not respond to the Senior Hall arrangement proposed by the Committee on College Government and for that reason that arrangement cannot be carried out this session, and the Seniors will observe the closed study hour.

Upon the report and recommendation of the House Government Committee, after conference with a Committee of the Senior Class of last year, the following rules about the holding of offices have been adopted and will be in force this session, except that a member of the Senior Class of 1909 may be elected to offices provided they do not give her more than two points above the limit set by the Student Government Committee:

All offices shall be divided into three classes to be known as degree I, II, and III respectively. An office of the First Degree shall be valued at six (6) points; an office of the Second Degree at three (3) points; and an office of the Third Degree at one (1) point. No student shall at one time hold offices amounting to more than ten (10) points; nor shall she hold more than two Second Degree offices.

No student who has a condition shall be elected president of a literary society or of a class or editor of any College publication.

No student who makes a failure on any subject during the year can hold any office whatever during that or the ensuing year.

The girls will go to church and Sunday school in a body a heretofore. Two teachers will go with the whole body.

The rules of the College require that all students shall be vaccinated. No pupil will be allowed to remain at College who refuses to be vaccinated. If any student has been exposed to any contagious disease, she should report this fact to the resident physician at once.

It has been our attempt to assign all of you in the dormitory to rooms and with room-mates of your choice, so far as possible. It has not been possible to do this, however, in all cases, because, oftentimes, we did not know your choice and frequently because others who had a prior claim had asked for the same room you did, and because, in some cases, students not taking music wanted to be in the South Dormitory. It is our desire and purpose to place in the same room students who are mutually agreeably. If you find your room or room-mate unsatisfactory, you will have the privilege of moving out by permission and under the direction of the matron, if another place can be secured for you. It is not fair, however, to ask us to move your room-mate out because you may not like her. The fact of being the first in the room does not give you a permanent claim on it. We reserve the right, at all times, of course, of moving any student wherever we think it to her interest or the interest of the school to move her.

Daily hours: See printed schedule blank.

Dinner to-day at 1:30. First bell at 1:15.

Groups of ten, arranged according to the preference of those composing them, in covered passage ways at ringing of bell. The house-keeper, Mrs. Cochran, has authority to select and appoint those in charge of the tables.

You will be interested in knowing that we have had 1,047 applications for admission to Winthrop this year and places in the dormitories for only 428. 693 tried the entrance examination last July and only 107 passed.

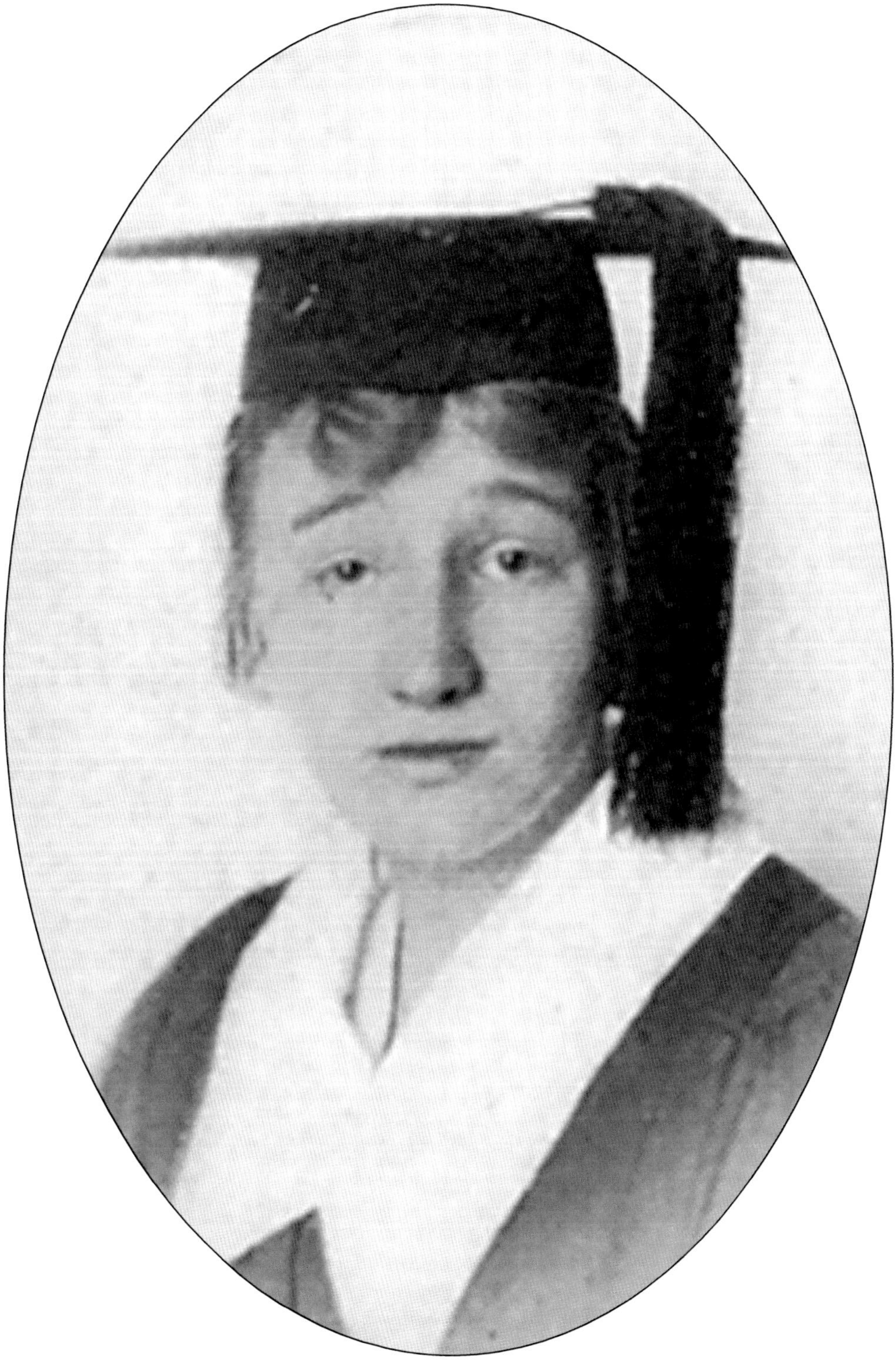

MARGARET MARSHALL'S PHOTO FROM THE 1919 *TATLER* *"Who is it that makes witty remarks in class?"*

I Remember the Class of 1919. *Margaret Marshall, Class of 1919, wrote this memoir in 1954. Throughout the pages, the author's affection burns brightly. The memoir is typical of the many others housed in the Winthrop Archives.*

I found my old leather Winthrop memory book in the attic. Turning the pages I thought of the opening words of one of my favorite TV programs—"I remember San Francisco and the house where I was born . . ."

For I remember Winthrop College and four happy years there, I remember the professors and our beloved "Debe," but most of all I remember the girls.

Their pictures fill the pages of the old scrapbook. College girls in dark blue skirts that came to the top of their high-laced shoes, with hats set at rakish angles, uniform hats issued with little regard for head size or becomingness. Here's a request from the Dean of Women, "Please, girls, wear your hats a little tilted if you must, but not perpendicular!"

I remember the amazing athletes of 1919! We won everything—hockey, basketball, track meet. Headlines cut from the college newspaper read, "Freshman team wins again." "Class of '19 wins Track Meet." "Freshman Defeat Seniors."

How could we help winning with Sara Godbold, Sarah Bailey, Madge LaBoom, Ethel Mace, Mary Sullivan, Helen Shirley, Jimmie Shelor, and other stars? What a team!

One picture shows this triumphant crew wearing the most fetching tams, (we made them ourselves of garnet and gray sateen). When our team ran out on the floor in black bloomers made from three yards of 54-foot serge, white middy blouses, garnet and gray ties and every girl with a white rabbit foot in her pocket, we really wowed them.

I had gone to Winthrop thinking I was one of the world's best basketball players, having played for fours years on the dirt court at the York High School, and having run in many county athletic contests. But the day Sara Godbold banged in to me and I slid across the hardwood floor of the gym on my middy blouse tie, I gave up all hopes of making the team and was glad to be a substitute or a cheerleader.

We were a really cocky crew and even beat our sister class of '17. One of our yells was "Sister class, we love you, sister class, you're sweet,/We don't want to hurt you, but we sure want to beat!"

I remember when the beautiful new gym was dedicated and the marvelous pool. Really, we did wear those bathing suits , baggy and voluminous. We did have to swim the length of the pool before we could graduate.

Track meet programs and news reports that say, "Four World's Records Broken at Track Meet." Sarah Bailey, I remember, broke the record for the discus throw. This is a picture of Miss Boggs and Miss Kolb, popular gym teachers. Miss Boggs in the long smock with a tennis racket, Miss Kolb is the one in the baggy bloomers and middy. Miss Boggs dismissed a gym class after a stiff workout that left us panting and red in the face with a cheery, "Thanks for the day comrades!"

I remember these Very Important People—Martha Woods from Darlington, freshman class president. Lovely, gracious Martha. Mary H. Sullivan, from Honea Path, president when we were sophomores, wonderful athlete, brilliant student, president of Curry Literary Society, active on YW cabinet. Mary Lewis, from our junior class president, of Mary we say, "Behold the winner of A. Markley Lee, We're proud of her as we can be!" Mary was a commencement speaker and the winner of tennis doubles, and for two years a member of the varsity hockey team.

And this is Melle Beard from Charlotte, popular, gay, friendly Melle, our senior class

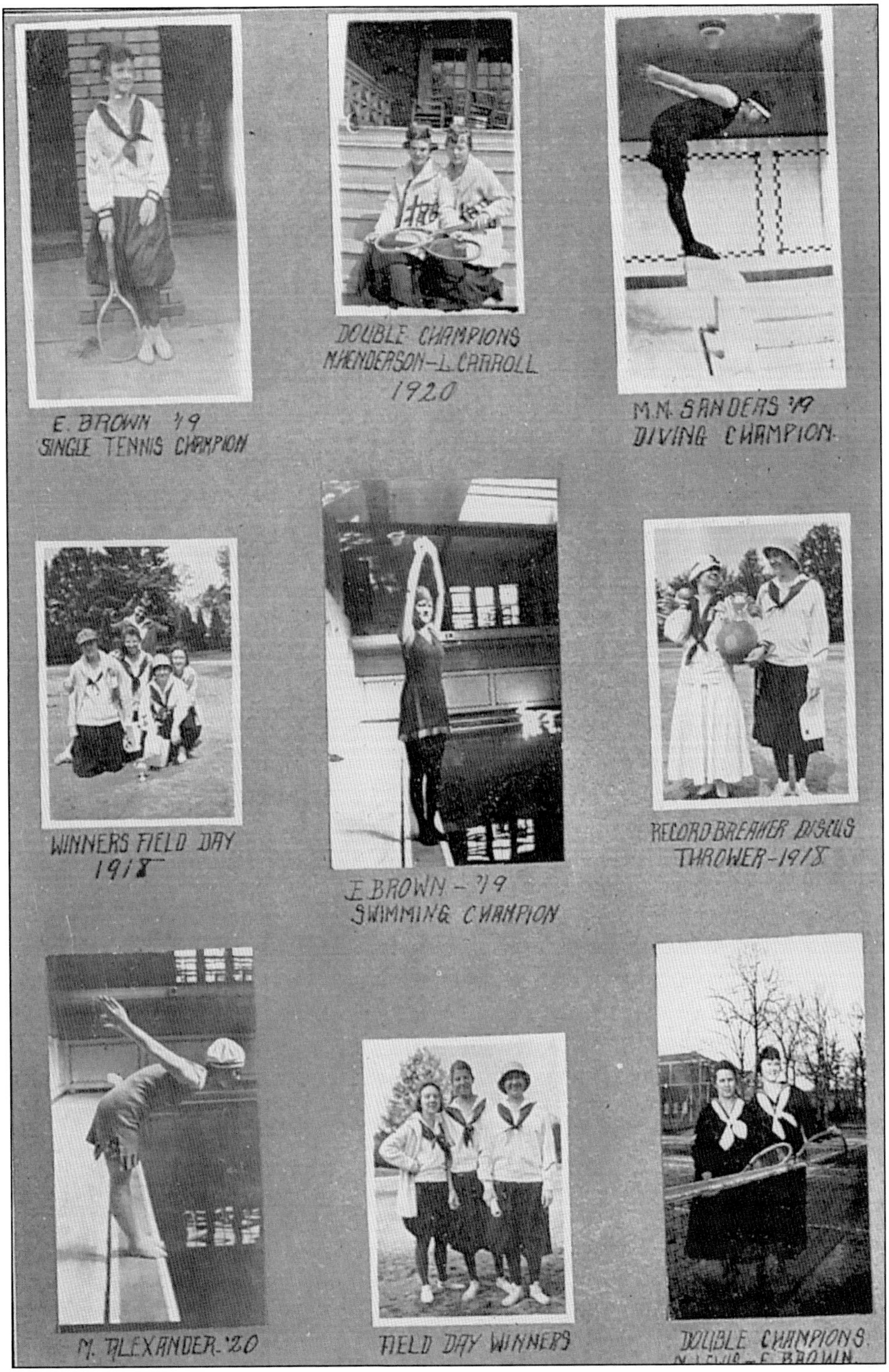

WINTHROP CHAMPIONS, 1918–1920

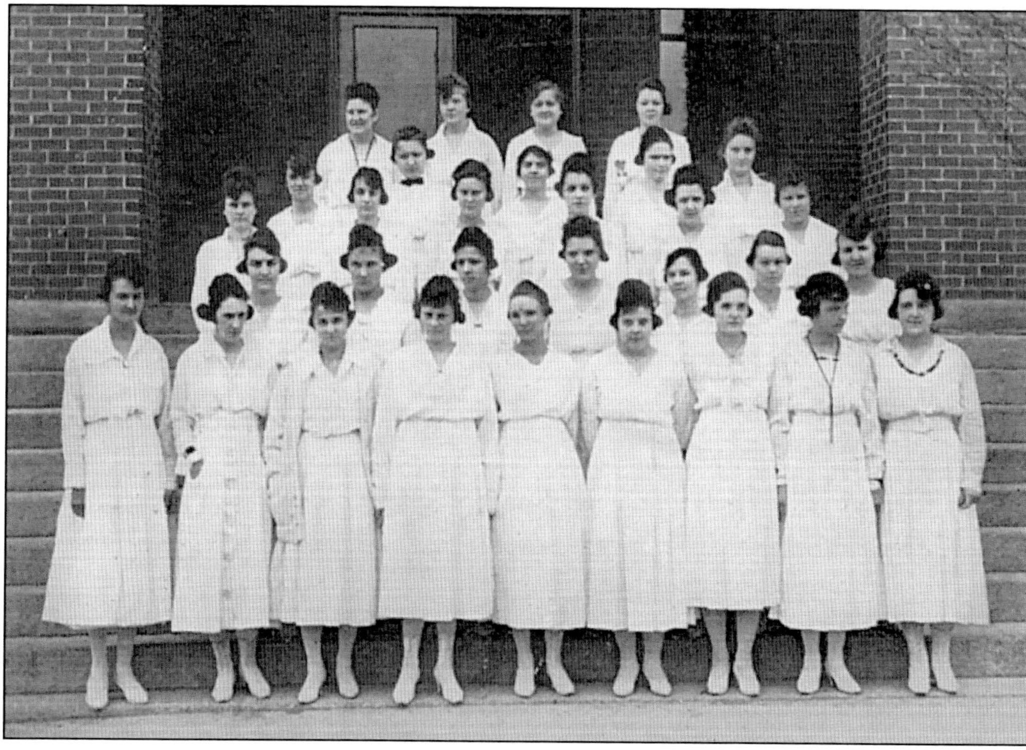

The 1918–19 officers for the Winthrop Choral Society

president and our president now.

This lovely girl knitting a sock and holding a big flowered knitting bag is Annie Laurie Maynard, president of YW. A very wonderful person, she was married soon after we graduated and went to Africa with her husband as a missionary.

This is Virginia Thomas, president of Student government "wise, and sweet and good, and kind, the finest in the land." "Ginnie" became Dean of the Woman's College and Professor of English at Furman and one of the outstanding educators of the state.

Sara Godbold with a list of honors in every field of college life, athletics, student government, commencement speaker, YW cabinet—"'19's best old sport, here's to you." Claire Kearse, the class artist who drew these gay little illustrations, Claire's career in the field of psychoanalytic therapy and psychological services at Columbia University was a brilliant one.

I remember Choral Society and the fun we had singing in operatas. This picture is of Martha Marie Sanders as "Dead-eye Dick, seaman" in *Pinafore*. One Sunday night after we sang in chapel, the young Baptist preacher said, "Girls, I hope you will go to Heaven, you will add so much to the singing of the angels!"

I remember how patriotic we were, for our class lived through World War I. The old scrapbook shows the little service flags that we tacked on our doors, the letters with "A.E.F." stamps, pictures of Elise Smith as the lovely spirit of America in the patriotic pageant. We wept when Esther Robinson sang, "My Buddy—your Buddy misses you." We thought wistfully of our friends and loved ones in France and we wrote little verses in chemistry class. These pasted in the scrapbook are some of "Lish" Goodings: "'Tis weary I am and sad in my heart / For my Laddie had gone over there" And an even sadder one—"We sat up in chemistry and /

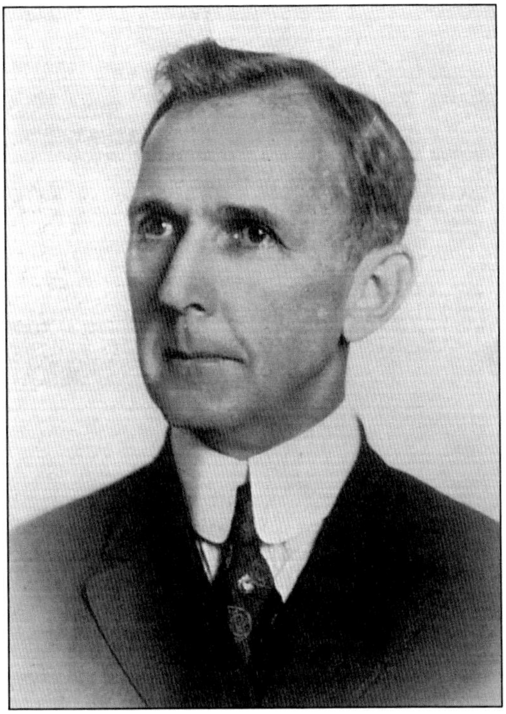

PROFESSOR J. THOMPSON BROWN

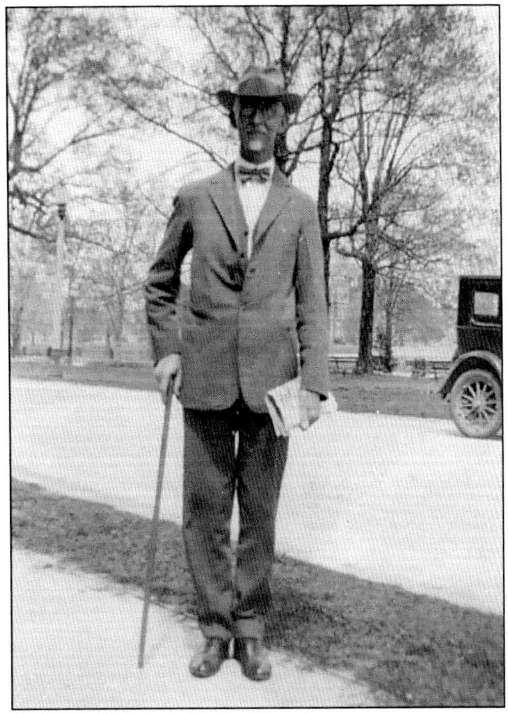

WINTHROP'S BELOVED JAMES P. KINARD

wrote a little rhyme, / Exams told the story that / rhyme left us blind."

Having no radios to give us the daily news we met our history teacher after supper and she tried to keep us informed about what the news of the day was. I remember asking the question, "What does making the world safe for democracy mean?" (We are still trying to answer that question, aren't we?)

These are pictures of the "Victory Parade" we had on Armistice Day, when we joined all Rock Hill to celebrate. For our class day we presented a program in chapel that was a howling success. We as a class were being discharged from the army of Winthrop. This is Madge LaBoom as "General Nuisance." This, Mutt Bratton, a casualty, "choked to death on red tape trying to get permission to go home." We had a wonderful time.

I remember how hard we worked to raise money for the Student Building and for the Red Cross; how we struggled to edit the *Winthrop Journal* and how marvelous Miss Margaret Jane Ketchin was about helping us.

These little notes were written by her on articles that we took for her approval: "This has promise, but needs more work" or "Keep trying, I believe that you will learn to write an editorial after all."

I remember the South Carolina Press Association meeting at Coker College and the honors we won. I remember the YW Conference at Blue Ridge. I remember "Morning Watch" before breakfast.

This handsome gentleman in the white linen suit is Professor J. Thompson Brown and we call him "The Godfather of the Class of '19" and we dedicated our annual to him.

This is Dr. Kinard, Dean of the College. I remember the day we had prepared our cooking class luncheon and the Kinards, our honor guests, did not arrive. Desperately, we tried to keep the baked fish hot and finally telephoned over to inform Dr. Kinard to tell Mrs. Kinard that they were invited. We watched from the windows as they ran across the campus hand in hand arriving breathless and full of apologies.

I remember Mrs. Alexander Long, the beloved and inspiring teacher of the Episcopal College Bible Class. I remember the dinner parties she gave for us and her constant interest in all of "her girls."

I remember Model Home. Our gang went over late in the spring and behaved so outrageously that Miss Simons reported us to the President. We made fudge over the open fire in our bedroom, the delightful odor filling the house while Miss Simons sniffing disapprovingly entertained guests in the parlor after supper.

We overslept one morning and dashed down to start breakfast only to realize that the menu, which could not be changed listed cheese souffle, which could not be hurried. Martha Glenn tried to save the day by conducting "Morning Watch" in the parlor, piously insisting that we sing every verse of "Onward Christian Soldiers."

Here's a picture of one of us feeding the chickens. They had to be counted every night, and the record of eggs gathered on the daybook. Did we really have to milk this cow, or is that picture taken just for fun? Miss Simons informed the President that we should never make good homemakers, but I remember what fun we had those two weeks.

I remember so many things, so many wonderful people. But these are the last pages of the scrapbook, commencement programs, lovely pictures of Daisy Chain, and friends in caps and gowns. The old book closes with my last report with "Very good, D.B. Johnson" written on it. Then a letter confirming my election as a teacher in the schools of Hartsville and another Winthrop girl goes out into the "wide, wide world."

This is our year to have our 35th reunion. I am looking forward to it with great pleasure. Winthrop College holds a place in my heart that nothing can replace. I am proud of my school and grateful for all Winthrop meant to my gay college days and has meant since I left school.

MY WINTHROP YEARS. *Pauline Marion Worthy, the author of this well-written memoir, was a 1920 Winthrop graduate. In 1986, she gave the memoir to the university's archives. In her cover letter, which she addressed "Dear Winthrop," she wrote "Now that you are celebrating your hundredth birthday, I thought I would like to remind you what life was like in those ancient days."*

I did not graduate from high school. There were eleven grades in our school. After I had completed the tenth my grandfather suggested that I take the entrance examination for admission to Winthrop College. I jumped at this idea. I longed for broader horizons. It did not occur to me that because I was such a problem at home Mama Jones was just as anxious for me to go away as I was to go.

The thrill of anticipation and all the preparations to go were very exciting. I had to have a trunk to take, so for the first time since My Mother's death, my grandmother unpacked the big trunk in the upstairs hall which had belonged to "Dear Rosa."

At rare intervals, as I was growing up, I had peeped into the trunk when Mama Jones was not at home. I had handled the beautiful ostrich feather fan with its mirrored spokes, had sniffed the dainty handkerchiefs of lined and lace still redolent of lavender, and coveted the cut glass powder box with its silver top. I examined the wedding veil, the wax orange blossoms and the oddly shaped little satin shoes. But the tray was very heavy and I had never seen what was underneath. Now ten years after her death I saw my Mother's clothes. There were beautiful dresses of blue and green. There were two wedding dresses, one of heavy cream colored silk and the other of lavender

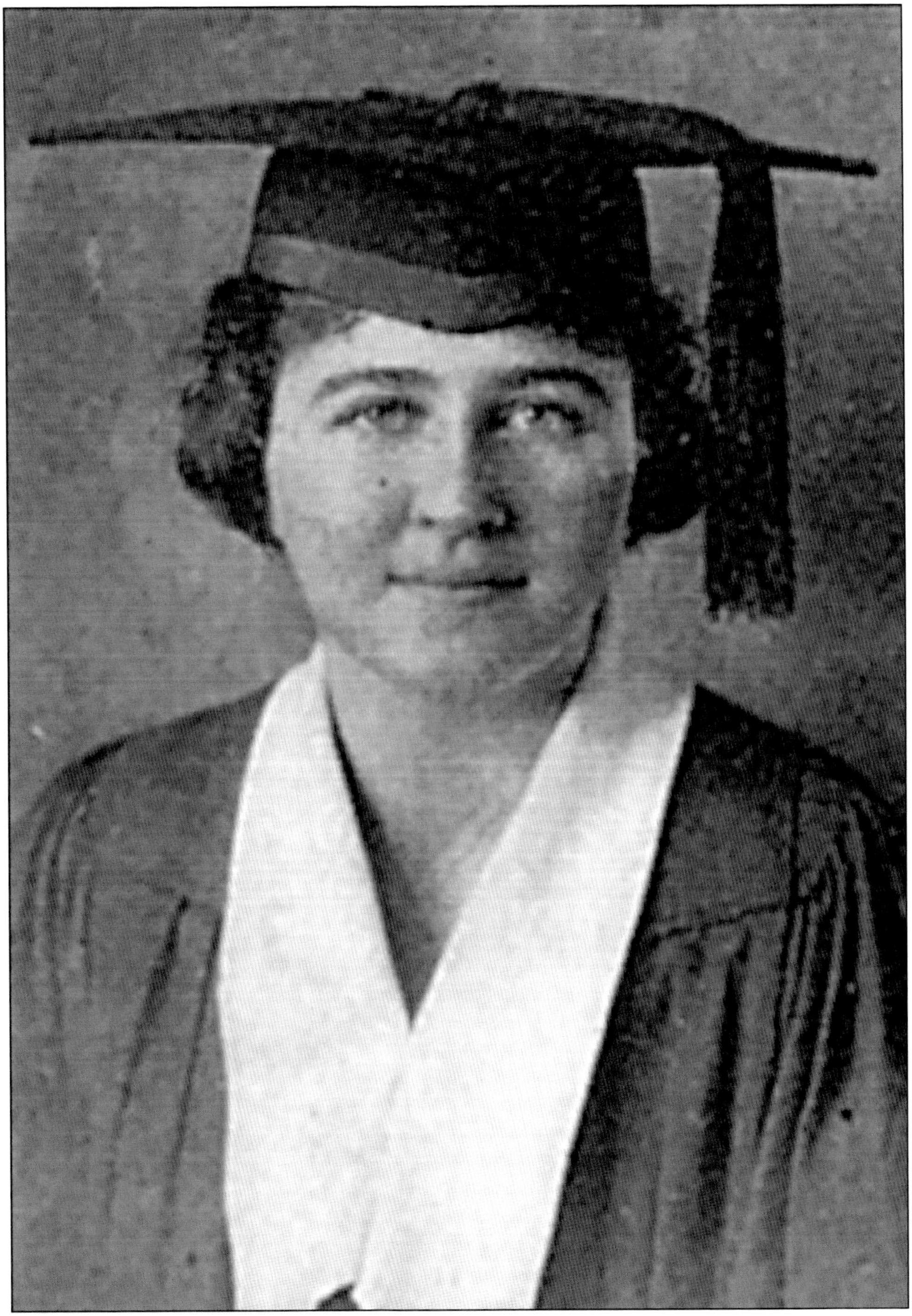

PAULINE MARION WORTHY AS SHE APPEARED IN THE 1920 *TATLER*

chiffon. I hated to leave these things behind but we had to empty the trunk so my own things could be packed. However, I took the cut glass powder box, my father's first gift to his only sweetheart, to college with me and it has stood on my dressing table these many years.

I entered Winthrop in September 1916. College life was not at all as I had imagined it. I had read entirely too many stories about the larks girls had at boarding schools. Though I was never actually homesick. I was about as miserable as any freshman who ever was.

My living conditions were uncomfortable, three girls, not very congenial, in a band box of a room. The food was terrible, the classes hard, and the regimen strict and strange. Besides I did not know anybody. What was that play in which the little girl went around singing "Nobody knows my name?" When I heard it afterward I remembered myself as a freshman at Winthrop.

The President's welcome to the freshman was not very comforting. "We are glad you are here!," he announced to the class assembled a few days after matriculation, "but one thing we don't want are any cry babies. If you are not happy here and want to go home, come by my office as soon as possible and we will arrange for your transportation back home. Hundreds of girls in this state are waiting for your place and for the privilege of being a Winthrop Girl." There were nearly four hundred girls in that class and not one of them went home, no matter how much they may have wanted to.

My sophomore year was better because I had found friends. By the time I was a junior, I had hit my stride. I helped edit the *Journal* and won an honorary scholarship. (No money, only academic recognition.) My senior year was all roses and I squeezed a lot of juice out of being a Big Man on Campus.

I had wanted very much to go to college, but I did not want to go to Winthrop. It was not a stylish place to go. Dorothy went to Agnes Scott, Katherine went to Converse, and Mary Heath went to Sweet Briar, all more popular schools. My other friends scattered here and there. Winthrop had the reputation of being very difficult and the idea of wearing a uniform all the time was not attractive.

Looking back on the experience, I am glad that I went and proud that I graduated. It was a hard and thorough training school where everything was regimented. I am glad I was tough enough to survive along with all those hundreds and hundreds of other tough "gals," who both survived and profited to the enrichment of South Carolina.

I met some lonely girls and made some devoted and lifelong friends. Though a few were boring and lackluster on the whole, I was fortunate in my teachers who did a great deal for me.

I went to Winthrop because Papa Jones had wanted me to go. He had been in the Legislature when the school was started as a State Teachers College. He had been active in steering through to final commitment the bill which created the College. And as Speaker of the House, he had made the Dedicatory Address at the laying of the cornerstone on May 12, 1894. I have his copy of this address here on the desk beside me as I write. It reviews the steps which led from the founding of the tiny Winthrop Training School in Columbia in 1886 to the selection of Rock Hill as the site of this to-be-great institution. There was fierce competition between towns to acquire the college and I note the final gift which made Rock Hill the winner.

I knew that Rock Hill gave the site consisting of more than thirty acres, but I didn't remember, if I ever heard before, that the town not only delivered 375,000 brick to the site but gave the use of a brick and clay quarry with the right to quarry all necessary granite. All this in addition to a cash gift plus $60,000 in six percent bonds sold at par, an investment on which the city has capitalized many times over.

In his address Papa Jones paid tribute to David Bancroft Johnson's zealous advocacy of the education of women and to his able

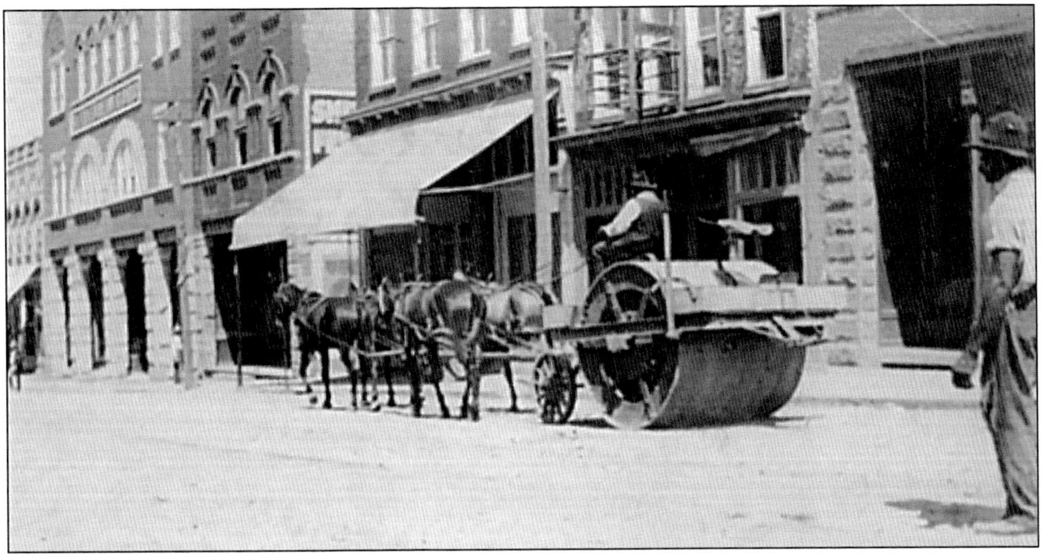

ROCK HILL IN THE EARLY 20TH CENTURY

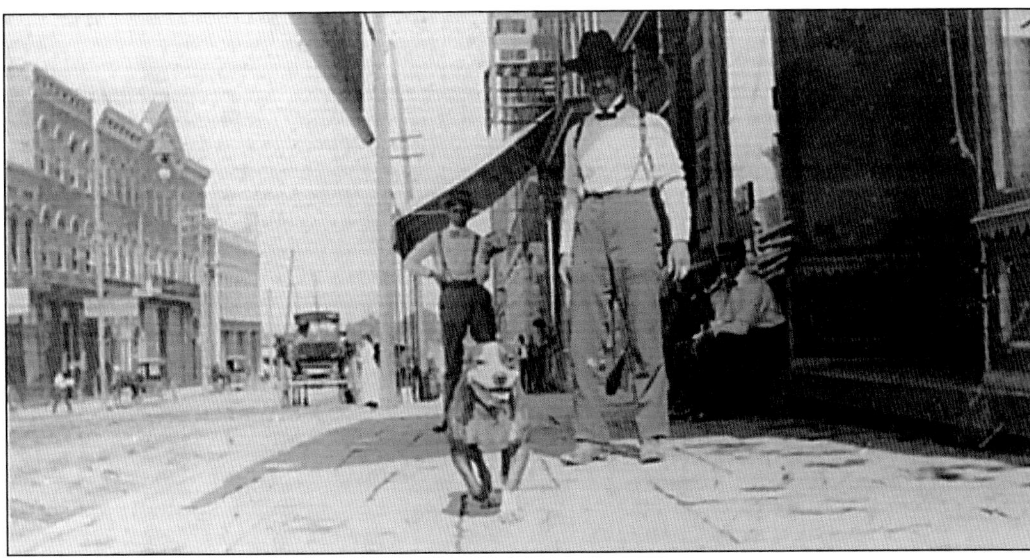

coadjutor, Dr. Edward S. Joynes. He spoke of the financial assistance obtained from the Peabody fund through the assistance of Mr. Winthrop, and of the official endorsement of Governor Tillman.

But this is the paragraph which interests me. I quote: "The duty of the state to afford her daughters similar opportunities for intellectual culture as afforded her sons, seems clear. The matter for surprise in the long delay of according women to her right in this regard. There should be no voyage on the intellectual sea which a woman may not, if she will, undertake. Those who think woman not capable of as high mental attainments as man, are mistaken. I have taught school and I can testify that the boys showed no superiority over the girls. Where ever woman has been given the opportunity she has proven herself a formidable competitor with man in every intellectual field. The ordinary comparison is faulty in that it fails to take into consideration the environments of women, which have shut her from so many fields of competition. For my part, I say open up more doors of employment to women, and then when she performs work equal to man's give her the pay of man. Preserving always the purity of women, and preserving always the home life, strike off every shackle, remove every obstacle and let woman be as free as man is free."

This is the kind of grandfather I had! I wish I had been there to clap for these sentiments expressed ably nearly a century ago. And to think after all these many years, we are still trying in 1976 to get the Equal Rights Amendment passed.

In 1920, a quarter of a century after this speech, I graduated from this South Carolina College for Women. Papa Jones was there, clapping for me.

In this search backward through time, my years at Winthrop are a blur, a blur of a thousand girls in navy blue, a blur of bells. Bells waked us at 7 a.m. Rolling out of bed at the last possible minute and sticking hair pins in our long hair, we raced to breakfast as fast as we could, for one must be in one's assigned place in the dining hall before the 7:30 bell stopped ringing. You had to be in your place fully dressed three times a day on the dot, hungry or not. I remember yet the sound of knives and forks clicking away as a thousand girls, ten to each table, ate their meals in a huge dining hall, And what meals! Terrible! There were no snack bars or tea rooms, so I lived on Hershey bars and gained fifteen pounds between September and Christmas.

We rushed to classes to the sound of those bells, difficult classes with demanding and impersonal teachers. I had nightmares over Math and Science and barely squeaked through, but History and English I found extremely interesting. Windows were actually opening.

Added to my other grievances as a freshman, I developed mumps and had to spend nine days in quarantine in the college infirmary. This was in April and I had learned by this time that all the teachers were not remote and impersonal. My English teacher, Miss Davis, sent me roses, and one day I waked from an afternoon nap to find a copy of *Browning's Poems* under my pillow with the following couplet from "Evelyn Hope" underlined: "The good stars met in your horoscope / made you of spirit, fire and dew."

The date of my birth was written in the margin. When I wrote to thank Miss Davis, I told her that I was spending most of my time in the infirmary planning a beautiful wardrobe. She promptly sent me a copy of *Vogue*. I really loved this sweet understanding woman who introduced me to Wordsworth and Shelley and Keats.

This matter of planning a wardrobe grew out of my intense aversion to wearing a uniform. From my present vantage point, I can see how sensible uniforms are for school girls, but I hated them then. Being required to wear a navy blue skirt (hem line six inches from the floor) and a white shirt waist (blouse) for four solid years affected my lifestyle. It was so impressed on me that navy was a sensible color that to this day I can hardly pass a navy dress on the rack. And nobody knows how I love color: beautiful blues for dresses, red coats, pink nightgowns, green rooms, and yellow flowers. The gorgeous golden daffodils, whole sheafs of them, spreading across the campus in early spring first began to endear Winthrop to me.

Miss Davis is one of the half dozen teachers in a long line whom I remember with affection. The finest, I think, was Dr. Walmsley, head of the History Department. During my Junior and Senior years I took every course he taught. A really magnificent teacher, he had the magic ability to inspire students with enough genuine curiosity to investigate for themselves. To him, gratitude for a golden question mark.

There was Miss Wysor, whose subject matter later was anathema but whose personality intrigued me. I can see her

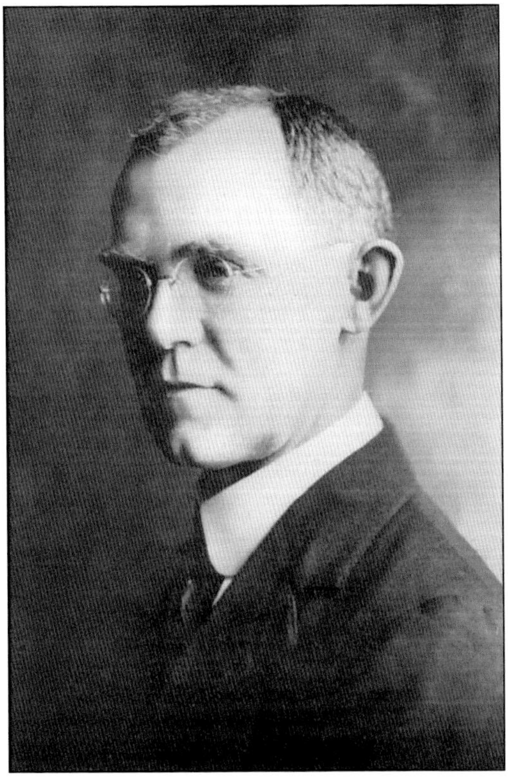

James Elliot Walmsley of the History Department *Mr. Walmsley was the finest Winthrop teacher, according to Pauline Marion Worthy.*

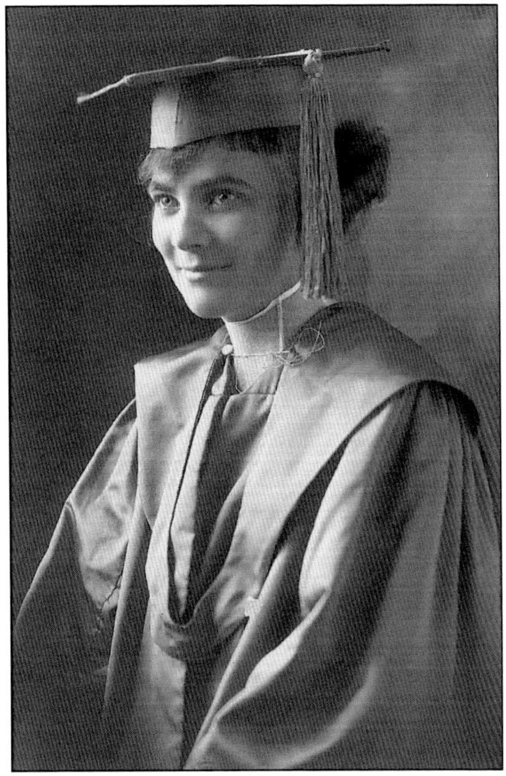

Mattie Henderson, second term president in 1920

now, sweeping into the auditorium on some dress-up occasion, long necklace of real amber swaying as she walked, and she walked always as if she wore a coronet.

There was Mr. Brown, gentle scholar, talking of the Transcendentalists among whom he, himself, belonged. There was Clifton Gray, who said to me one day, "You have a mind with wheels in it, girl." While the imagery was distracting, I had a warm feeling that this was intended as a compliment, and above all things I craved approval.

Perhaps closest to me of all, because her friendship carried over into a later period of my life, was Carolyn Hastings. She was crippled by polio but her mind had wings and she made her subject come alive. She was only a year or two out of Wellesley when she taught European history at Winthrop and we became great friends. Later she was at Columbia University working on a graduate degree while I was there and I saw her often. She married an artist, Glen Henshaw, and, when his biography was written a few years ago, his biographer wrote me that my address had been found among Mrs. Henshaw's papers. He wanted to know what I could tell him about her personality. It was a request that I was delighted to answer.

Another teacher that I remembered with pleasure was Mademoiselle Moudy. She was small boned and dainty and looked like a Dresden figurine. Each day she came to class in the quaintest of costumes. These beautiful dresses

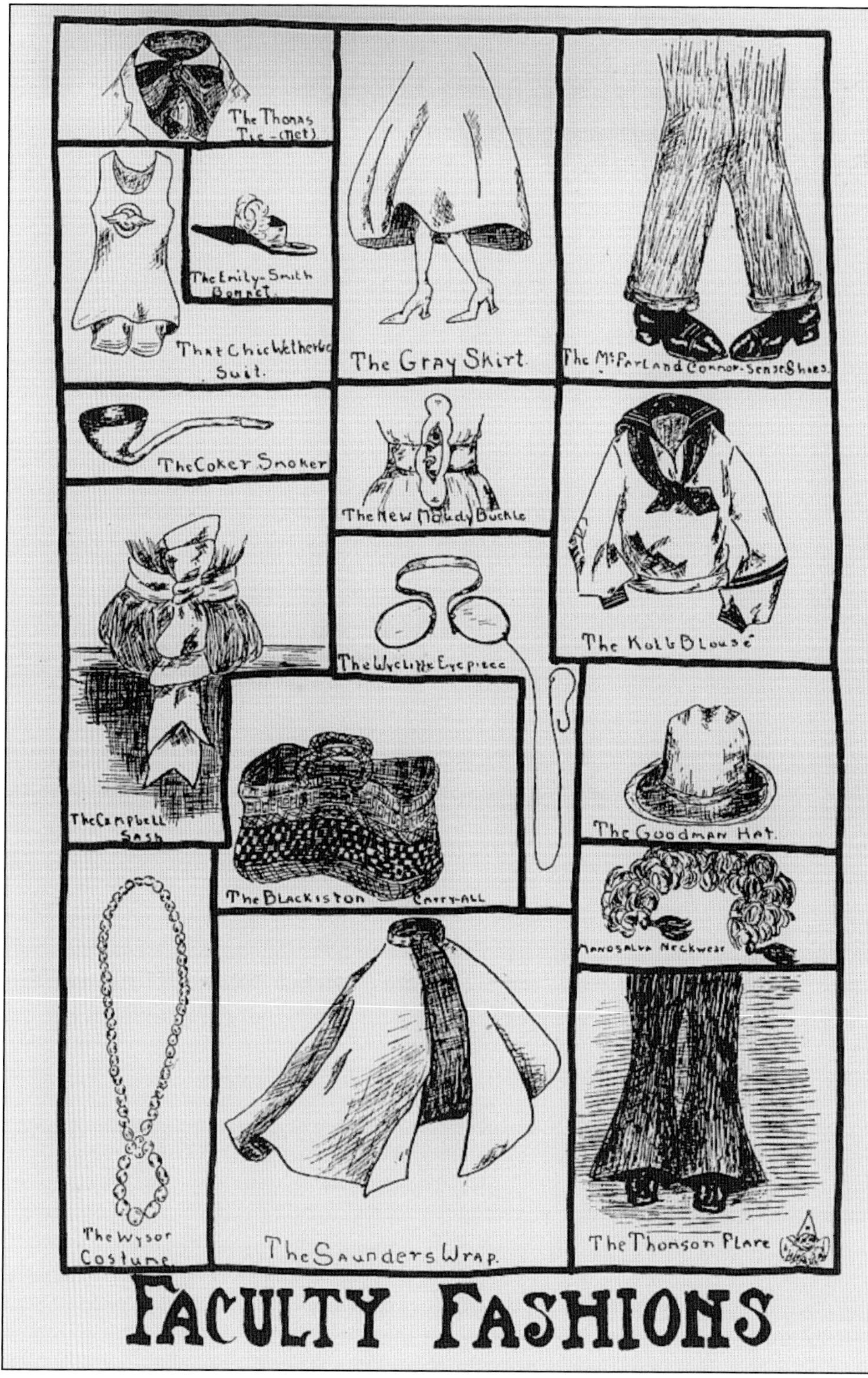

Faculty fashions, 1919

made of exquisite materials in turn-of-the-century styles, had been her trousseau twenty years before. Her lover had been drowned at sea and she had never married. She taught French to generations of students.

It was in French class that I first met Mary Lewis, a diminutive blonde with lovely hair and soft brown eyes. She looked like a brainless butterfly, but she was the farthest thing from that than can be imagined.

She was not only brilliant, but she was a person of great integrity, straight forward and determined. We met every day in the library, which was "My refuge and my stay." It was a wonderful library and Miss Ida J. Dacus, the librarian, was my first real friend at Winthrop.

Mary Lewis was a Sophomore, two years older than I and already becoming a Personage on campus. Mary became president of the Junior class, chief marshall, tennis champion, and winner in her Junior year of the Markley Lee Scholarship, given for the best all-round girl in school.

I lived in the same room with her for nearly three years and profited greatly from this association. No element of rivalry ever entered our relationship. I recognized and appreciated superiority.

There were other friends, of course. Fannie, quaint and old fashioned, and Elizabeth, and dear little Mae. There was Maida, beautiful, reserved, and somewhat withdrawn into a delicate shell of unhappiness; Maida, who did everything precisely and was satisfied with nothing short of perfection. And Helen, who first swam into my line of vision in a Freshman Math class, fair hair flying and "great soul shining in her eyes," Helen, who was sweet and gracious and so transcendently unselfish that she could be the most exasperating person alive. Oh, those long, long talks with Helen, "the bitter hurt, the tramping in the rain"!

The relationship of the student body to the president of the College was one of affectionate awe. Dr. Johnson had been instrumental in founding the college and he felt responsible for every detail of its operation. He personally planned the curriculum and because he thought that there were certain qualifications every woman should possess, everybody had to take a course in cooking, sewing, and manual training. The latter in order that a wife might put up a shelf in case her husband didn't know how to drive a nail.

At Chapel every morning (compulsory), Dr. Johnson called "Debe" by everyone, read the Bible and preached us a mini-sermon, designed obviously for character building. Some of his little stories were delightful. I remember the day he told us the love story behind the hymn "Love Divine, All Love Excelling," one of his favorite admonitions was "Dare to be Daniel,/Dare to stand alone,/Dare to have a purpose/Dare to make it known."

Because Debe was afraid one of "his girls" might drown some day, there was a requirement that in order to graduate, every student must swim the length of the pool (90 feet.). I am ashamed for my swimming, skiing, scuba-diving granddaughters to know this requirement nearly proved my *bete noir*. Just as it embarrasses me for my sports writer grandson to know how I loathed all forms of athletics. Since Debe was a fanatic on the idea of a sound mind in a sound body, Winthrop had a handsome gymnasium and every sort of sport was available. You had to play one. I chose hockey but never enjoyed a minute of it.

Debe was bald, roly-poly, and sixty when I was a freshman. He cultivated in the State the idea that he was a father figure who loved everyone of "his girls." Actually he had very little personal contact with his girls. The only time I every really talked to him was when I went to his office not long before I graduated. I was editor-in-chief of *The Tatler*, the college annual. After paying all expenses, the annual staff had cleared nearly a thousand dollars. We wanted to use this to make a gift to the college in the name of the Class of 1920. I went to see Dr. Johnson to discuss the use of this money,

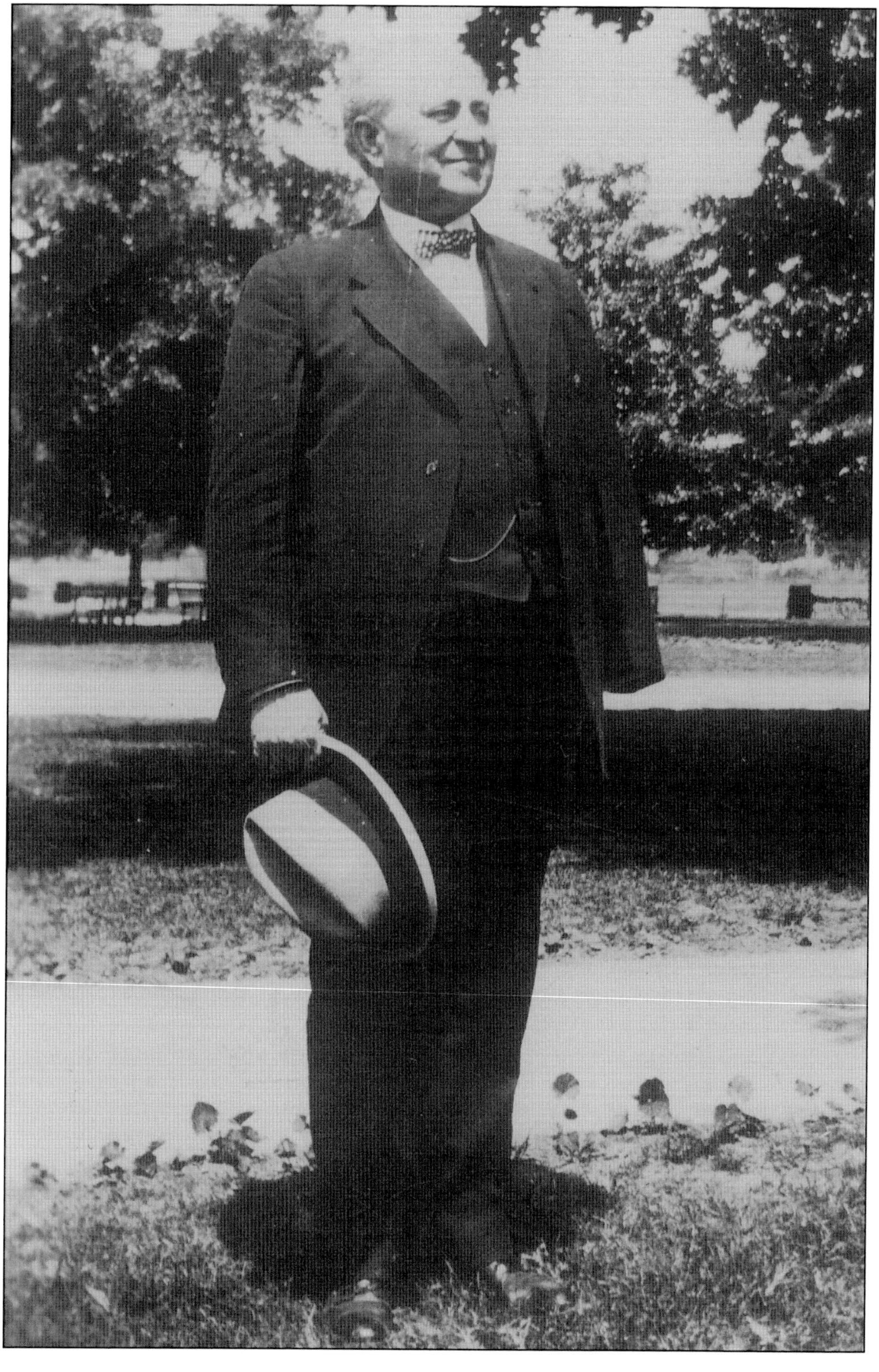

D.B. JOHNSON IN HIS LATER YEARS

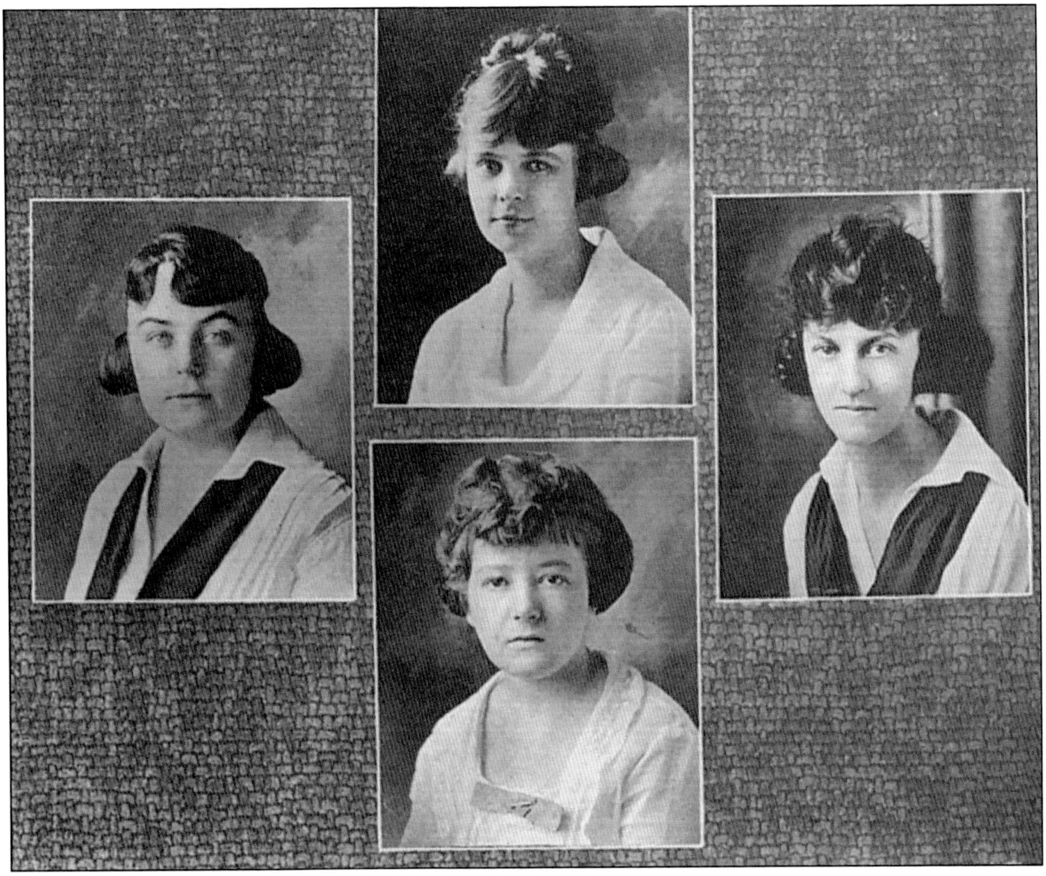

The officers of the Class of 1920

to ask him what he could suggest that the college would most appreciate.

He told me that he had wanted for a long time to activate the clock in the tower of the Main Building, but that ready money was always scarce. Ever since the construction of the building in the 1890s, the clock had been a dummy, its hands pointing to twenty minutes past seven. Somebody suggested that might have been the time Mr. Winthrop died. As a result of that conversation, the Class of 1920 installed a running clock in the tower and it has been running ever since. I doubt if anyone in the student body today knows the history of the clock.

Dr. Johnson planned a number of nice things for "his girls" and would probably have done more had the lean years of World War I not intervened. Once he chartered a train and took us all to Columbia to see the State Fair.

Hundreds of identically clad girls running around the State Capital on that occasion inspired one reader of the Columbia *State* to write a letter to the editor saying, "Please write something in the paper about these sweet Winthrop girls who are passing through here today. They look so much like real girls in their white waists and blue skirts and their blue and white hats and their clean faces with no vanishing cream or rouge—so unlike some of these city girls in their satins and georgettes, their transparent silk hose, and their rouged faces."

The highlight of my Senior year came when "Debe" took our class to

Charleston to see Magnolia Gardens, the most breath-taking beauty to which I had ever been exposed.

One of the most surprising things Debe ever did was to take us to see Buffalo Bill's Wild West Show. A few months before William F. Cody died in 1917, he brought his famous Wild West Show to Rock Hill. The show had been all over the world since its organization thirty years prior to that time. It had sparked the proliferation of the Western "hero" business and has been credited with being the forerunner of the thousands of Western stories and motion pictures with cowboy heroes, whose popularity seems endless.

We were thrilled to have Debe announce in Chapel one morning that Buffalo Bill was coming to town and since he represented a phase of life the girls would never have an opportunity to see again, he would take anyone who wanted to go see the show. That was a real experience. I remember Buffalo Bill vividly. He was a distinguished looking individual with the white goatee of a statesman. His cowboy riders were unbelievably skillful of all being the women who had ridden through the West with Theodore Roosevelt. Buffalo Bill himself gave a wonderful exhibition. He was as great a rider now in his seventies as he had been when he had ridden for the Pony Express when he was in his teens. He got his nickname because he was famous as a buffalo hunter. With him that night he had the buffalo who had been the designer's model for the buffalo nickel, a new coin then only recently issued.

We were much more excited over seeing him than we were over seeing President Taft, who visited Winthrop when I was there. Mr. Taft was no longer President by that time, but all the girls were excited over the prospect of entertaining a character out of history and great preparations were made. Imagine their disgust when the local politician, who introduced the eminent visitor, talked for a solid hour and the ex-President spoke for less than ten minutes.

A number of interesting visitors came to Winthrop during my time, but the two I remember with particular interest were Emmeline Pankhurst and Anna Howard Shaw, two pioneers in the battle for Woman Suffrage.

During my high school years, I had heard much of Mrs. Pankhurst's exploits in London, of the violence in which she participated, of her jail sentences and her hunger strikes, and I expected to see an Amazon. I was stunned when she stepped out on the platform, a small grandmotherly little creature with a little lavender shawl over her simple black dress.

The story Mrs. Pankhurst told was a thrilling one, but she was not in the class with Mrs. Shaw, who was then president of the National American Woman's Suffrage Association. Mrs. Shaw was a notable speaker and a very, very charming woman. I consider it one of the privileges of my life to have been detailed by the College as the marshal to take care of Mrs. Shaw while she was Winthrop's guest. It was my responsibility to escort her everywhere and to see that she arrived promptly at the proper places at the proper times. As we walked across the campus, we talked as if we had always known each other and it was nice to be able to tell her that my grandparents were advocates of women suffrage, and that, while in high school, I had marched in a "Votes for Women" parade.

Not too long after that interesting contact, President Wilson appointed Anna Howard Shaw chairman of the Woman's Division of National Defense. Her work in that capacity paved the way for the founding of the Woman's Division of the Department of Labor.

The Nineteenth Amendment, giving women the right to vote, became the law of the land in August 1920, some months before I, personally, was old enough to exercise that right.

Dr. and Mrs. Johnson lived in a handsome brick house on the edge of the campus, and we saw Mrs. Debe everyday. We really felt

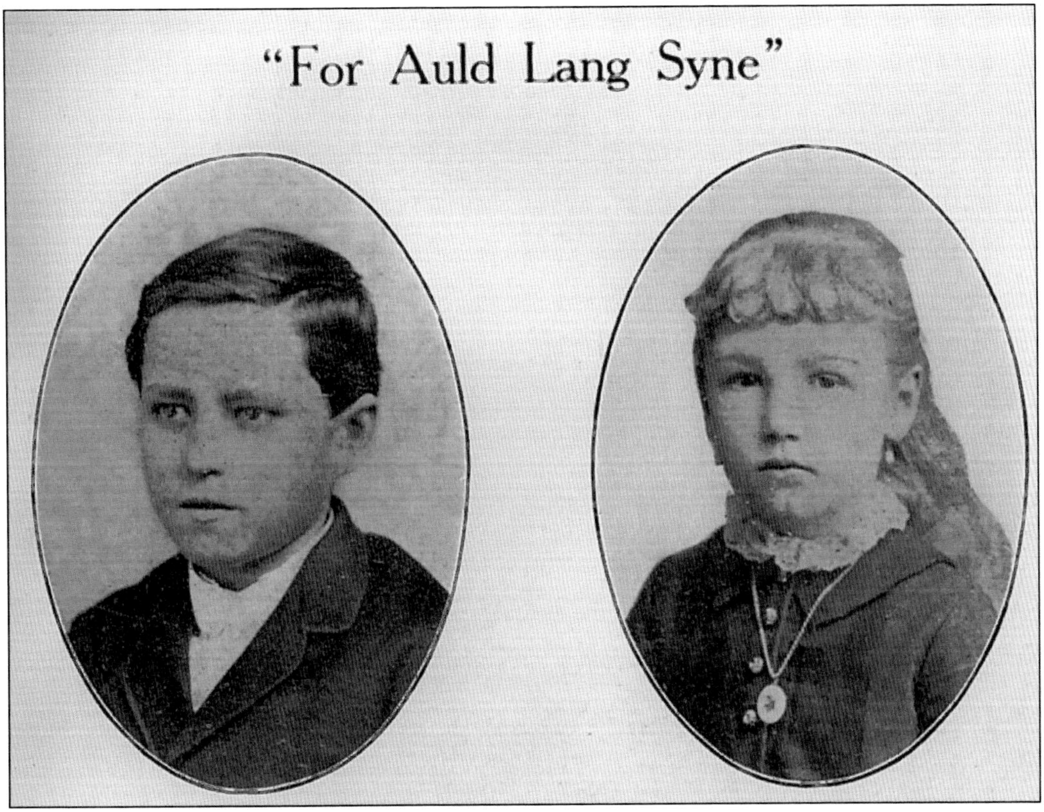

D.B. AND MRS. JOHNSON AS CHILDREN, FROM THE 1919 *TATLER*

closer to her than to her husband. She was both pretty and charming and a number of years younger than her husband. A gift for remembering names and faces made her know personally practically every girl in college. The girls in turn were fascinated by her romantic story. She had been a student at Winthrop in earlier days. After an escapade which was regarded as such a serious infringement of the rules, the President himself had her hauled on the carpet for his personal reprimand. I don't know whether this was their only meeting or not, or whether he asked her to marry him on sight. At any rate, by the time I got to Winthrop, she was the mother of his two small sons. When their daughter was born, the entire student body felt personally involved.

Certain "attractions" came to Winthrop with the Lyceum course, attractions such as the Russian Symphony and the great Metropolitan opera star, Frieda Hempel, both remembered because they were my introduction to great music, but for the most part we lived a Spartan life with no social activity whatever.

Until the Study Period bell rang at 7:30 p.m., the hour after supper was free. Many girls went to the dance hall, but the girls had to dance with each other. Boys were an unknown quantity on that campus. Having a date was so hedged about with restrictions that few had dates and those rarely.

The campus was surrounded by an iron fence, and it was against the rules to even wave to a boy on the other side of that fence. Even if you met one face to face down town, you were not supposed

Answer to "Flanders' Fields"

Sleep well, ye heroes brave, who lie
In Flanders' fields; we hear your cry,
And though where waving grain has grown,
Where poppies' crimson flame has blown,
The earth is stained with hero blood
Redder than ever poppies stood;
Though those sad crosses side by side
('Twas on a cross our Saviour died)
Stand o'er the bravest sons of France,
Fallen in a great advance.
Sleep well—for where your feet have trod
We fight for peace—for France—for God.

FAYE FORD, '22.

POEM WRITTEN BY FAYE FORD, CLASS OF 1922, FROM THE 1919 *TATLER*

to speak beyond "Hello." The occasions on which you went to town were very, very rare. We were told that girls had gone more often in the days of public transportation. When Nanie and Betty were there, the city had a streetcar drawn by two mules, one facetiously named "Elec" and the other "Tricity." Automobiles had arrived by my time, but it was against the rules for a Winthrop girl to accept a ride in one.

The temptation to communicate with the opposite sex was removed during the War. After the spring of 1917, all boys who were not lame, halt, or blind were drafted and so vanished from the local scene.

In April 1917, the United States officially entered the War against Germany. No one was surprised. Diplomatic relations had been broken in February and everyone had been emotionally involved with France and the Allies for sometime. What we were surprised about was that there should be a war at all in our civilized twentieth century.

It had been nearly three years since Gavrillo Prinzip had killed Arch Duke Francis Ferdinand at Sarajevo. In August 1914 I was at a house party at the Haile Gold Mine and was out in the woods swinging in a grapevine swing when I first heard the unbelievable news that there was a war on in Europe. Unbelievable because wars were things fought in history books long, long ago but certainly not now in our modern world. The United States stayed out of the war as long as possible but when it began to look as if civilization would crumble without us, Woodrow Wilson and the Congress declared war.

The draft calls went out, and men and boys were rushed into uniform, some of them were my friends. Before Christmas 1917, a thousand American boys were in France. By the time summer of 1918, there were two thousand. By the time the Armistice was signed on November 11, 1918, more than one fourth of all the men in the United States between eighteen and thirty-five were in the Armed forces. Many of the girls at school had brothers and sweethearts who were involved. Sometimes the news was very bad, and with no radio or T.V., the news took a long time coming.

Everything and everybody in the entire country was focused on the war effort. The nation was committed whole heartedly to this war which we were told was to save Democracy, a War to end all Wars.

In this time of frantic conversation and scarcity of all commodities, our meals became even worse. Every week wheatless days, meatless days, and sugarless days were on the schedule. A particular type of tough, gray, tasteless meat was served so often that we had a joke at our table to the effect that if all the goats eaten at Winthrop were made into one goat, that goat could stand in Rock Hill and butt the Statue of Liberty down. Although we were very much aware of the war everyday in all our activities, there was practically nothing that we could really do no matter how much we would have liked to. Everybody tried to knit. Knitting needles even clicked in classes. One wonders what happened to all those shapeless sweaters and socks which were turned out. We bought War Stamps out of our allowances and helped with Liberty Loan rallies, and every night at nine o'clock, the lights went out for two minutes so everyone could pray for our boys overseas.

The news of the Armistice came late at night. All the bells began to ring and all the whistles began to blow. Lights had long been out and most of the girls were sound asleep, but as the news spread like wildfire, the entire student body, one thousand strong, erupted into the dormitory halls. Such yelling and screaming and noise making as was never heard within those walls before or since!

My most vivid memory is of Mrs. Funkhouser, that most dignified of matrons (housemother), trying vainly to restore order. Her gray hair up in curlers, and barely half dressed, she rushed up and down the hall shouting "Nothing but Peace, girls! Don't get so excited! It's nothing but Peace!"

The most exciting thing that happened at Winthrop in my time occurred when the boys came home from the War. On April 1, 1919, the City of Rock Hill had a great celebration of welcome for South Carolina's returning soldiers, sailors, and marines and had it at Winthrop. All those man-starved girls and girl-starved men nearly lost their minds at the sight of each other. The Banquet that night was a gala, which I shall never cease to remember.

I went back to Winthrop on a visit some years after I graduated. It was a mistake. It made me more homesick than I had ever been when I was actually there.

This was My college. The tie had been knit through long years whose slow growth was part of me. My college! Yet in no far away city did I ever feel so alien. The clock striking in that tower was the gift of my class. Here on this campus I once knew joy in Spring, once sat on the grass during long twilights with other girls who twanged ukuleles and sang "It's a Long Way to Tipperary" and "There's a Long, Long Trail A-Winding into the Land of My Dreams."

In this gymnasium I had danced, in this pool learned to swim, in this Infirmary suffered with mumps, and survived influenza in the great epidemic of 1918. In this auditorium I had felt breast lift and throat contract in a burst of breath-taking patriotism when the boys came home from France.

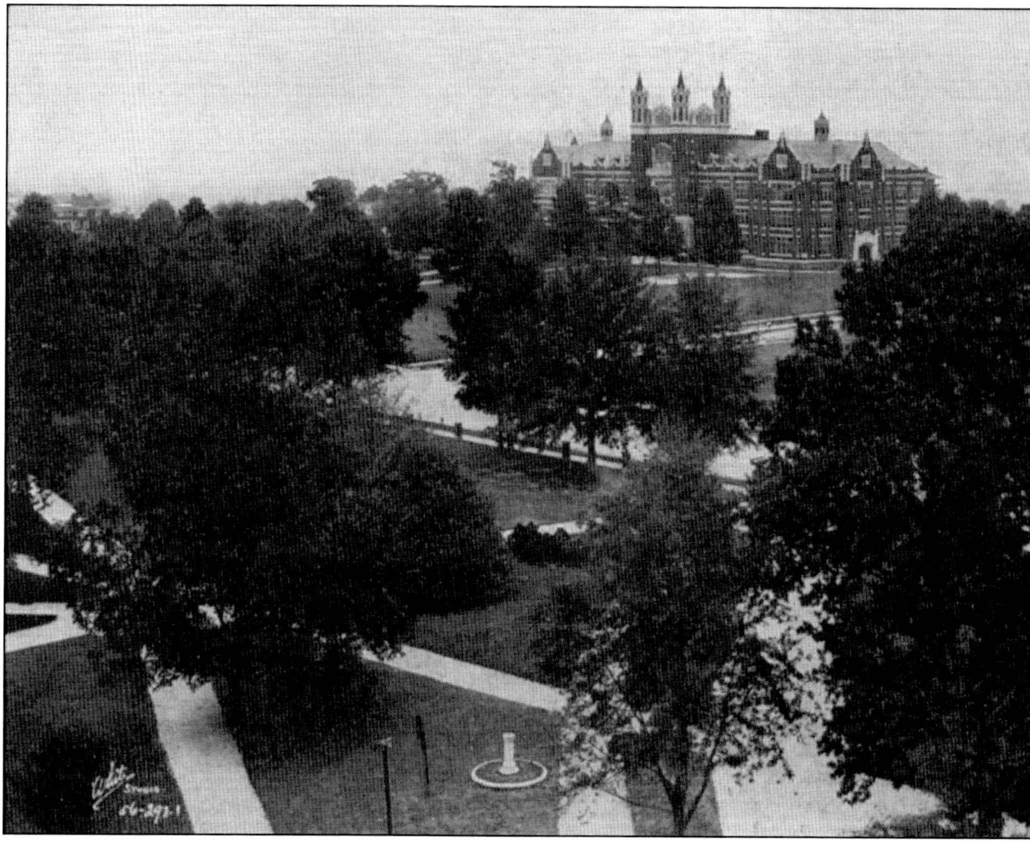

The Training School, 1920

Beside this fountain I waited for Helen, on this porch, heard first the story of Maida's engagement, in yonder room, lived with Mary, the greatest single influence I had in college.

There, beyond that great pine on back campus I produced my first play, a strange medley of ideas unconsciously appropriated from *A Midsummer Night's Dream*, *The Land of Heart's Desire*, and the fairy tales of infancy. Daffodils still bloomed near the tree beneath which I had wept for Tess of the D' Urbevilles. Girls still munched Hershey bars as they strolled along the campus walks. How young they seemed. Could I possibly have ever been so young?

Here was the Library, more truly mine than all the rest. This was my corner. Here I discovered Christopher Morley and Rupert Brooke, here read "The Everlasting Mercy" and "Red Rock," here learned to love the old "Bookman." The stacks! They were closed to students now and the poor deprived book-lovers of today can never learn the look and "feel" of hundreds of volume they don't know enough to ask to see. Miser's gold to me, those hours spent sitting on a small ladder between the stacks, just taking books off the shelves, looking through them, reading a paragraph here and there. This was where I got my real education. Students took history notes as frantically as ever at the same old library tables. Did they still read John Fiske and Charles Hazen? And was there one among them who loved Kenneth Grahame or sympathized with Marie Bashkirtseff?

Everything looked the same yet everything was curiously different. Only the Winged

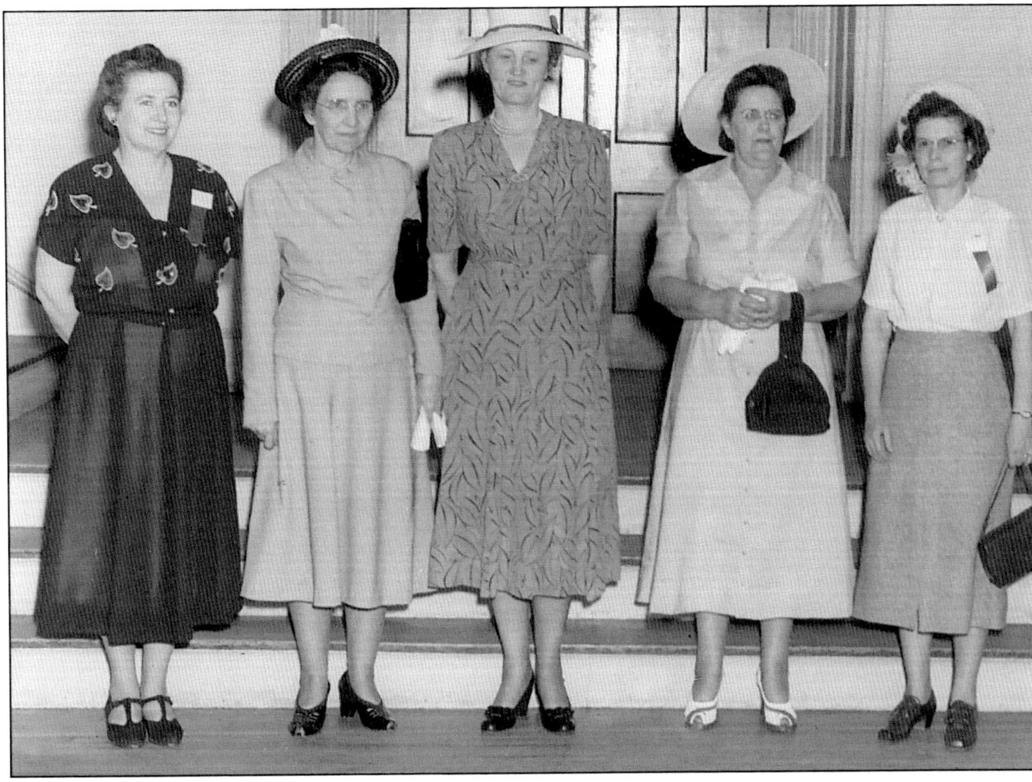

Pauline Jones Worthy and members of her graduating class *They returned to the college for alumnae activities during the college's annual commencement program in 1955. From left to right are Mrs. Pauline Marion Worthy of Washington, NC; Mrs. M.S. Lewis of Charleston, SC; Mrs. M.T. Williams of High Point, NC; Mrs. W.T. Hemingway of Hemingway, SC; and Mrs. W.T. Weir of Kings Mountain, NC.*

Victory, still standing at the foot of the steps in the lobby of Main Building seemed her usual self. For the first time I really looked at the Nike, classic draperies streaming behind her. During the four years I had lived in the shadow of her wings, I had never felt particularly fond of her. Now, at least, I mentally embraced her as my own. Every line of her body was straining forward. What a marvelous symbol for a Woman's College. It told me something about D.B. Johnson.

Our Ludy Comes Home. *Lucile Godbold was Winthrop's greatest athlete and one of the greatest in South Carolina history. Ludy, as she was affectionately known at Winthrop, broke the women's world shot put record and brought home six medals from a 1922 international track meet in Paris. At the time, women were barred from Olympic competition. Our heroine returned to Winthrop after her remarkable performance, and on October 7, 1922, she stood on the newly constructed stage on Winthrop's front lawn and addressed a cheering crowd of students. After her speech, President Johnson suspended classes so the entire college could celebrate "Ludy Day."*

Lucile Godbold's remarks, which follow, were published in the October 20, 1922 issue of The Johnsonian, *the student newspaper.*

President Johnson was standing where he has stood all these years. The hymn

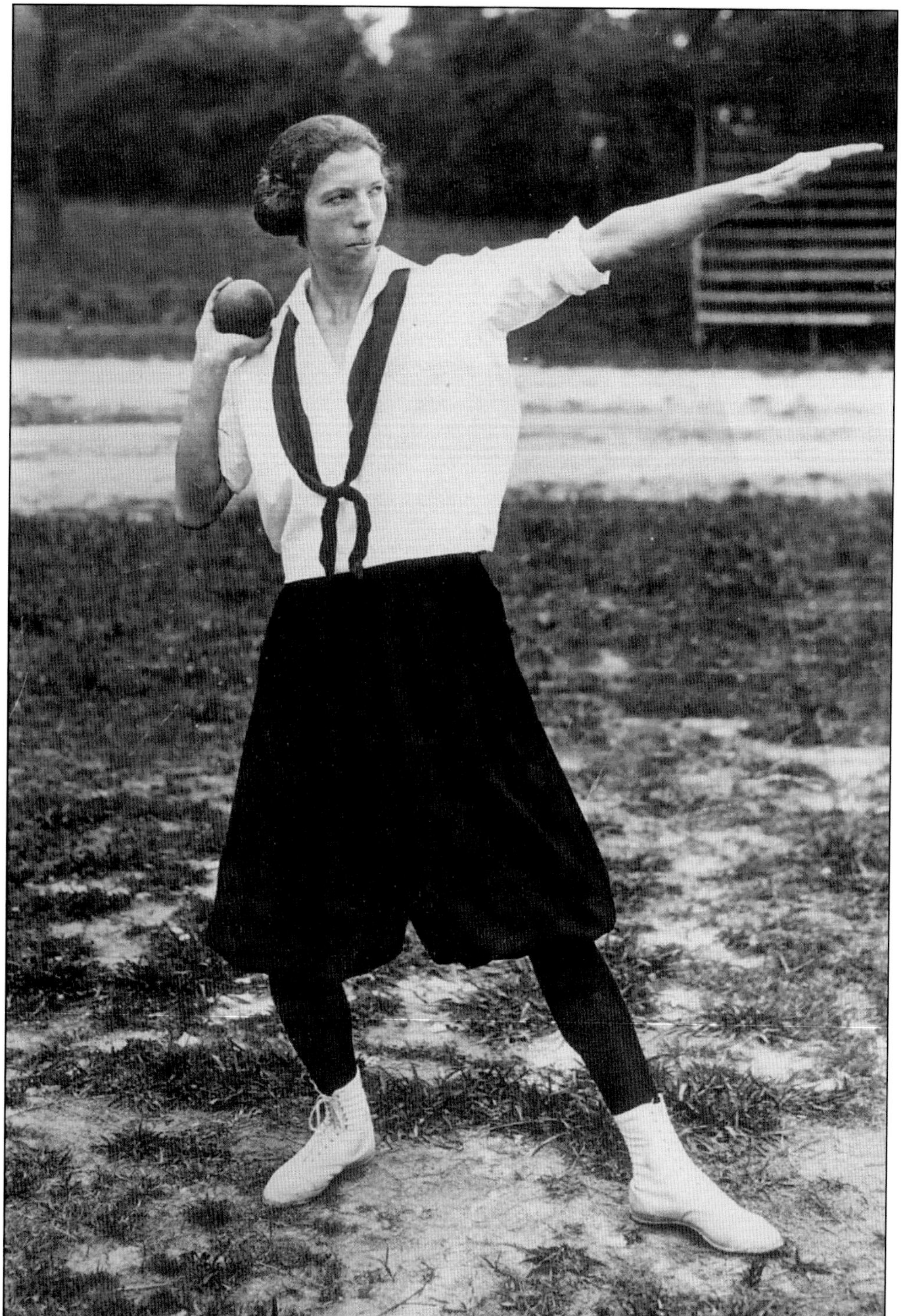

LUDY GODBOLD, WORLD CLASS ATHLETE

was announced, the Scripture read, the Lord's Prayer was repeated as usual, and then the announcements but just as Dr. Johnson had begun to tell that the movie that night would show Our Ludy in action at the Paris Olympic, the marshals with their beribboned staffs appeared in the rear, and with their entrance a roar, a storm, a thunder storm, of applause swept down the student crowd. It was deafening, overwhelming. The newcomers, especially on the platform, wondered what it was all about, but soon someone said, it's Ludy! And so behind the marshals there came a tall, graceful young woman tastefully dressed in dark blue, and evidently overwhelmed by her roaring reception. And how they did roar! They would have roared more had thirteen hundred girls possessed other means of roaring besides feet, hands and lungs.

Finally, the marshals reached the platform, where they presented the heroine to the president, who seated her in his chair and then with his masterly directness and terseness told of his trip to Paris, of the Olympic contest, and of the Winthrop victories. It's good to see Lucy in the movie, concluded Dr. Johnson. But it's better to have her here in the flesh, so it gives me special pleasure to represent her to you this morning.

As the modest, self-possessed young woman stepped to the front, the storm again broke loose, the storm of twenty-six hundred hands trying to tell in one volume the welcome that was stirring in thirteen hundred hearts. But it was trying to say something that after all could never be said, even by twenty-six hundred hands and thirteen hundred hearts. When the storm subsided in a voice full of individuality, Our Ludy began to speak and here is what she said, but as you read put in roars of applause at every telling point:

Dr. Johnson, faculty and students of Winthrop College: before I begin talking about myself I want to take the time to thank each and all of you, as well as those students who finished Winthrop last year, for the most wonderful and most pleasant trip of my life. Not just because you people raised the money to cover my expenses, but the way in which you did it and knowing that you wanted me to enjoyed my trip as well as represent Winthrop college at the first international track meet for women. I shall always think of you people and Winthrop College with pleasure. To you I owe a debt greater than I can ever pay, not a debt of money, but a debt of love and a debt of thanks. There is no finer college, nor finer people in all the world. I am proud to say that I have been a student of the South Carolina college for women.

Now, as I had to get up before five o'clock this morning because I had to leave Columbia (where I am teaching gym at Columbia College) on the 5:10 train, I'm not exactly myself, and I'm going to ask all of you to put up with what I say, whether it's interesting or not. If you get bored, please don't do anything worse than yawn, stretch, torment your neighbors or raise the roof. You better get fixed—for good, too, because I'm going to talk till sunset. You know people who get up on time to hear dawn crack are long-winded, and remember that when I got up this morning I met myself to bed. As you know, early in the spring, Winthrop College had her annual track meet. At this meet I broke the American record in shot put and as a result, at the suggestion of Mrs. Bartlett, our physical director, you raised enough money to send me to Mamaroneck, N.Y., to take part in a try-out track meet which was held to select a team to complete in the international meet. I had the luck to be chosen as a member of this team. [In New York she broke the American record in shot put, came first in basketball, second in hop-sky-jump, and second in the hundred-yard dash.]

Then you raised the necessary money for my trip to Paris. I was told to practice four events, shot put, and javelin throwing with hands, the 300-meter run and the 1,000-meter run. I came to summer school and

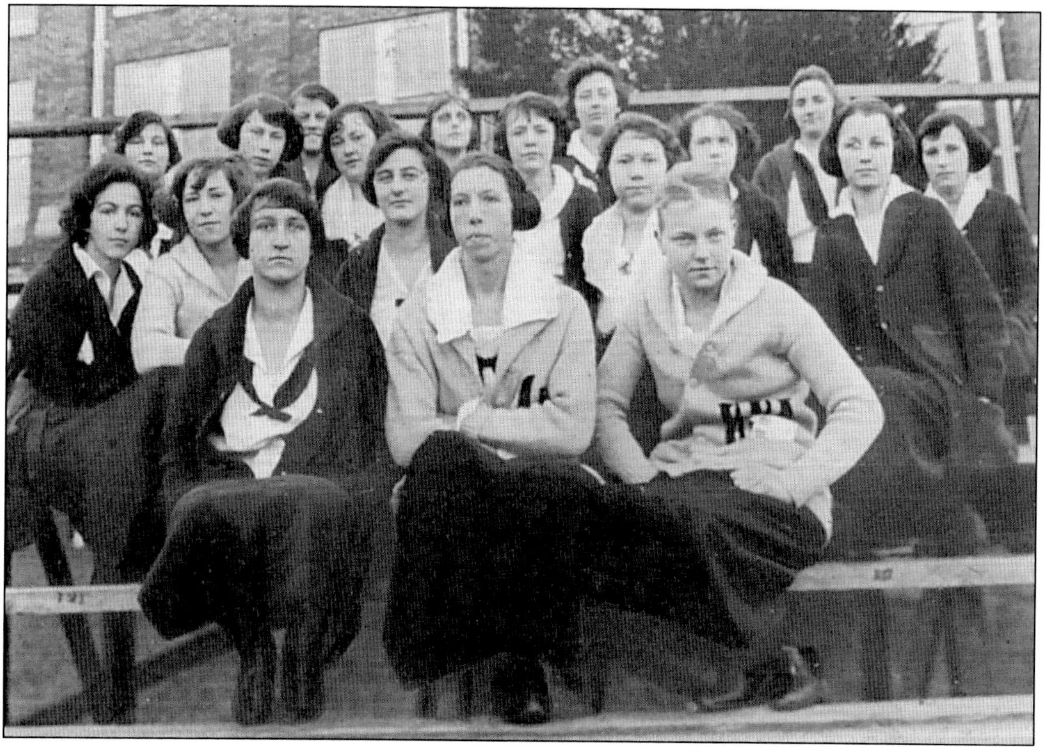

Ludy (center, front row) and the rest of the 1922 Athletic Association Board

got up early every morning to practice these events. It wasn't so much fun practicing by myself with nobody for except the dew and the birds that use to sit up on the grandstand and laugh at my attempts to throw the javelin. However, I stuck to it and after I had broken a couple of javelins and run round the track field so much till I could shut both eyes and run around backwards. Then the time came for me to go to New York.

We stayed in New York about a week, going over to Newark, N.J., every day to practice. We had a grand time in New York, and the members of the team got to know each other before we sailed.

On August 1 the team, with coaches and chaperones, sailed from New York in the *Aquitania*. It took us just six days to cross and we had a wonderful trip. We enjoyed it so much that we hated to leave the ship. We got up every morning before breakfast and practice on deck, one of which the captain let us use. To practice the 1,000 meter run I had to go round the deck three times, which gives you some idea of the size of the ship. Right here for Mr. Cooker's benefit, I'll say that a meter is a little over 39 miles—inches, I mean.

On August 7 we landed at Cherbourg, France. We had time getting through the custom house. They wanted to know if we had any tobacco or cigars in our baggage. Of course, they wouldn't take our word for it, so we had to give our clothes a coming-out party. I had a funny experience. I got a porter to carry my baggage and when he put it down I gave him a tip. Then he began jabbering some kind of lingo at me and after a time he got me to understand (Bright Ludy— that it wasn't enough. So, wanting to see the last of him, I tipped him again—and once more he started jabbering. I told him in good English that if he thought he was going to get any more money from me, he was having a dream. Both of us would have been standing there yet if I hadn't turned my back on him and walked off. It made no difference how much we tipped a French porter he would demand more. I soon learned to give a certain amount and walk off.

We went by rail from Cherbourg to Paris. We were in France two weeks. Every morning we would go to Colombes where we practiced for about two hours each day. In the afternoons or at night we went sight-seeing or to Grand Opera, etc. We saw everything that was worth seeing and a heap that wasn't. We took a trip to the battlefields and visited different cemeteries, and saw Quentin Roosevelt's grave.

We went to Versailles and went through the palace where the peace treaty was signed, and saw the flower gardens that are said to be the most beautiful in the world. After seeing all the beautiful things in Paris, the cathedrals, Notre Dame, the Louvre, etc., one doesn't wonder that certain French kings put France into bankruptcy.

The night before the meet I walked into the hotel, and whom should I see but Dr. Johnson! He looked good to me! Have you ever been away from America and a good while without seeing a soul you have known? Well it was a grand and glorious feeling, I'll tell you. The meet was to be next day and seen Dr. Johnson and knowing that someone from Winthrop would be there to want me to win out certainly did me a heap of good. I couldn't see him for long, but the next morning before the meet began, I talked to him a while. The meet was held in Pershing Stadium, and began early on the morning of August 20. In the morning we had the preliminaries. Only six of our team was chosen to be placed in the events. There were ten in each preliminary, because there were five countries represented and each country was allowed to have two contestants in each event. In the morning they were cut down to the four best. I placed in the shot put, javelin throw, the 300-meter run and the 1,000-meter run. The meet was run very much like our track meets, but on a large scale. Everything was announced in French.

We had lunch and Dr. Johnson ate with us. The meet began and each team marched around the field, with one member carrying her nation's flag. I was chosen to carry Old Glory, and, believe me, I was proud to lead that American team around the track. There were around 20,000 people to see us. The Americans were sitting in the center of the stadium, and I could see Dr. Johnson very well. It was a grand sight to see all those people from five countries yelling in five different languages.

My first event was shot put. I knew the French woman, who held the record was going to give me a hard fight, so I was all keyed up, so to speak. I was taller than the French woman was, but she was husky as an ox. She looks as though she could put that iron pill over the moon. Believe me, I was scared, too. Everybody knew she would win first. Her record with both hands was over 18 meters.

When I stepped into the circle our coach, Dr. Stewart, shouted, "now ole South Carolina mountaineer show 'em what the south can do!" I put the pill and I broke the world's record. I put it at twenty meters and more, twenty-two with both hands, and that it's sixty-six feet. This beat the French woman's record by more than six feet, six inches. She looked as though somebody has pulled a chair out from under her kind or sudden-like. But she was a good sport shook hands and congratulated me. The American flag was run up and the band played the "Star Spangled Banner" twice. I was one happy mortal!

The announcer took me around and introduced me to all those thousands of people (in French). He might have been crossing me out for all I know, but as everybody clapped, I reckon it was all ok. I can see those Americans yelling now.

They opened their mouths so wide I was scared to death for fear the sun will wrap their ribs or blister their tonsils.

Then when I looked up I was shut in by a group of men with cameras, about a million of them, as it seemed to me. I almost cast a fit grinning like a lunatic, and tried to make believe I was used to it. But you know better. The next event was the 300-meter run. My coach told me that it was just to trot around the track because that would give me fourth place, anyway, and he wanted to save me for the 1,000-meter race. I couldn't picture myself not running my fastest and I urged him to let me do my best, but couldn't budge him—worse than a balking horse! Before he finished, if he has said the moon was green cheese I would have agreed and thrown him a biscuit to eat with. That race was the hardest thing I ever did in all my life. The rest started off at a rapid rate and I have to just jog along I thought about Dr. Johnson and got tickled. I knew he must think I was crazy why anybody slower than a donkey could have gone faster than I did. I don't believe the judge knew whether I was last in that race or first in the next.

In the javelin throw I came third. I wish you could have seen the 1,000-meter race. Near the finish when you are supposed to speed up, the girl just in front of me fell sprawling. The big hunk of mud.! I could have murdered her. I was going pretty fast, and if somebody had offered me a million dollars to stop I could not have done it. I leaped over her (leap-frog-like) and in the leap thereof measured my length on that track of cinders. I thought I was through with this Old World. However, I dragged my carcass to an upright position, coaxed my bruised bones to work and took third place. That gave me two more points.

In the whole contest from the first, it was a tight race between England and America. We stayed ahead until two of our team was knocked out. Then England got ahead. She won first place, we got second, and France, third. After the international event, the American team had a meet of its own to present some events that were not included in the regular program. I took first place in hop-step-jump and second in basketball throw. I did not get points for this because the other countries did not go into them. Just our thirteen girls tried. If I had gotten points for these two events I would have had nineteen altogether, which would have been the highest number. After this all who won first places were given huge bunches of flowers. I thought I was a corpse.

We had lots of fun at the international banquet that night. Imagine five countries speaking five different languages, and you will make an idea of the fuss we made at that banquet. While in training we had to cut out all sweets, drinks, and so on, but at the banquet we turned loose. Did I drink wine? Can a fish swim? I ate so much French pastry I thought I would pop. In fact, I ate until there was no more.

A member of each team made a speech which was so much Hebrew to me. The cup was awarded to England. After we had eaten, the medals were awarded. I got six, three more than anybody else did. Each time a name was called—all in French—a girl went forward, got her medal and some other article from pictures to dishes. I am thinking of starting a hardware store.

The next morning we got up early and caught the train to Cherbourg. We sailed August 21 on the *Saxonia*. Who can keep from being seasick on a ship that thinks it's a cradle? About the third day out we got on a little gale and we began getting six meals per day—three going and three coming. One day I was leaning over the rail sightseeing, when a dumb-bell of a man came along and asked if I was waiting for the moon to come up. I told him I had seen everything else, but I didn't remember drinking any moonshine. Speaking of dumb-bells there were some on that tub. They thought Rex Beach was a bathing resort and Babe Ruth, a motion picture actress. Reckon they thought Billy Sunday was Easter Sunday's brother!

On *Acquitania* I had a room to myself, but coming back we existed four in a room. Our room was so small that half the furniture was painted on the wall. We

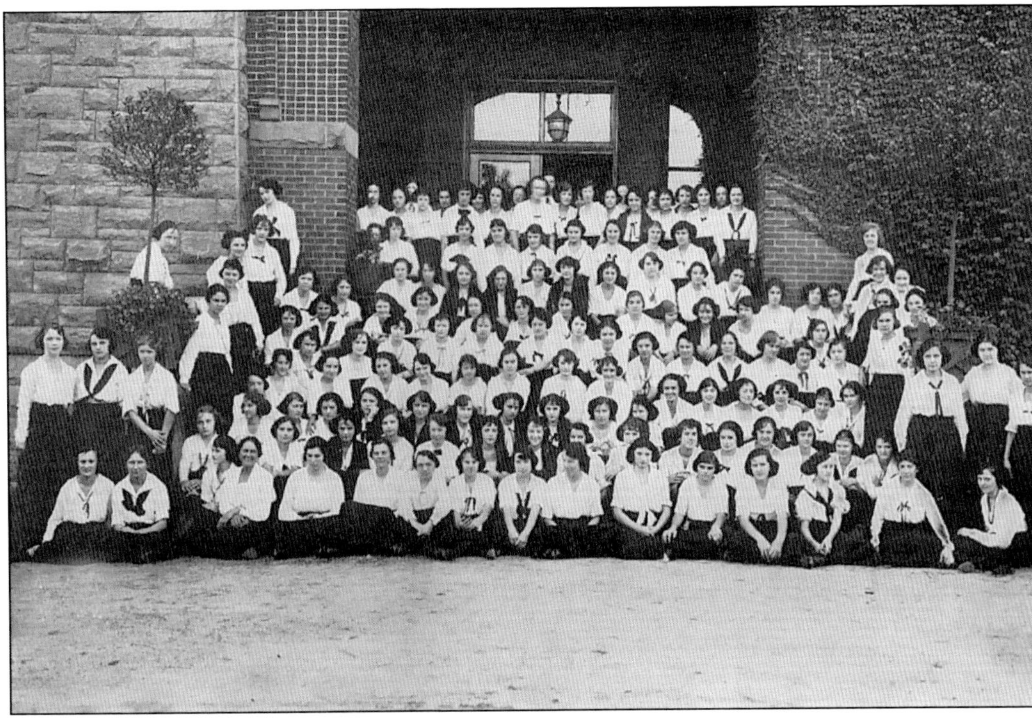

LUDY GODBOLD WAS A MEMBER OF THE SPECIAL CLASS OF 1922

had to back out in the hall to turn around and go on deck to even change our minds. As long as we stayed on deck it was all O.K. I cultivate the deck, and my deck chair and I were stonewalling buddies. I read so much I couldn't remember when I wasn't reading.

After creeping along for twelve days we got in sight of New York. Believe me, I was so glad to see the Goddess of Liberty as a Carolina mule is to see Sunday.

I didn't expect anybody to meet me and when I saw Mrs. Barlett I almost fell off the boat. I was so glad. I have to have my baggage searched, and I brought each of the men elements of the faculty a bottle of champagne straight from Paris, but I'm sorry to state it was taken away from me at the Custom House. After I had finished there I saw my father. Of course, I was tickled to see him, and after Mrs. Barlett had seen that I got my picture taken by everybody that asked me for it, we said good-bye and she went back home. My father and I stayed in New York a day or two, and then went to my home Estill, S.C.

The people in Estill were very nice to me and capped the climax by inviting Governor Harvey down and having what they called a Harvey-Godbold day. We had quite an exiting time. It was the first time a governor had ever spoken in Estill. I felt quite honored. Governor Harvey talked as though I had saved the country from small pox, or some such animal. Everything was decorated in garnet and gold and we had a lovely time. Before closing, I wanted to say once more how much I appreciate all that you people—the girls who finished last year, the faculty and officers, Dr. Johnson and Mrs.Barlett—did in connection with the trip to France. Especially do I want to thank Mrs. Barlett before all of you for the party she played. If she had not been a regular live wire, had she not kept up with what was going on in other parts of the country, I doubt if I would ever have gone to Mamaroneck to take part in the tryout meet in the spring. I have much to thank her for. As I said once before, what I did was done not for myself but for you people and for Winthrop, and because South Carolina and the south were looking to me to do my share in helping the U.S.A. win all she could in the first international meet for women. And after all that's what counts in all phases of life, knowing that there are people who want you to win out in whatever you undertake, whether it's doing track work, teaching or anything else worth while.

Possibly never before in its history did the old chapel ever see such a scene as followed Ludy's talk. In the thick of the thundering applause, Miss Mattie Sue Wofford stepped to the front of the stage and led the entire student body in singing the Winthrop Alma Mater Song, the college athletic song and Ludy Child. They sang out of one body and soul. Class demonstrations followed, entire classes rising spontaneously and in one way or another expressing their enthusiasm. And so it went, making an indescribable scene, which can occur only at a time of supreme exaltation. Dr. Johnson then introduced Mrs. Barlett, saying that it was to her training of Miss Godbold that owe the victories at Paris, that Miss Godbold had taken to Paris with her the spirit, the attitude and ideals which should always be characteristic of true athletics, which were at all times brought out here under the direction of our department of Physical Training, of which Mrs. Barlett is head. Mrs. Barlett then told how she meet Ludy in New York in response to a message from Dr. Stewart, who had a special message for Dr. Johnson and Winthrop, which was that Miss Godbold was by far the all-around athlete at the meet and that she established the morale of his party. Mrs. Barlett told of how when the boat docked everyone was asking and looking for Miss Godbold—that dozens of camera men were there trying hard to get pictures of her—that from the goodbyes of the party themselves it was not hard to see which was the most popular member of the American team. But best of all, said Mrs. Barlett, Ludy has come through world honors and is the same unspoiled Ludy. She then showed to the audience the six medals Ludy had won and also the suit, which she wore at the meet. Dr. Johnson said in conclusion: "Ludy has brought great honor to Winthrop and us all. Every leading newspaper in every civilized country in the world has made mention of her. We want to honor her"—but the students with their usual keenness, catching what was coming, drowned out the announcement which the president was about to make-and which he did make: "That today we will suspend work and celebrate in Miss Godbold's honor as Ludy Day!"

Chapter Three

Images of Winthrop's Campus

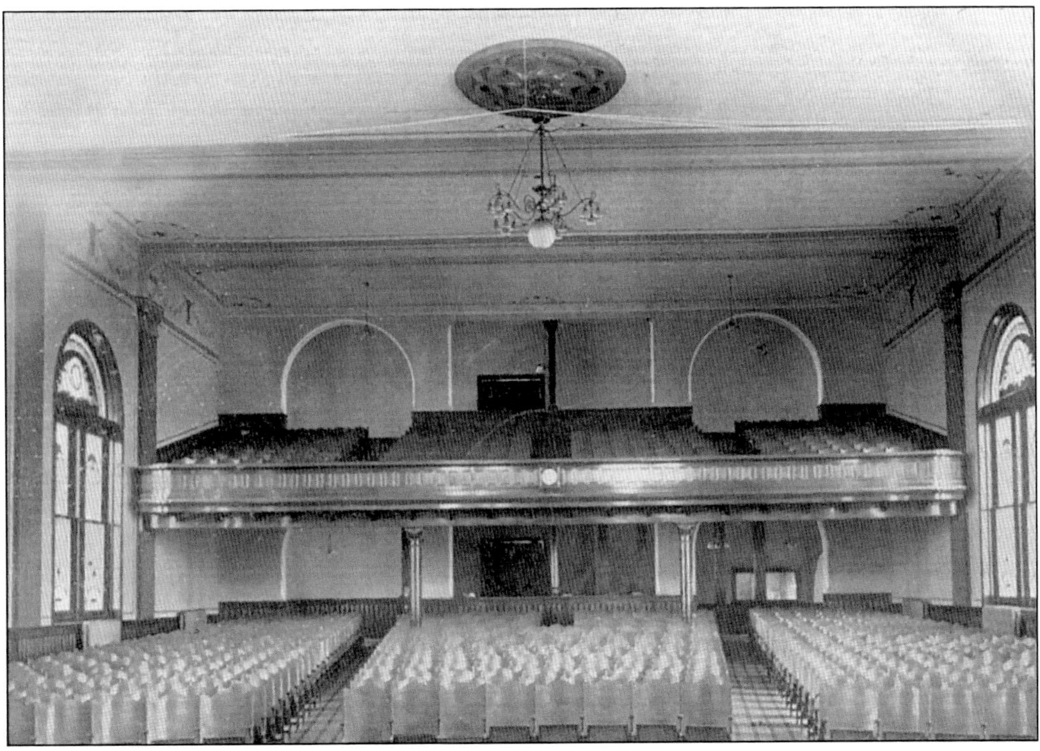

Auditorium, 1898

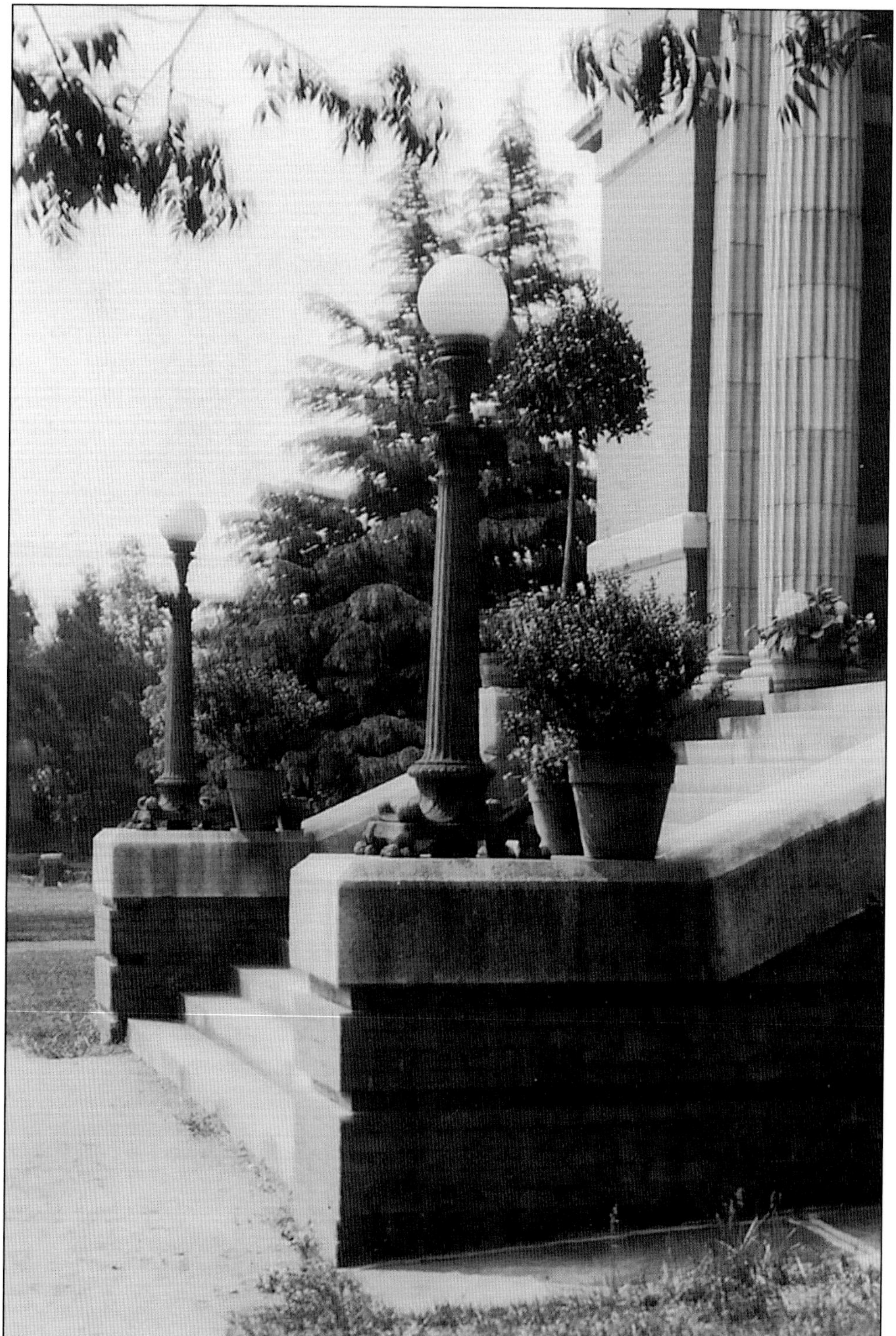

THE LIBRARY NEAR THE TURN OF THE 20TH CENTURY

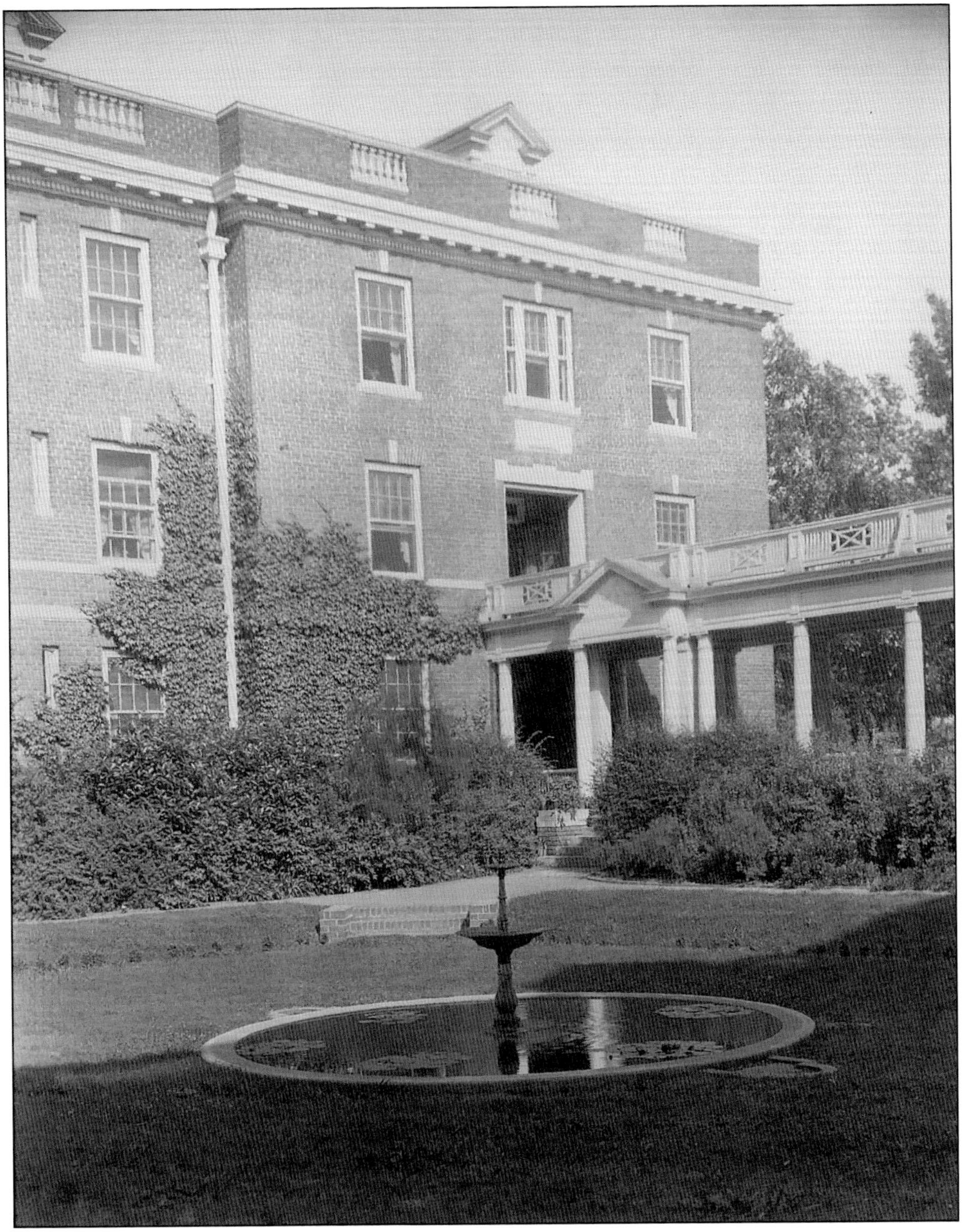

RODDEY HALL, BUILT IN 1920

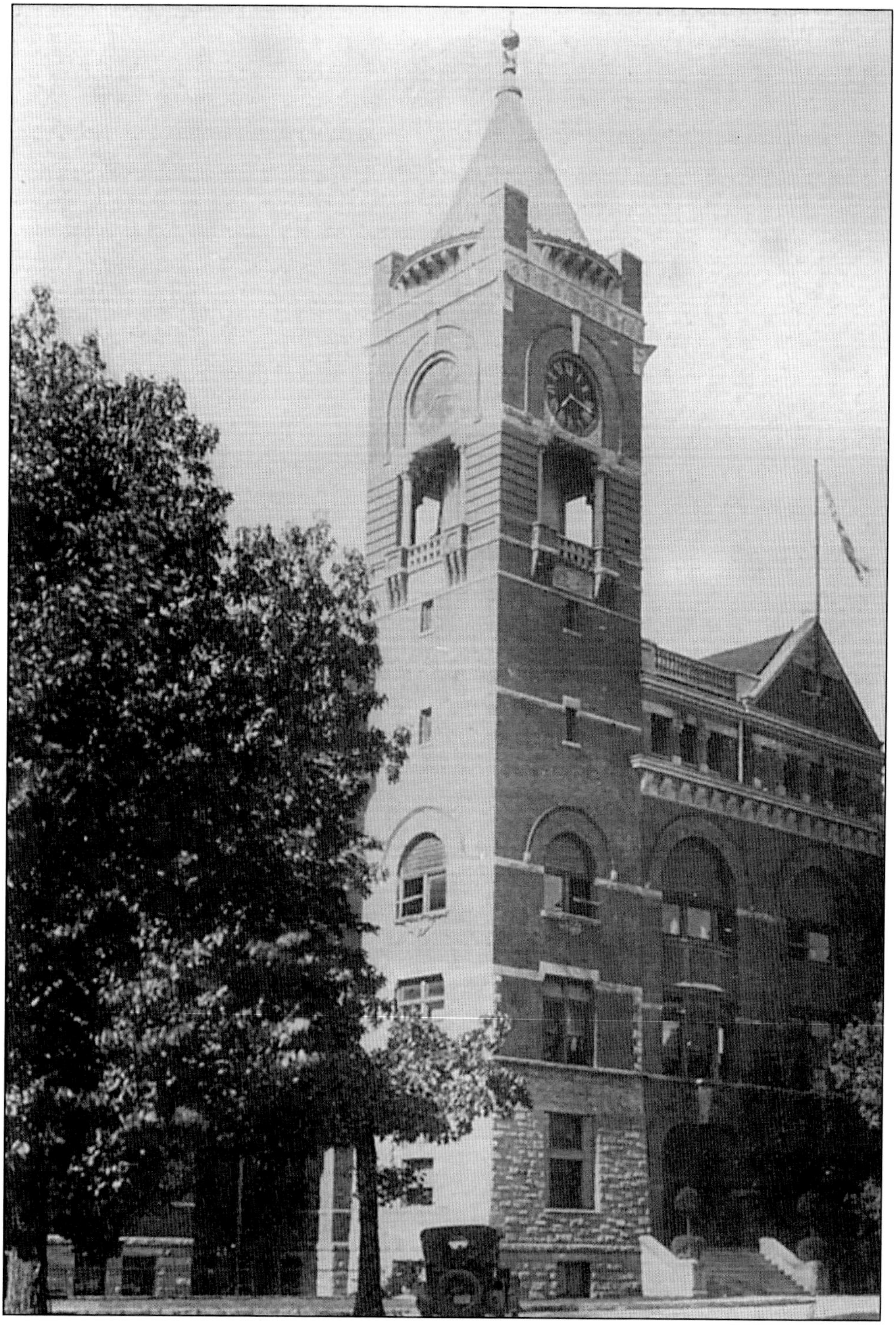

ADMINISTRATION BUILDING, 1920

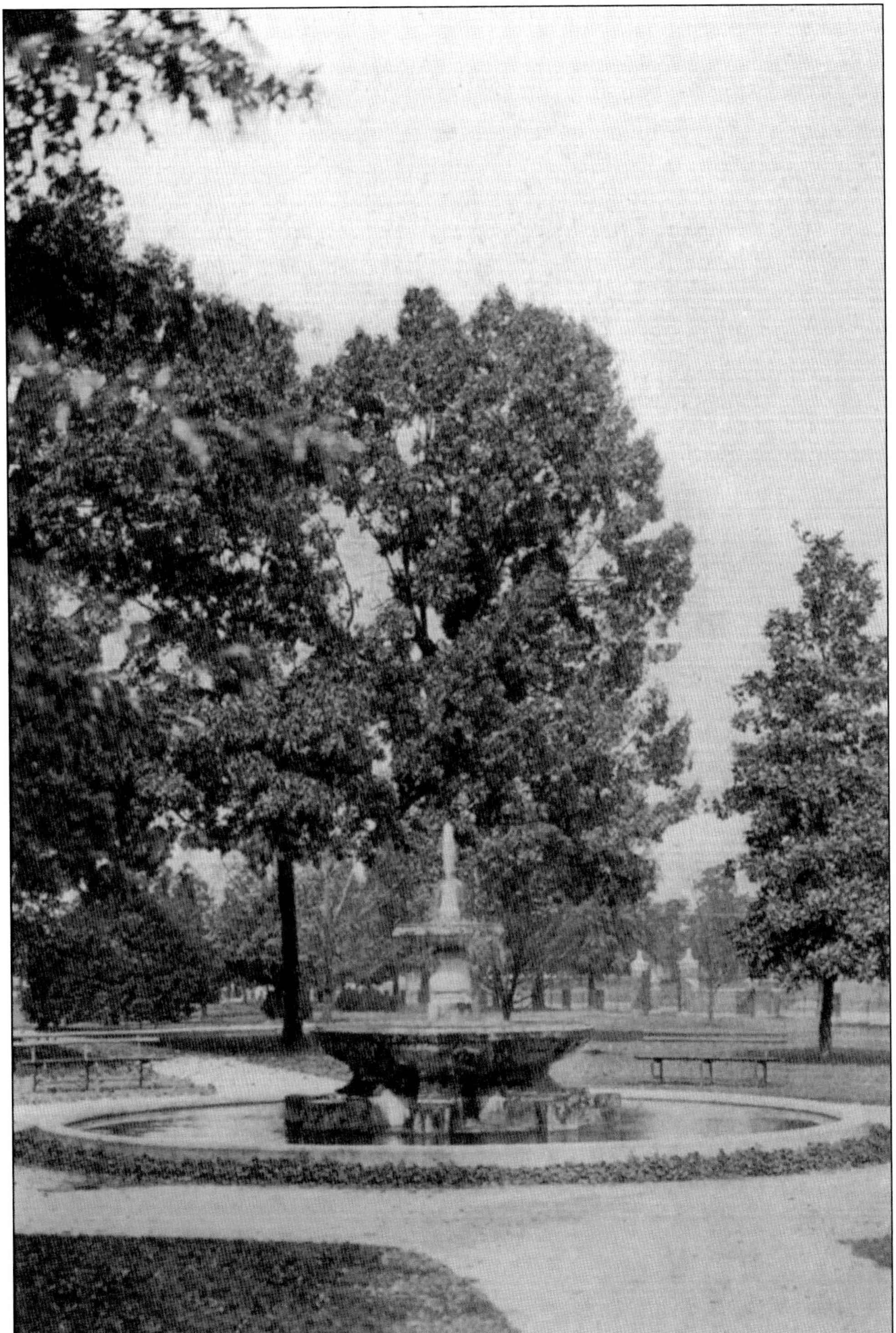

THE FOUNTAIN, 1920

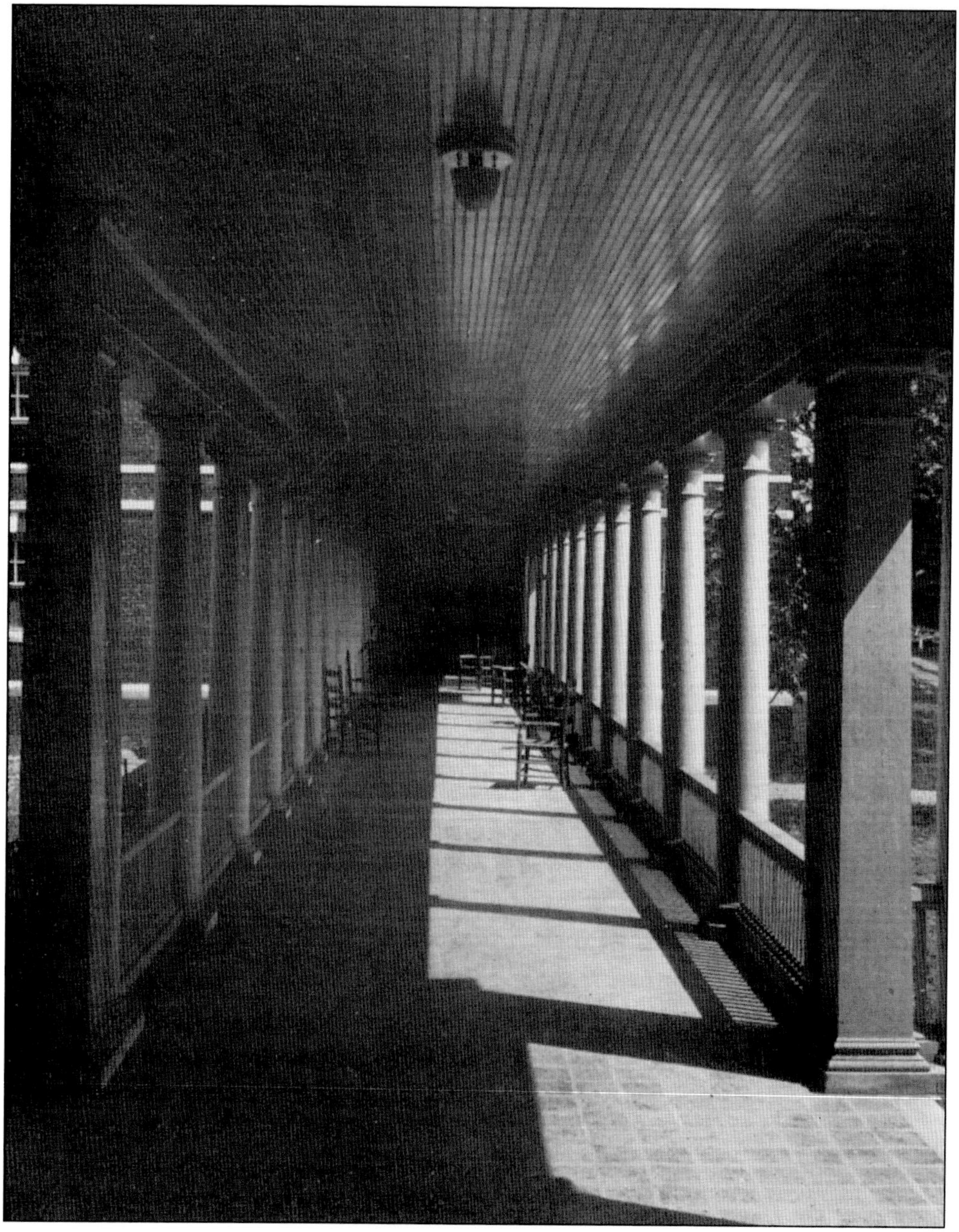

The college campus, 1922

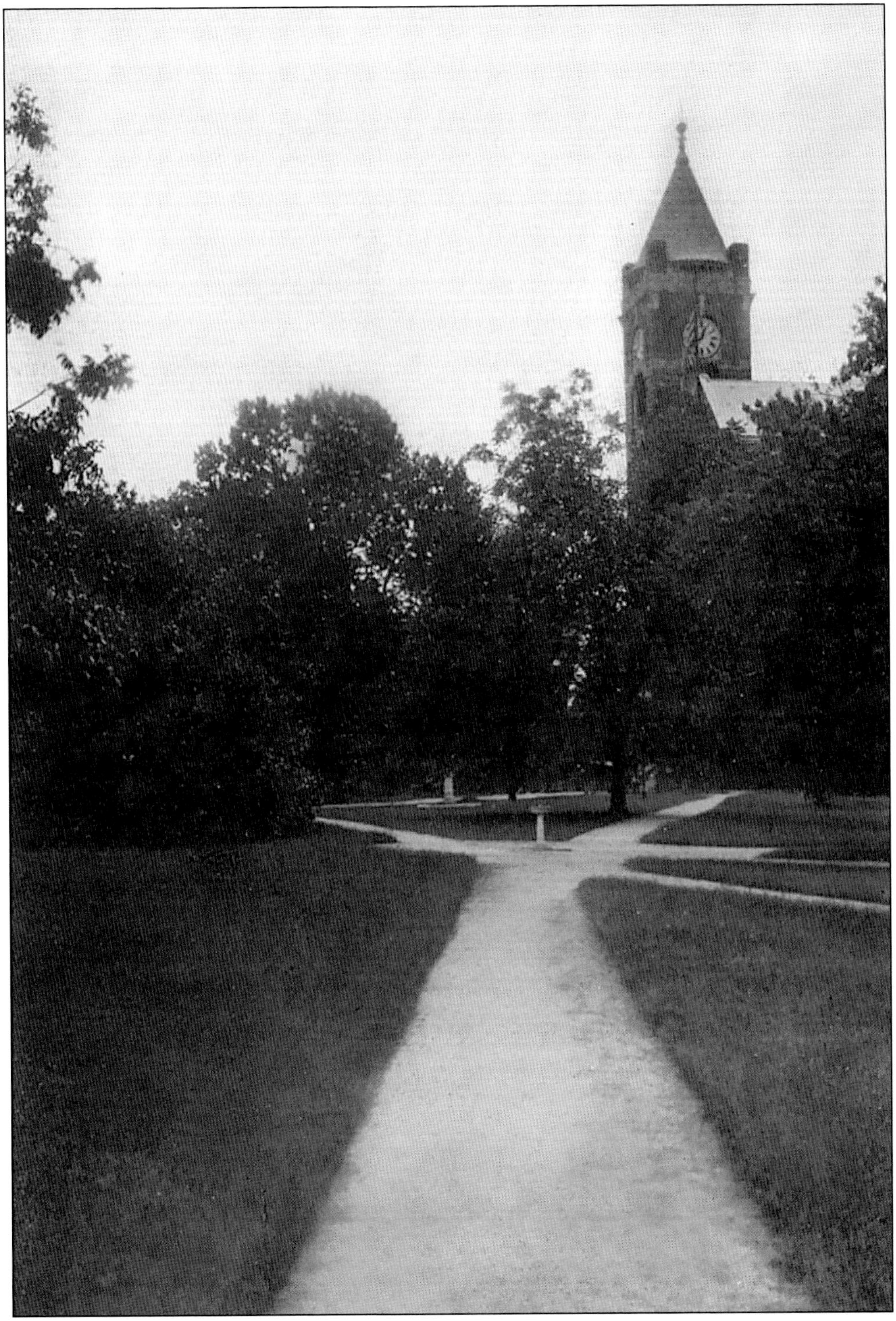

ANOTHER IMAGE OF THE CAMPUS, 1922

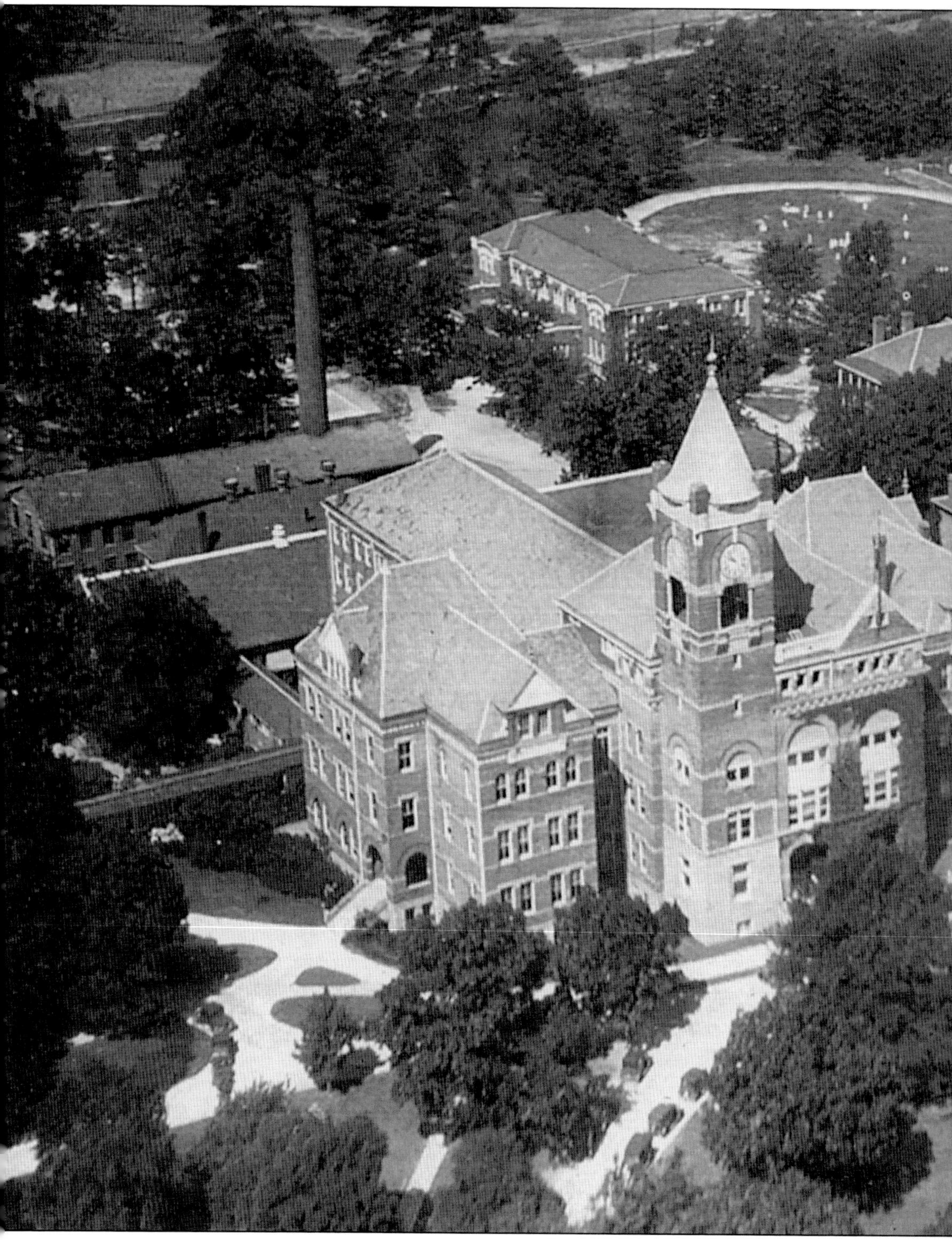

A bird's-eye view of campus, 1929

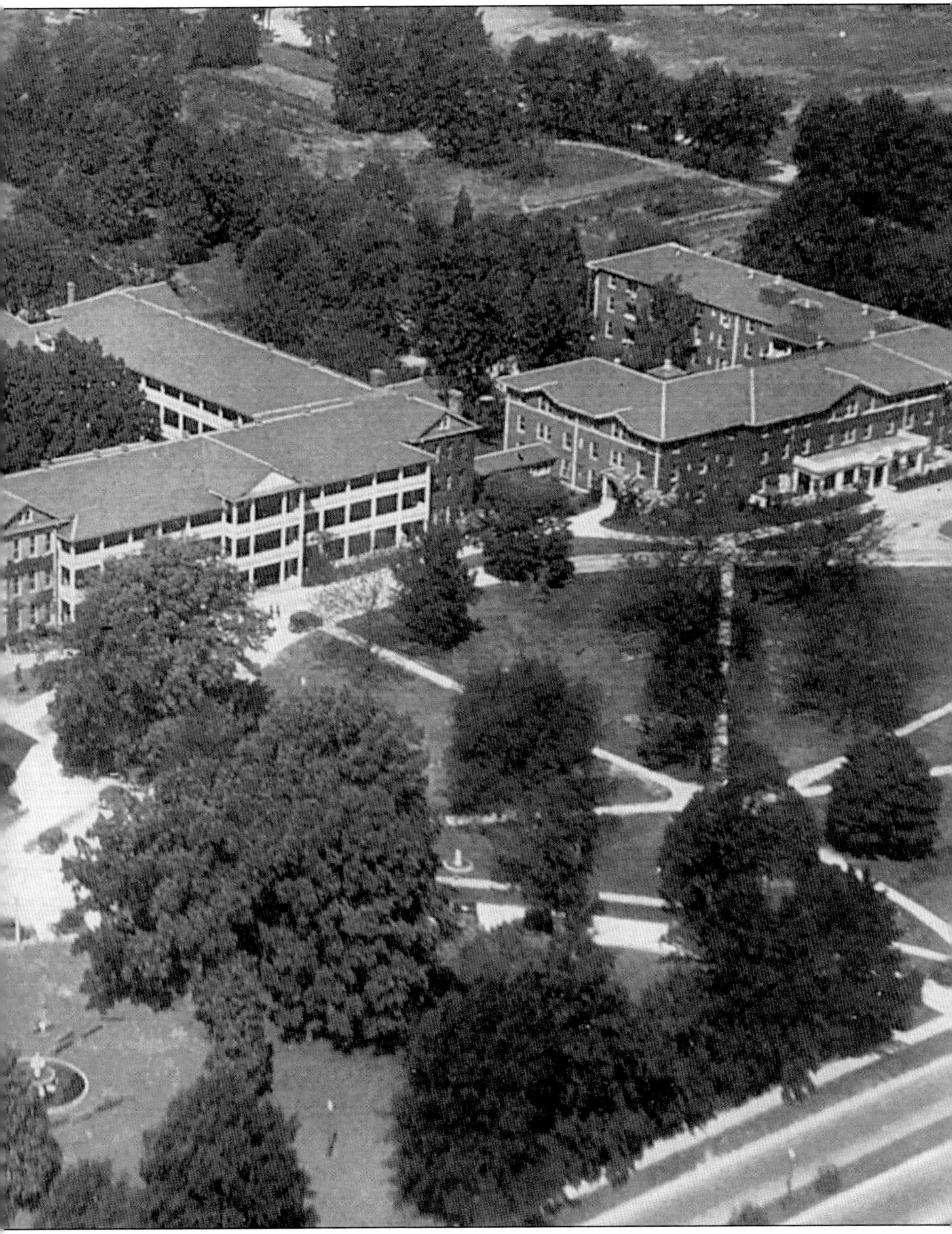

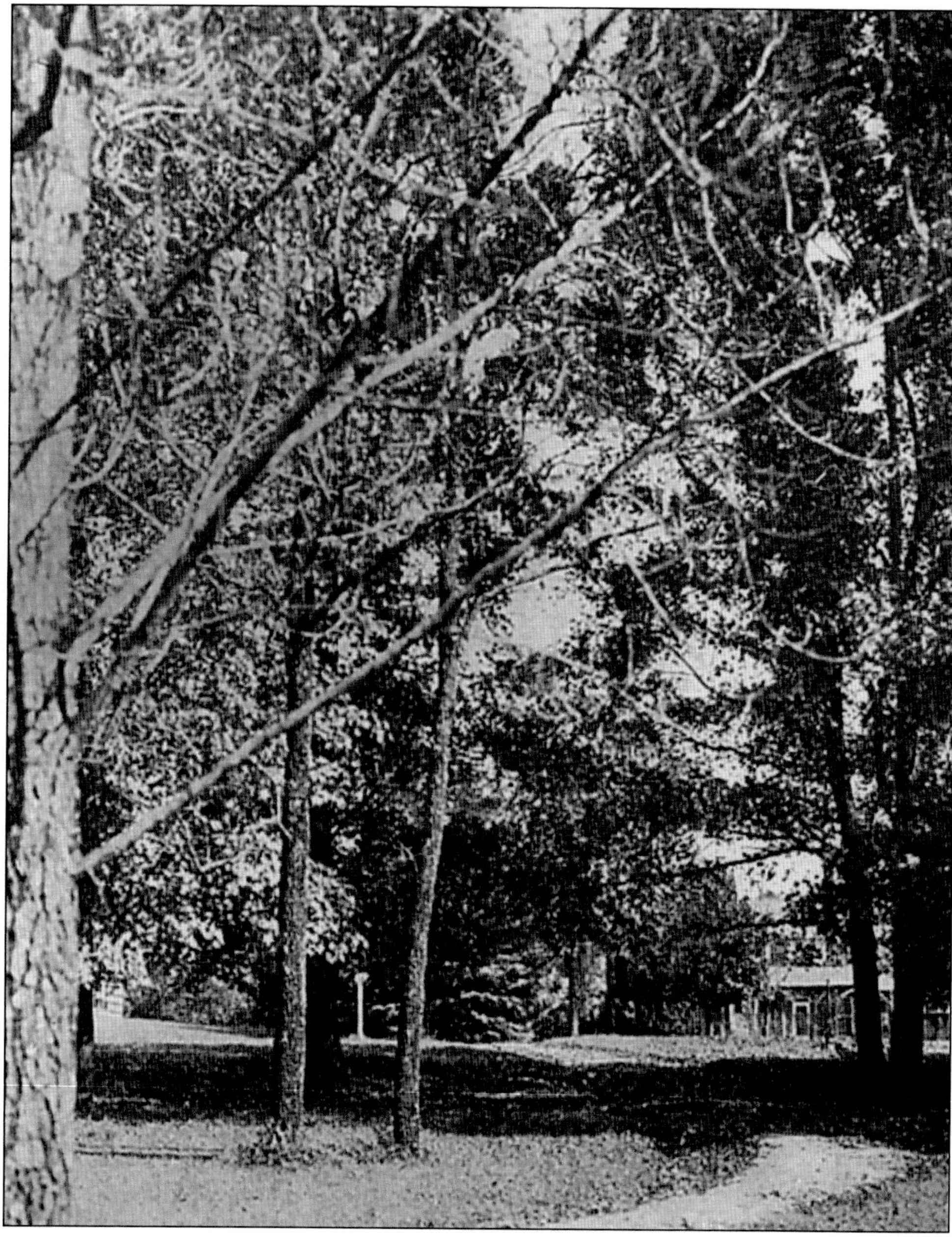

Long Lane, 1922

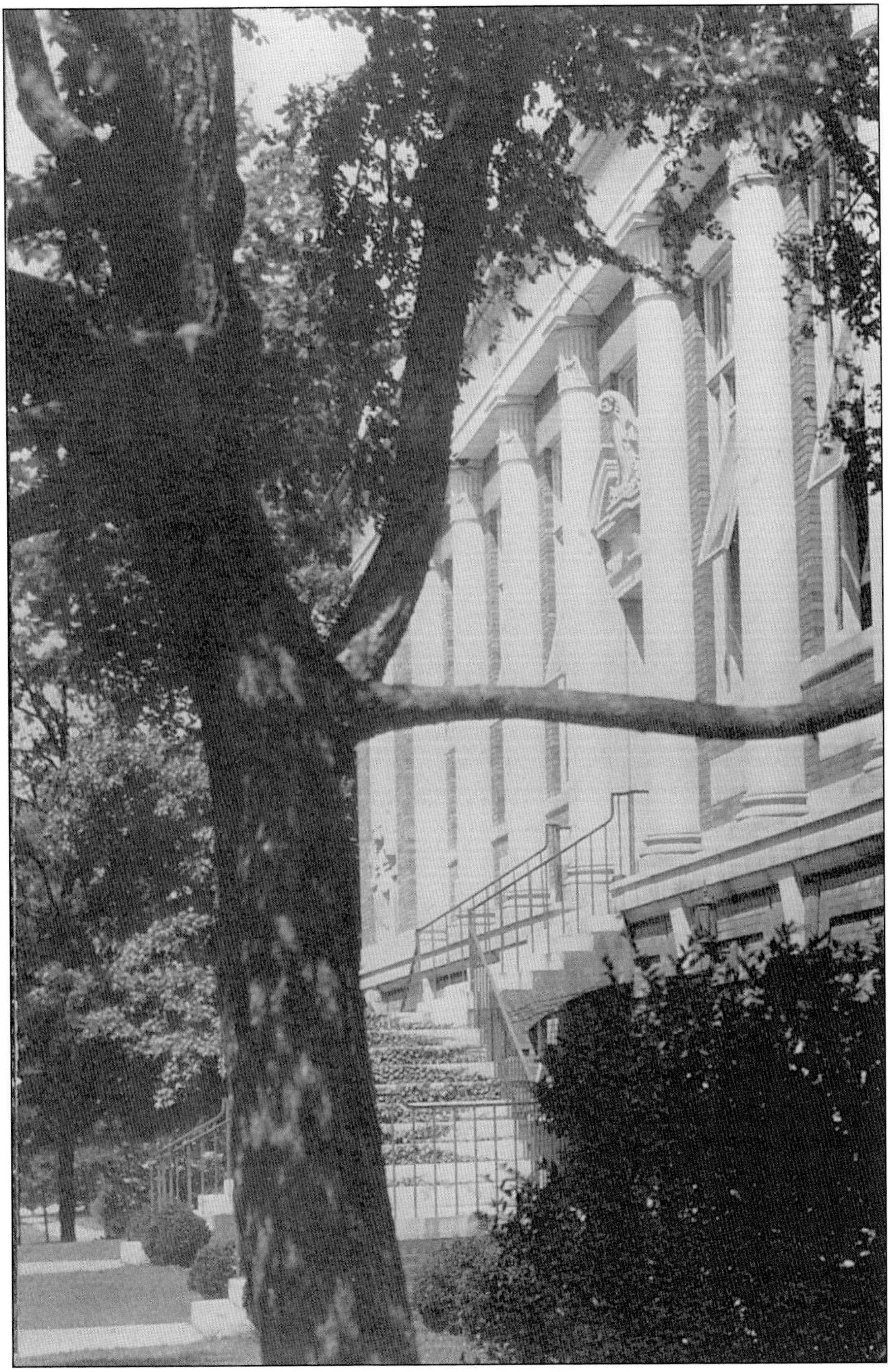

Looking down East Campus, 1934

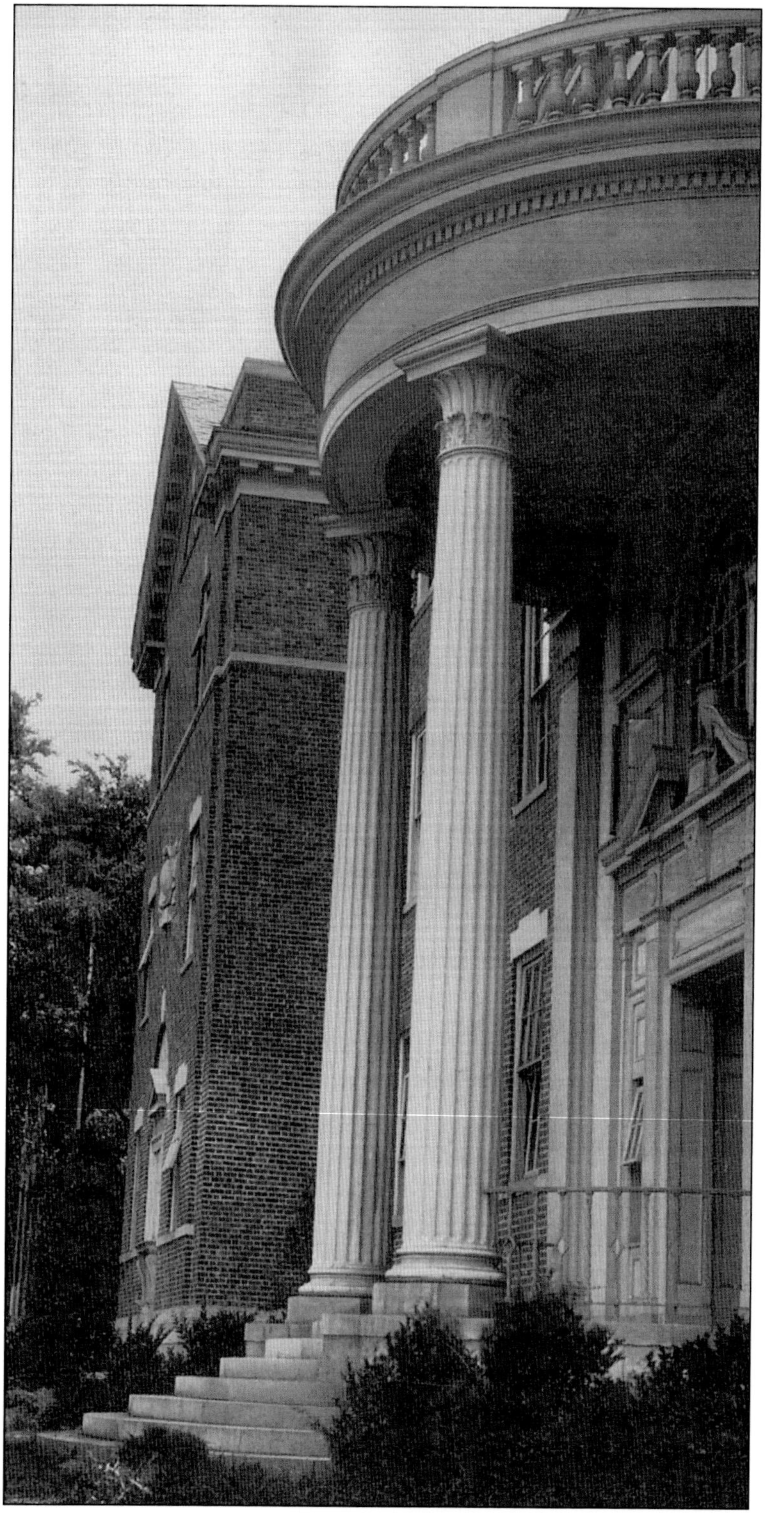

Kinard Hall, 1934

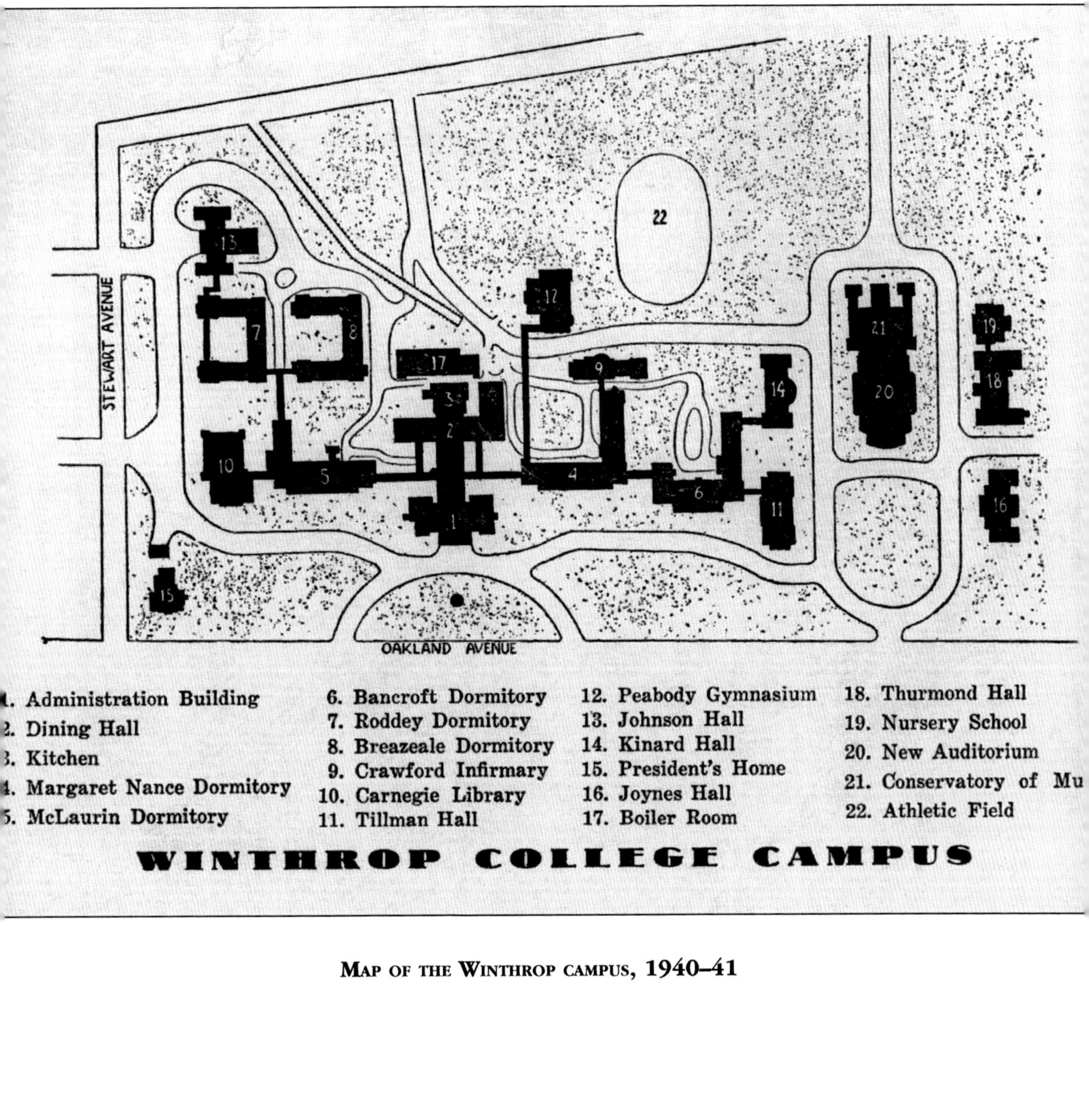

MAP OF THE WINTHROP CAMPUS, 1940–41

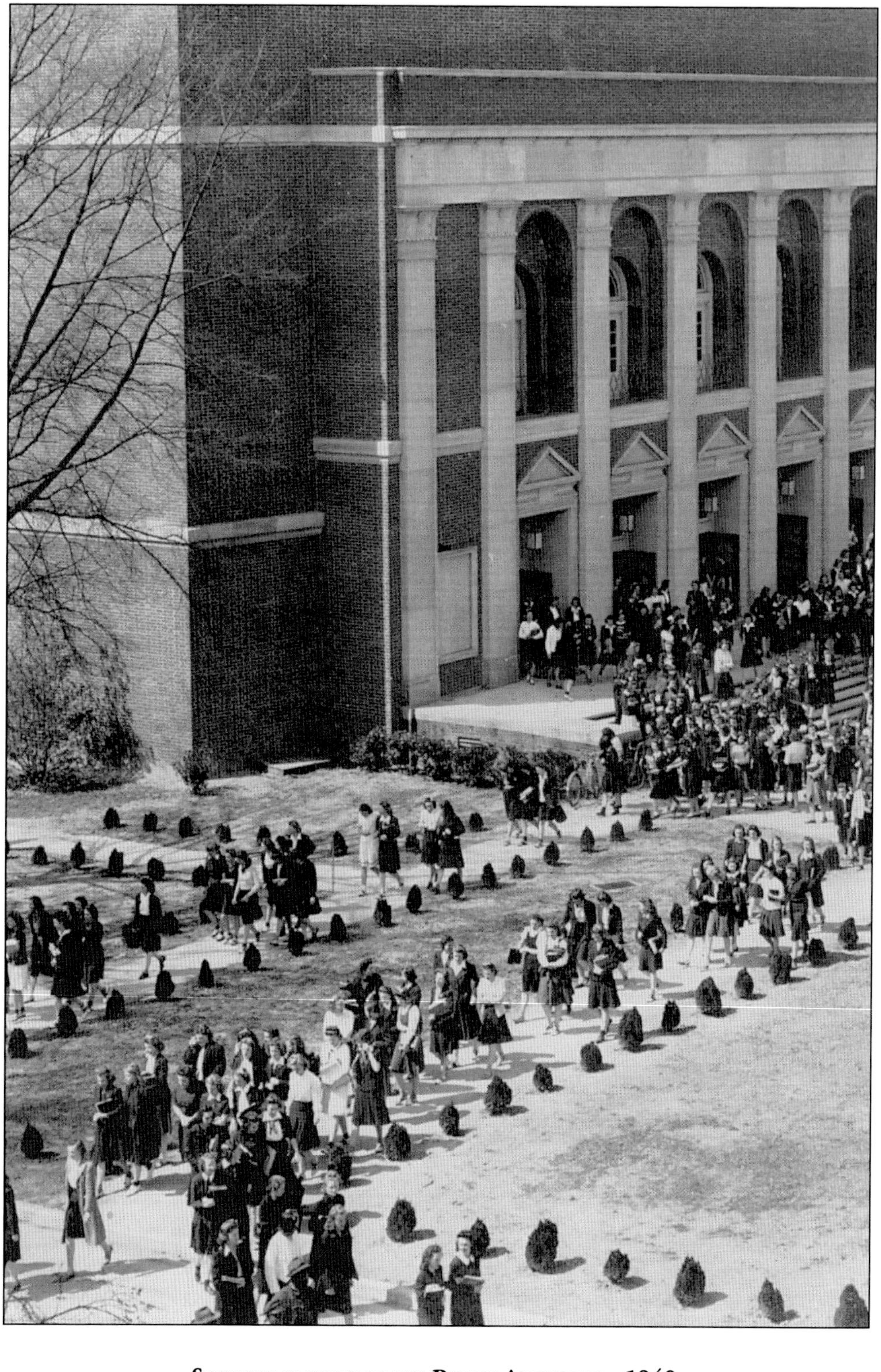

STUDENTS IN FRONT OF THE BYRNES AUDITORIUM, 1940

Chapter Four

Most Cherished Memories

A Most Nostalgic Look at May Day's Past. *This account appeared in the spring 1963 issue of the* Winthrop Alumnae Magazine. *In the university's pre-coeducation days, May Day was one of Winthrop's most venerable traditions. On the first Saturday in May, hundreds of Winthrop parents, alumni, students, and townspeople filled the brick tiers of the amphitheater. The May Court consisted of 16 handmaidens, 4 from each class. For many years, May Day was the last big celebration before graduation.*

Certainly on the occasion of Winthrop College's first May Day, most extravaganza was originated and sponsored by the senior class and directed by Miss Alice Allene Sefton, head of physical education; there was no hint that only five months later Wall Street would come crashing down and the Great Depression would settle over the land.

According to the April 27, 1929 edition of *The Johnsonian*, Winthrop was all a-twitter-making preparations for officially welcoming for the first time in its history the merry month of May.

On the first day of May the hockey field presented a scene far different from that of the exiting hockey game of last November, for Winthrop is, for the first time, inaugurating a May festival? "Mid folk dances, songs and light-hearted gaiety, she will crown her fairest daughter queen of the May. "

This fairest daughter was extolled for her beauty and charm in 108 lines of poetic prose, a few of which appeared below: Joy and excitement have full sway over our campus for the past few weeks.

Low whispers and thrilling silence have made mystery in our corridors!

Who Is the Queen, our Queen?
The lovely Queen of May
Whom all her subjects will adore
And reverently obey?

This lovely and delightful title has been bestowed upon an equally lovely and exquisite girl. Miss Mary Marvin, of White Hall, S.C., has been selected for the student

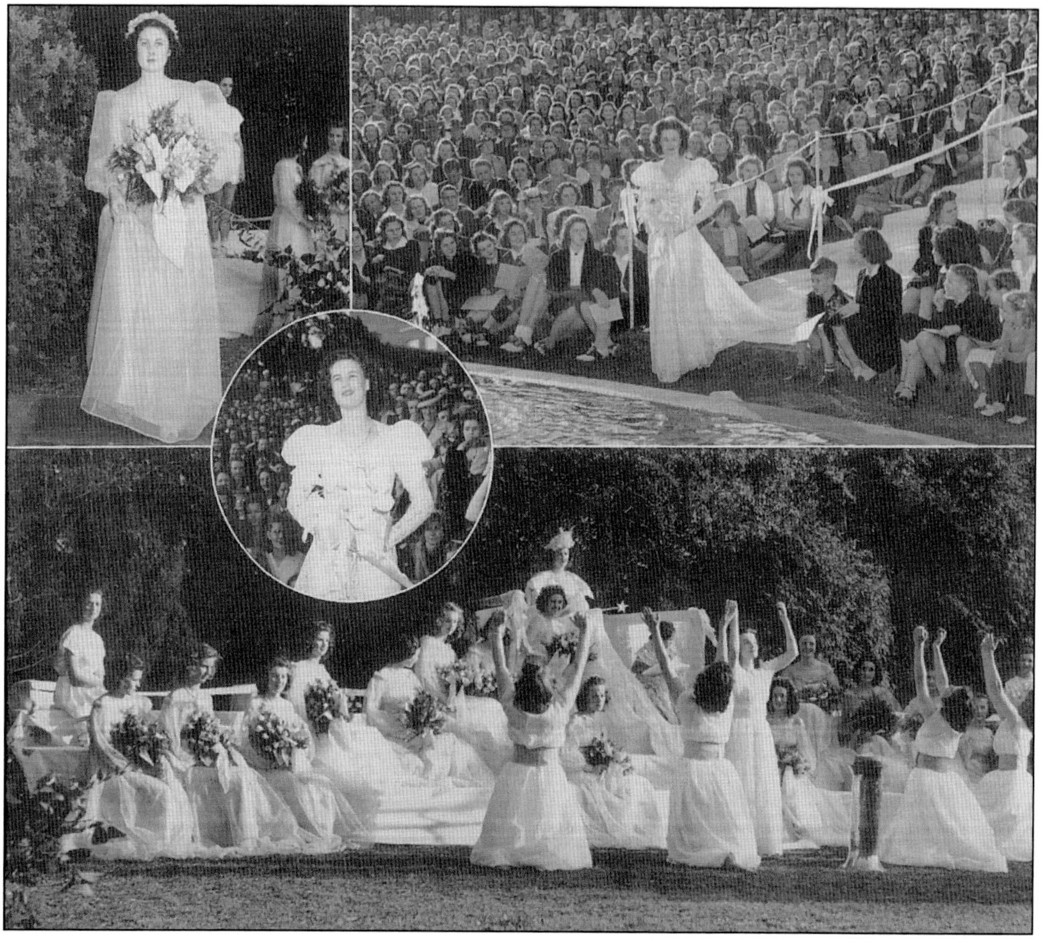

May Day at Winthrop, 1940

body as possessing all the charm required to become the queen of our first May Day.

It is known that the requirements for this honors were: that she should be regally poised, gracefully charming, and charmingly graceful, and should have the respect and admiration of her subjects. All of these and more are found in our queen-to-be and we congratulated ourselves upon such a splendid choice.

Besides the two columns wide, seven inches high picture of the queen-to-be in her royal dress of "white moire satin with a form-fitting Basque to the hips, then flowing gracefully into two circular godettes with uneven skirt up to the knees in front and to the heels in the back." *The Johnsonian* carried a picture of the sixteen maids who would attend the Queen. These Winthrop beauties from each of the classes of '29, '30, '31, and '32 were fashionably dressed in "organdy in pastel shades, made with tight bodices and skirts ruffled to the ground."

In the photo, Mamie Stackhouse Brooks (Mrs. David, '31), Georgia Townsend Sinkler (Mrs. D.L., '30), Genevieve Limehouse Thompson (Mrs. Ralph, '30), and Jamie Bland Roper (Mrs. Robert, '30) all wore their long tresses pulled demurely behind their ears, probably into neat buns at the back. Elizabeth Lowe Koon (Mrs. Sam, '31) added originality to her hairdo by braiding it

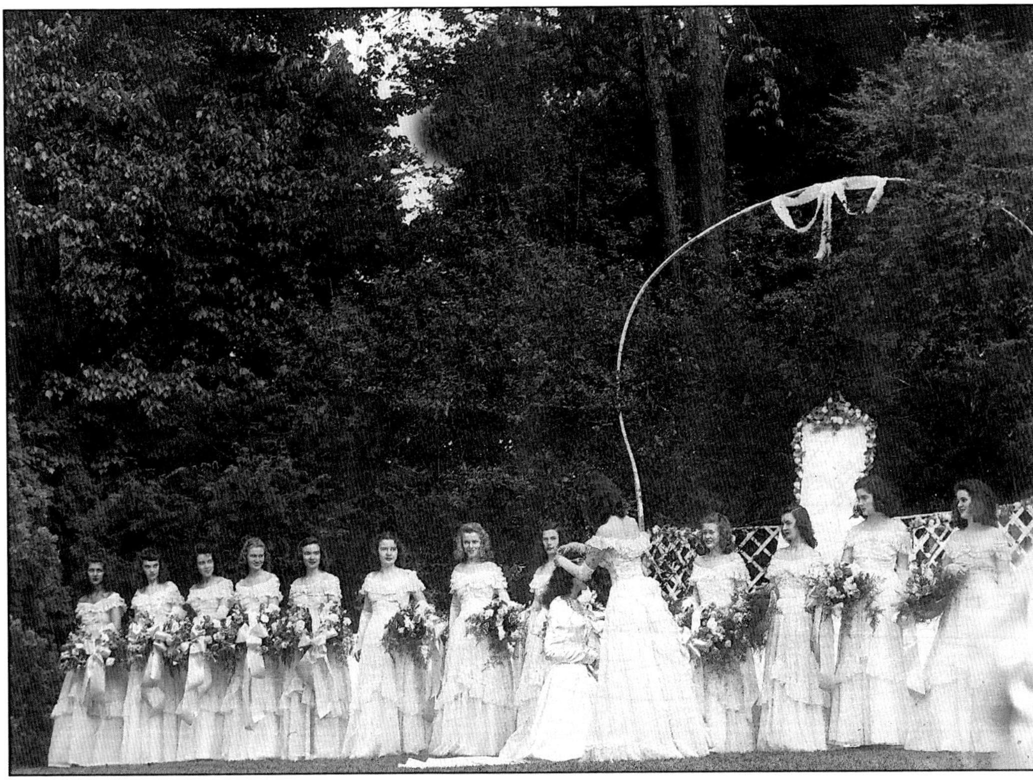

Crowning La Neele Smith, the May Day Queen for 1947

across the top of her head. Katherine Knight Coe (Mr. Richard, '32), though pulling hers back behind the ears, added a coy touch by making a large pin curl on the side.

Florence Croft Stone (Mrs. Eugene, '30), from the picture, at least, appears to have been blessed with naturally curly hair. Most of the others, which include Lena Miles Wever Todd (Mrs. Leonard, '31), Allie Smith Spencer ('29), Thelma Hodge McCollum Jackson (Mrs. Jay L., '29) show evidence of having been marcelled at the beauty parlor or, at least, to have had the benefit of hot curling iron artistically wielded by their roommates. Coiffures of Hilda Bingham Tiller (Mrs., '32), Katherine (Mrs. T.B., '31) and Martha Bryan Farmer (Mrs. Augustus, Ex-'32) for the year 1929, bear a remarkable resemblance to the strange bushiness so stylish today. For some reason, Mollie Blackwell DeLoach (Mrs. Serre, '32) and Ruth George Lott (Mrs. J. Neal, '29) were not present for the picture.

An editorial in the some issue of *The Johnsonian* called attention to some interesting May Day history:

The puritans, objecting to the celebration of this distinguished English costume, marched down in a body upon Thomas Morton and his group of gay followers, burned the Maypole and routed the company of merry-makers. So the old custom died out entirely, and not until recent years has it been revived. The American colleges have been largely responsible for the revival of this lovely custom.

The puritans might prohibit open demonstration of May Day pleasures, but they cannot prevent the unconscious nature of worship that springs up in every heart and will find expression in spite of creeds.

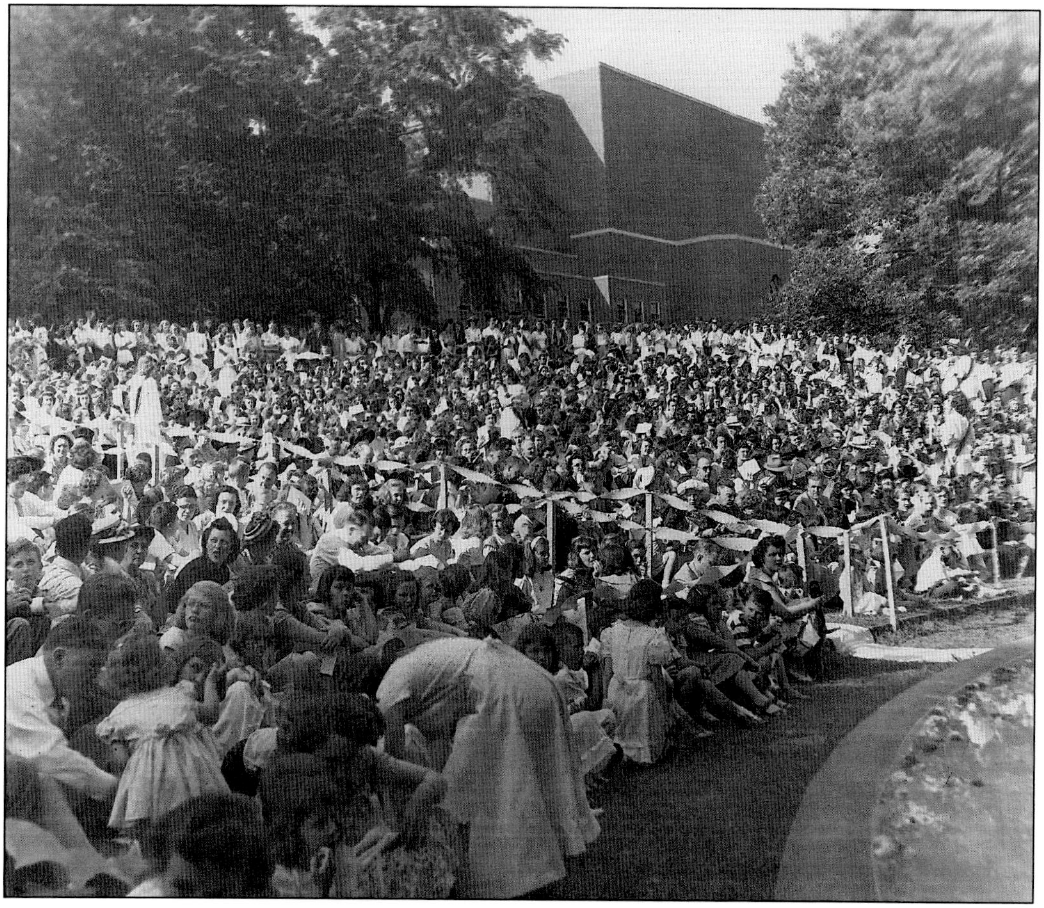

THE 1949 MAY DAY CELEBRATION *This huge crowd was typical of the crowds drawn by the annual celebration.*

This year Winthrop will have a May Queen who will preside over the festivities of May Day, while the students make an outward demonstration of that delightful spring feelings which communicates exhilaration to everything.

The 3,000 non- puritans from all over South Carolina who attended this first May day at Winthrop were handed expensive, lavender-colored programs of fine quality, deckle-edges paper with the title "Spring in many Lands" and a poem that began: "Hail, bounteous May, that doth inspire/Mirth and youth and warm desire."

A count of the names listed in the program as being participants in the Winthrop's first May Day indicates that a whopping 421 people portrayed Greek maids and athletes; danced favorite Swedish folk dances; played the parts of witches, little fairies, and Irish dancers; fluttered about as butterflies in a forest in Russia; sang as they cleaned out the wells, an ancient German custom; performed "A flirtatious French dance"; and welcomed spring with singing and dancing, Spanish and Italian style or with coyly waving Japanese fans. Sixty-four girls danced around the Maypole; 22 girls played in the orchestra and 37 sang in the chorus. Professor Walter B. Roberts directed music.

The tremendous amount of thought, originality, and plain hard work that

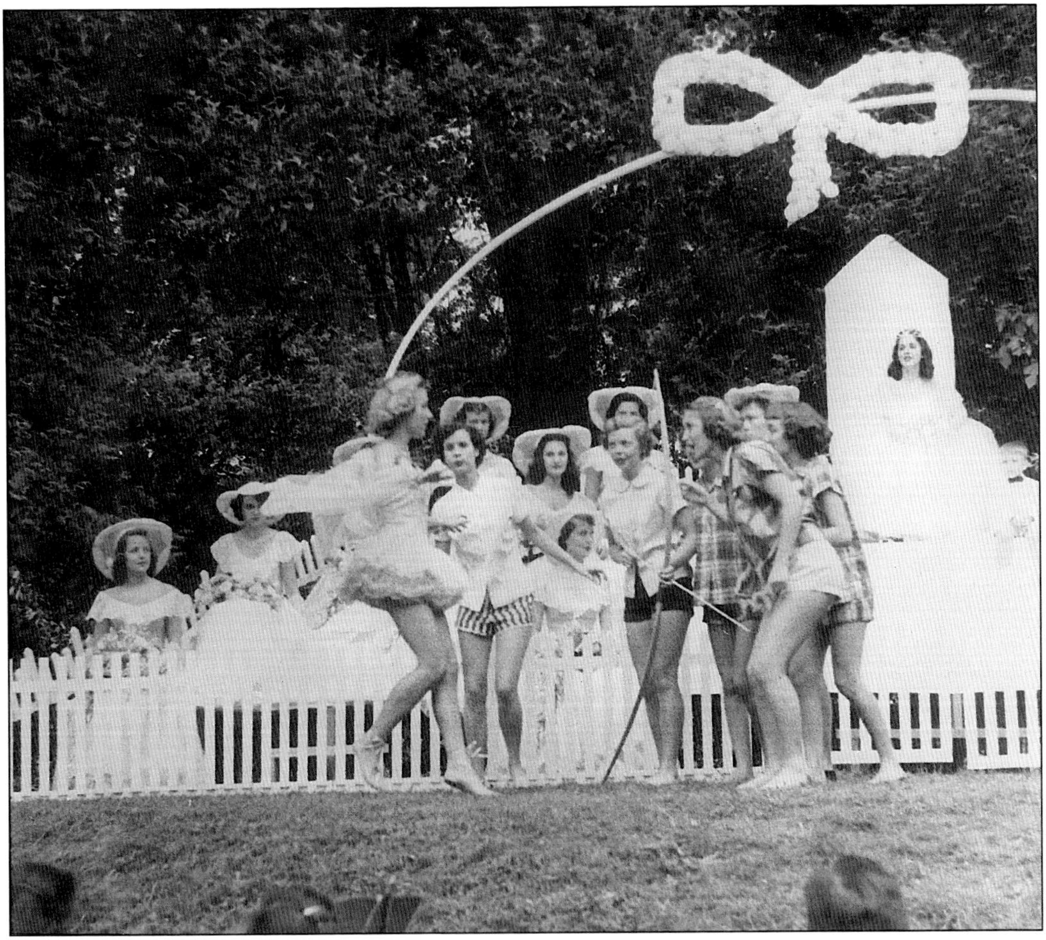

FUN AND FROLIC AT THE 1951 MAY DAY CELEBRATION

went into Winthrop's first May Day was appropriately recognized and applauded roundly in the next issue of *The Johnsonian* and in papers over the state. Many lines of print were devoted to descriptions of the extravagant artistry of this first May Day:

Fluttering forth from practically nowhere, a huge scarf fifteen yards square was borne by four graceful dancers before the throne. Rhythmically and musically, they billowed the lovely tinted silk into many shapes and ensigns, resembling more nearly a pale sunset cloud than a mere silken scarf.

The guiding force behind all this was duly recognize for her efforts and talent. Said one writer:

Too much praise cannot be given Miss Sefton for her interring work and effort to make this, Winthrop's first May festival, the success that it undoubtedly was. The program in every way gives evidence of her work, and is in itself an honor to her.

WINTHROP COLLEGE, 1934–1943: PEOPLE, PLACES, AND THINGS. *Stella Phelps was the wife of Winthrop's third president, Shelton Phelps. The period covered by this essay includes the years that Mrs. Phelps's husband served as the president.*

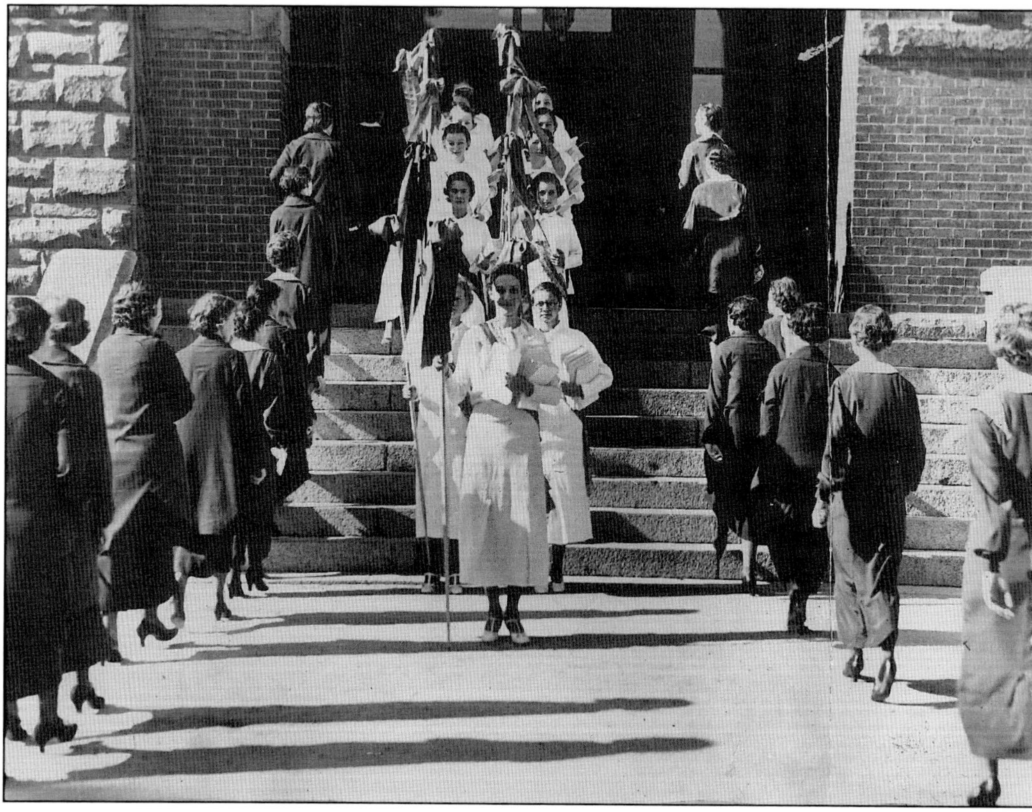

Inauguration of Shelton S. Phelps

I shall reverse the order in my attempt to remember Winthrop as it appeared to me when I first came to the campus and the changes which took place while my husband was its President, and what a beautiful campus it was with its historical buildings, wonderful old trees and attractive grounds.

The very first change as I recall was the removal of the wooden porches from the dormitories and the installation of a sprinkler system, making the fire hazard less dangerous.

Later came the new buildings: the auditorium and music conservatory; the home economics building and the nursery school; acquiring of, removal and on the campus of Winthrop's first home as a chapel and shrine in the memory of Winthrop's Founder and first President, Dr. David Bancroft Johnson; and the last of the buildings was a senior dormitory, later named Phelps Hall. All of these buildings not only added to the beauty of the already beautiful campus but also made the College more efficient and adaptable to the growing college. There is no more beautiful college campus than this lovely spot but it took the able and loyal assistance of many groups and individuals: the board of trustees, the legislature, the administrative staff, but also many friends of Winthrop.

Winthrop may have passed her 75th anniversary but she is not seventy-five years old, but seventy-five years young and growing younger each year with its new and vigorous members being added, who will carry on the dreams, the hopes and the traditions of all who have had the privilege and the opportunity of being a part of Winthrop.

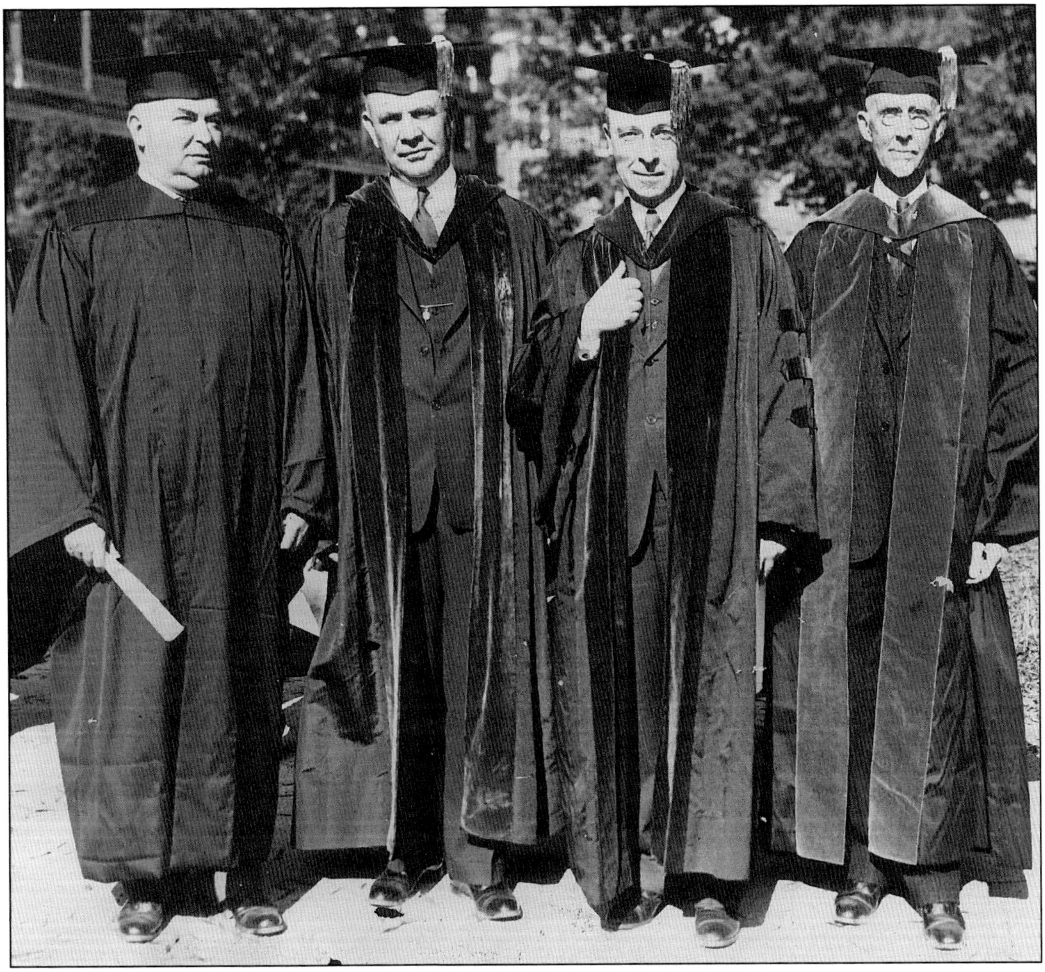

SHELTON S. PHELPS, INAUGURATED THE PRESIDENT OF WINTHROP COLLEGE, NOVEMBER 9, 1934

Along with the changes in the appearance came other changes: added curricula such as the nursing program in co-operation with the York County Hospital, and the department of journalism. There were increases in the faculty as the enrollment climbed.

Next there comes to my mind the memory of the places which meant so much to us in becoming acquainted with Winthrop, with its rich background and tradition. This meant trips all over the State and brings back vivid memories of Charleston, Beaufort, Summerville, the Gardens, and the many, many trips to your Capitol for meetings with the board of trustees, the finance committee of the legislature, and the other groups, in the interest of Winthrop College. On many of these trips I accompanied my husband, not in any official capacity, but as Mrs. Kinard once said as excess baggage, but I think perhaps the most vivid in my memory of these trips are those we made to the towns and villages when we were guests of the alumnae groups at their district meetings. I never ceased to be thrilled by the gracious hospitality, the enthusiasm and devotion of those whom we met and the pleasure of seeing these same people when they returned to Winthrop.

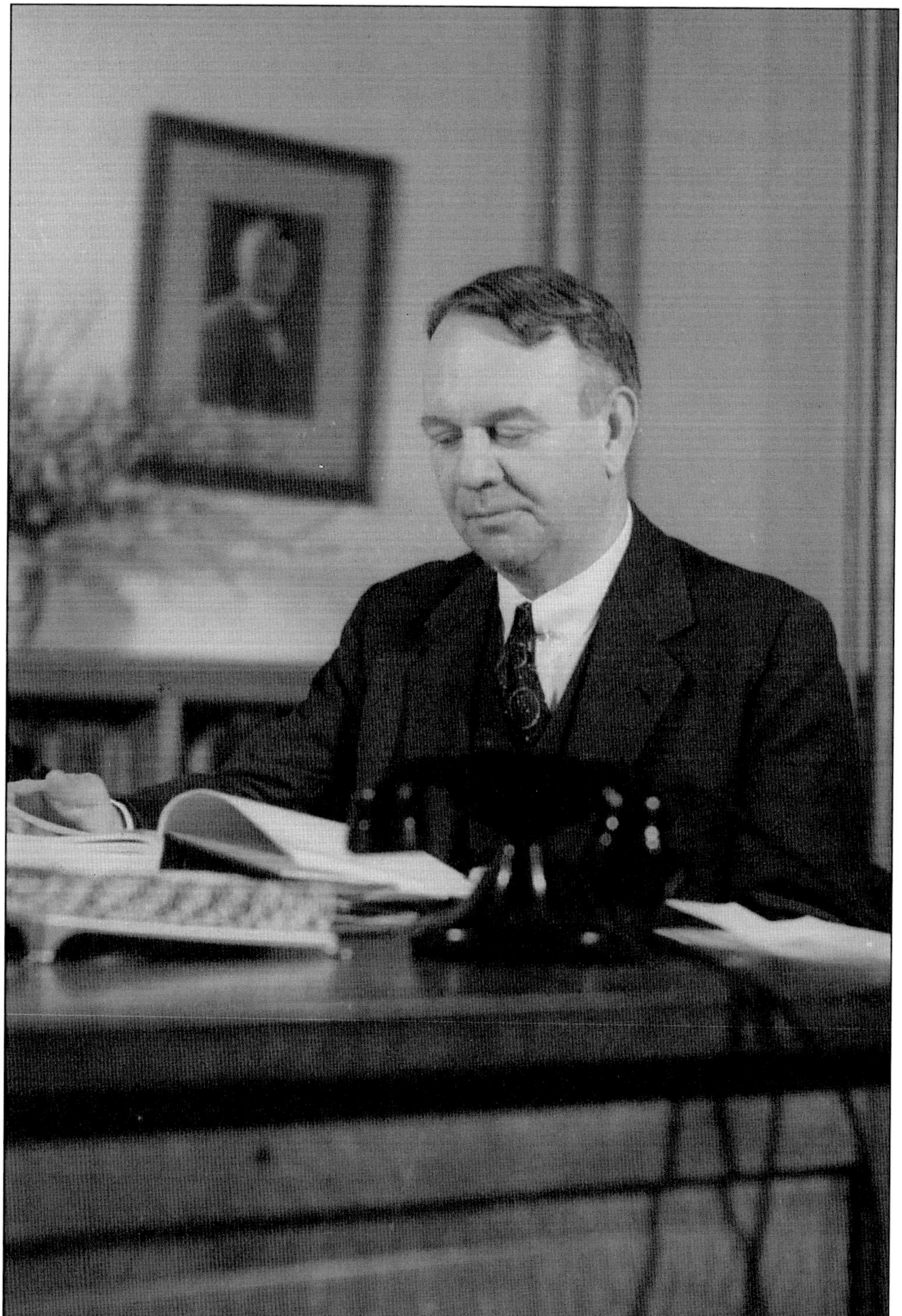

President Phelps had at work in the 1930s

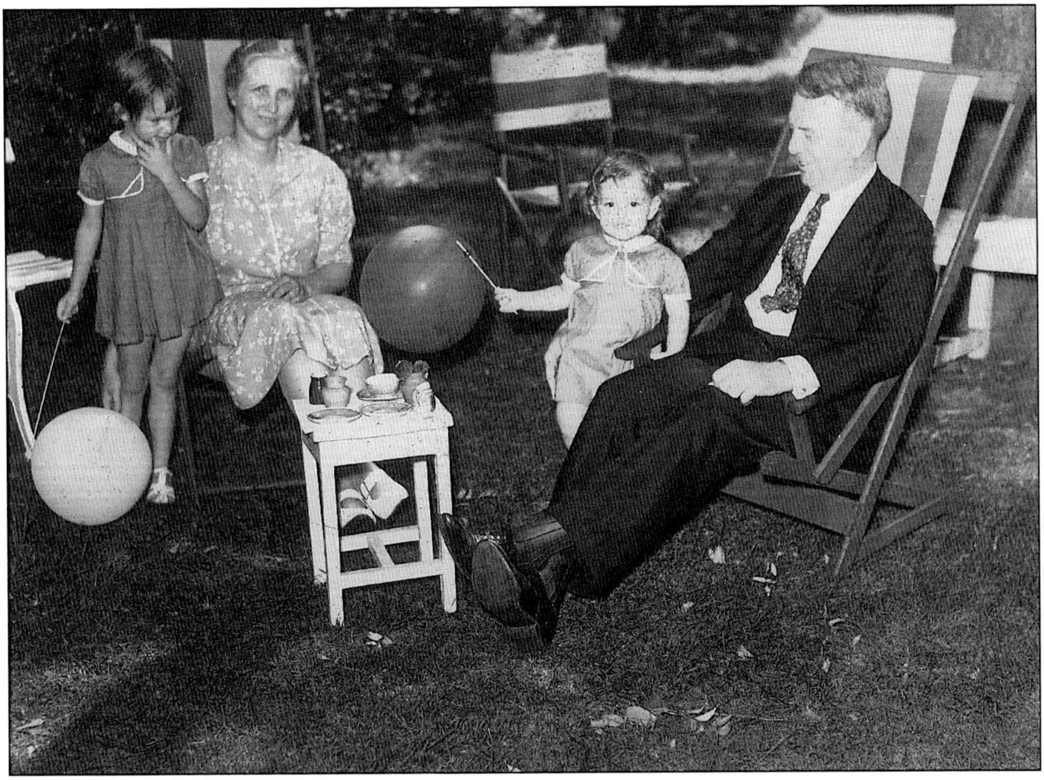

President and Mrs. Phelps with their grandchildren in 1939

The trips reminded me, also, of those who went with us to these gatherings—sometimes faculty or members of the administrative staff and often some of the students. Especially do I recall the members of the Sextet who added so much pleasure to any gathering.

And now I am remembering people, who after all are the college. When we arrived in July of 1934 to take up our life at Winthrop, the President's home was not quite in readiness for us and we were guests in old North Dormitory. Since it was summer vacation time the students and most of the faculty were absent from the campus and I remember we felt a little lonely and strange at first, as one does in a strange and unaccustomed place. But then one day a lovely lady called to bid us welcome and to offer her friendship and hospitality. That gracious person was none other than Winthrop's real First Lady, Mrs. D.B. Johnson, and there forthwith cemented a friendship that has lasted not only throughout the years we were here but is still as deep and fresh as then. Many, many pleasant memories cling to and around that friendship, understanding, and gracious hospitality.

I recall, too, the many courtesies and kind offers of friendship of Dr. and Mrs. Kinard and the trips around the State we shared. Others come flocking to my mind: the Roddeys, the Andersons, the Cobbs, the Huckles, the Angus Macaulays, the Will Rileys, the Rion McKissicks, General and Mrs. Summerall, and scores of others, too numerous to mention, all friends and wellwishers of Winthrop College.

Here on campus there are so many faces I could never name them all but there are some whose friendship and courtesies are so dear and so vivid I must needs mention a

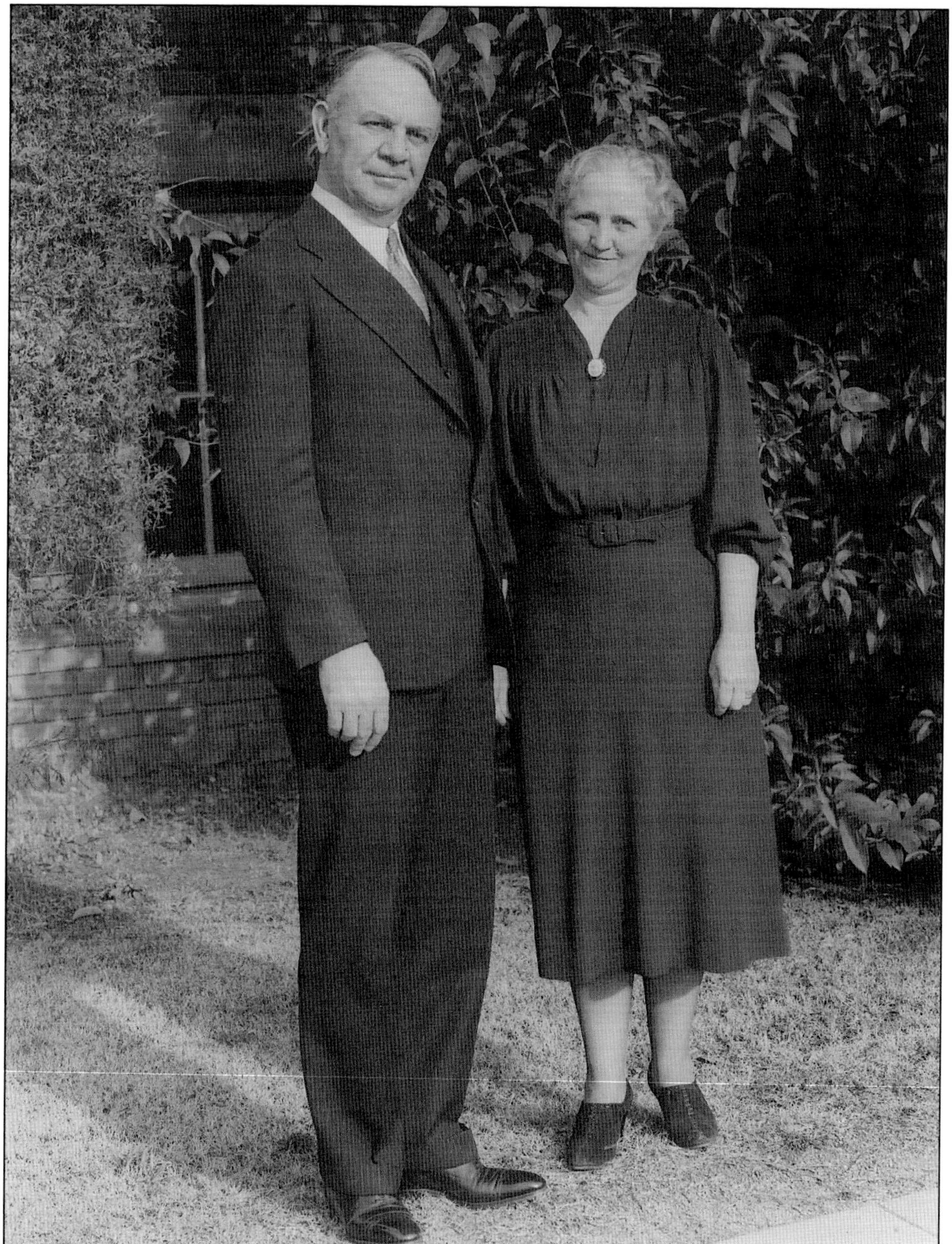

President and Mrs. Phelps in 1939

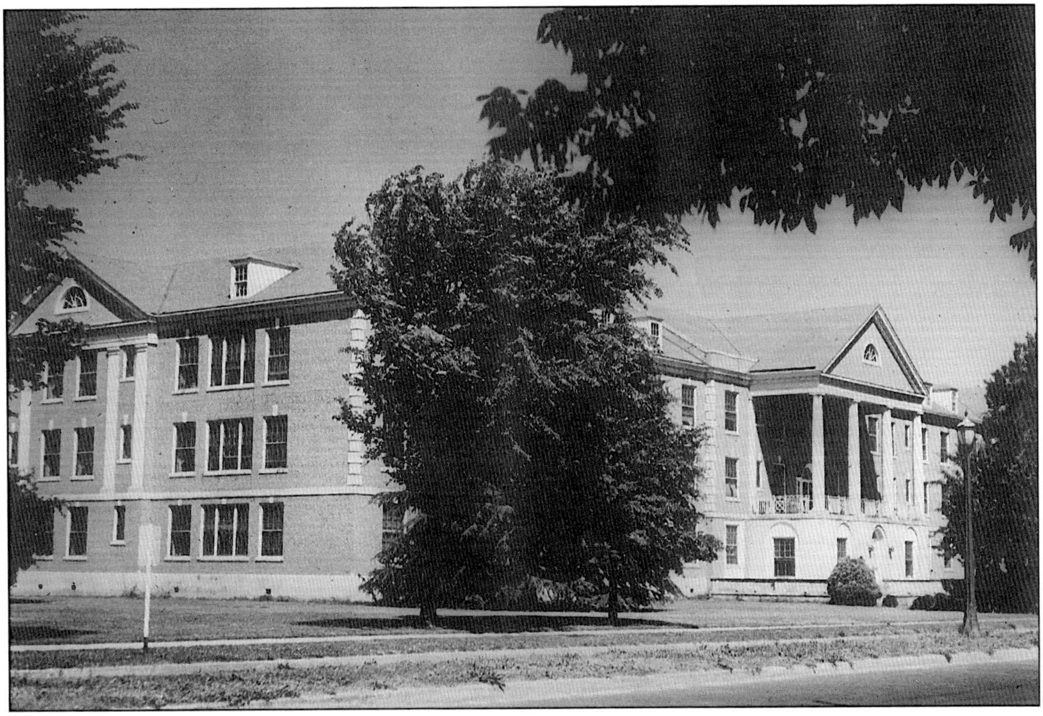

PHELPS DORMITORY, NAMED IN SHELTON S. PHELPS'S MEMORY

few: Dean Katie Hardin, Miss Leila Russell, Miss Ida Dacus, Mrs. Cora Hargrove, Mrs. McBryde, Dr. Donnis Martin, Dr. Elizabeth Johnson, Mr. Frank Harrison, Dean Fraser, the Grahams, the Kelleys, the Jarrells, the Roberts, the Keiths and so many more to whom I shall ever feel a debt of gratitude for the many ways in which they showed their loyalty to Winthrop and their friendship to us.

But after all I think was our help and bulwark through the years, Miss Iva Bishop, whom I am sure holds the record of having not only the President's right hand but who faithfully served as wise counselor, reminder and friend of all the wives of Winthrop's Presidents. She is still my source of news of Winthrop and my very good friend.

At Winthrop the President's home is not only the dwelling place for the President and his family but also the proud guest home of many notable persons who come to Winthrop for some event or occasion, such as members of the Artist Course, or Vesper services, or in another official capacity, and it was always a pleasure and a privilege to have such people in our home. To recall just a few: South Carolina's Governor Maybank and his lovely wife, your own poet laureate, Archibald Rutledge, Dr. Holmes of Harvard, John Erskine, Governor Keen Johnson of Kentucky and his family, and even the wife of the President of the United States, as well as numerous college presidents, government officials, and people of lesser note but equally welcome as guests.

I cannot fail to recall the many happy years we enjoyed in this lovely home, nor can I forget the happy memories of the personal friends who were our guests, nor the dear grandchildren who made the home happy with their fun and laughter. I remember, too, our daughter's wedding

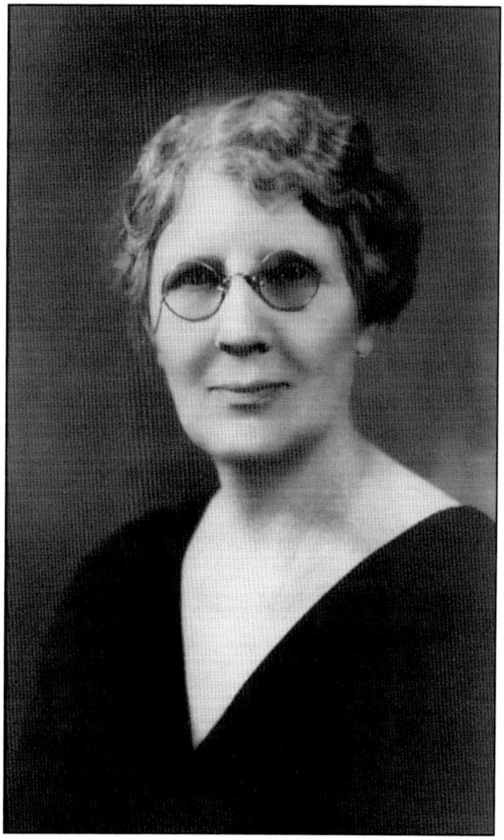

Leila Russell

and friends who were there. These were happy and rewarding years and "thanks for the memories."

If I may turn poetic for a bit and paraphrase and misquote, let me say:

> You may break, you may shatter the vase when you will,
> But the scent of the rose will cling round it still.
> Where'er my path lies be it gloomy or bright,
> My soul, happy friends, will be with you that night.
> Too blest if it tells me that mid your gay cheer
> Some kind voice will murmur—I wish you were here.

The College Seal. *Leila Russell (1871–1963), a 1889 graduate of Winthrop University, was instrumental in Winthrop's early development, serving as alumni secretary from 1895 to 1945 and an organizer and first president of the YWCA, a prominent organization at Winthrop during the college's formative years. This history was written on January 7, 1941.*

An effort to secure information brought forth from numerous persons at Winthrop the remark, "I don't know. If you don't, Miss Russell, then no one does."

It has given me pleasure to look up all available information possible concerning the Winthrop college seal. Its history reaches back almost a half-century. A seal could not be designed until the college adopted a motto. Who was appointed on the committee to suggest a motto is not known, but Dr. James P. Kinard was chairman of it. Finding nothing in the library concerning the college motto or the seal, the catalogues and *Tattlers* were all searched for some mention of these two items. I next turned to Mrs. Mathews, secretary of the Board of Trustees, and requested that she look through the minutes of the Board. She found the bare mention of them. As a last resort I turned to the minutes of the faculty.

Some time prior to December, 1899, President D.B. Johnson appointed a committee to suggest a motto for our Alma Mater. The faculty minutes show that at a meeting on December 14, 1899, Dr. Kinard presented a long list of Latin mottoes. After considerable discussion, "Veritas cum libertate" was adopted. On December 20, 1899, President Johnson presented this motto to the Board of Trustees and it was adopted.

The faculty committee continued with instructions to report designs for a seal. The following May 14, 1900, the design now in use was adopted by the faculty. Professor Breazeale, who was then the head of the department of mathematics, moved its adoption; Mr. J.W. Thomson, head of

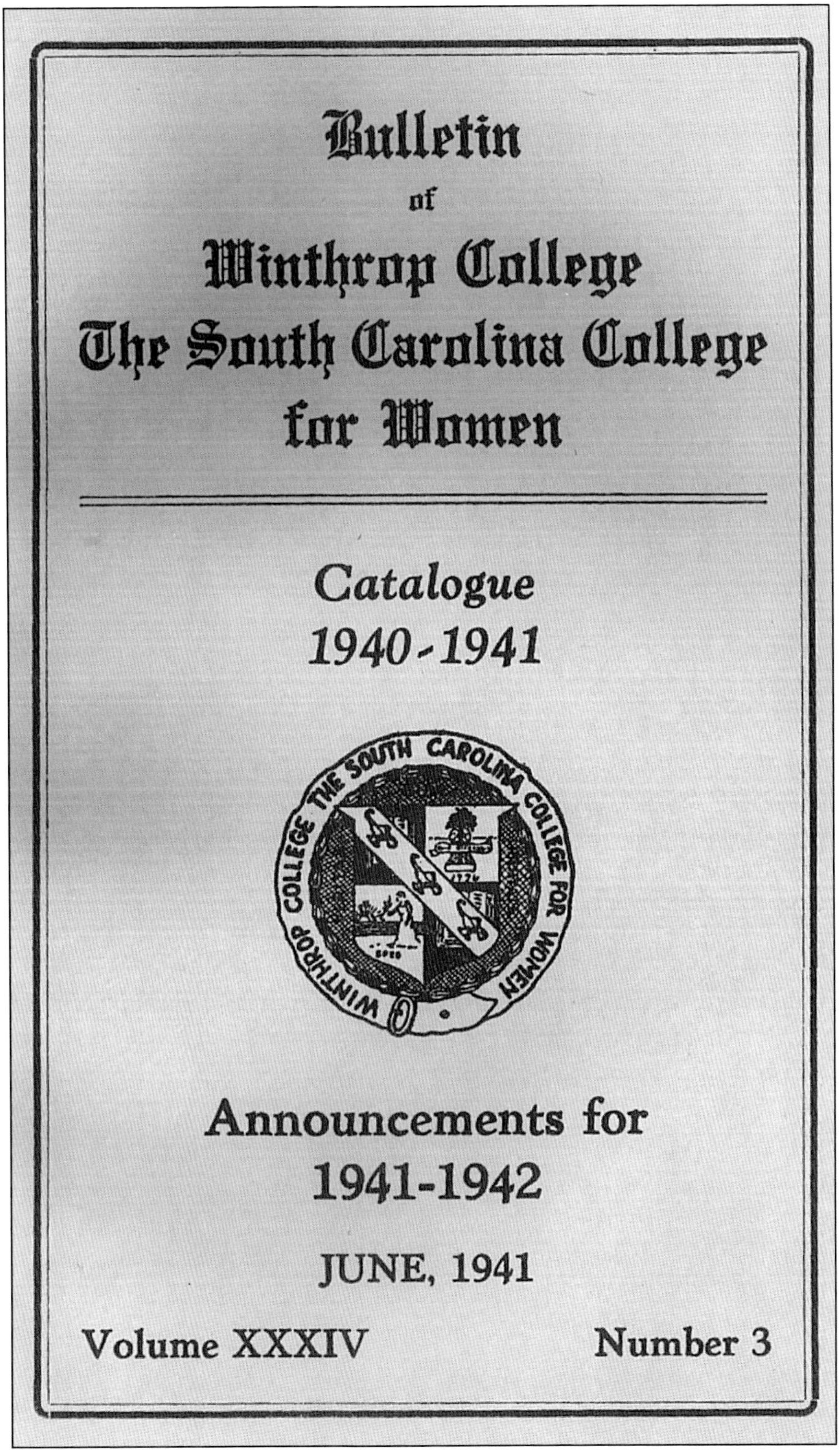

Bulletin
of
Winthrop College
The South Carolina College
for Women

Catalogue
1940-1941

Announcements for
1941-1942

JUNE, 1941

Volume XXXIV Number 3

THE COLLEGE SEAL AS IT APPEARED ON THE COVER OF THE 1940–41 CATALOGUE the department of education, seconded the motion; and the faculty unanimously adopted it.

It is based to a large extent on the great seal of our State of South Carolina. Of course, the liberal translation of "veritas cum libertate" is "Truth with liberty." The palmetto tree is the emblem of the State and is on her seal. This State seal, on which the college seal is based, was not designed until after Colonel Moultrie had defeated the British at the then Fort Sullivan, now Fort Moultrie. This fort was made of palmetto logs. Palmetto trees flourished on Sullivan's Island then as now. Thus the tree on our seal represents this fort. The date 1776 under the palmetto tree refers to March 26, 1776, when Moultrie defeated the British; and to July 4, 1776, when the Declaration of Independence was made by the Continental Congress. Twelve spears are bound crosswise to the stem of this tree, their points raised. The tree rests on a fallen log, representing a dead oak tree, and alludes to the British fleet as being constructed of oak timber and this dead oak tree represents the defeated British fleet.

The woman on the seashore and the rising sun and the Latin word "spes" represent the hope which is in the breasts of all daughters of Winthrop and all friends of the college—hope that the institution and the State creating her may ever go forward; hope that her daughters wherever they are may ever serve their homes, their communities, their State, and their God to the very best of their abilities. The small objects at the feet of the woman may well represent the difficulties overcome and the problems of life solved.

It will be noted that the woman holds a laurel branch in her hand and that there is a laurel wreath enclosing the shield. It is well known that laurel represents victory and honor—the honors won by our Winthrop Daughters; the honor reflected by them on their alma mater; honors which glorify the institution; and honors which the institution has brought to the State of South Carolina.

Crossing the center of the shield diagonally there is a band resting on two books and on this band are seen three small lamps, the lamp of learning, and of light. The whole signifies learning , knowledge, and wisdom. The rays from these lamps have reached the remotest corners of the globe for truly the sun never sets on the Winthrop Daughter. As someone has said her habitat is bounded by the aurora borealis, on the south by the procession of equinoxes, on the east by Kingdom Come, and on the west by the day of judgment, and wherever these daughters go they carry these rays of learning, light, and love.

Surrounding the shield and the laurel wreath is a buckle on which is the name of our college. This is emblematic of the strong union existing between the college and the State on the one hand, and the college and her daughters on the other.

The Civilian Pilot Training Program: A Memoir. *The Civilian Pilot Training Program operated at Winthrop from 1942 to 1944 and was designed to prepare World War II pilots, both physically and mentally, for pre-flight school training in other parts of the country. The pilots were housed at Bancroft Hall, which became known as "Fort Bancroft." The following memories were recorded by Carol Dillon.*

Army Air Force, 41st College Training Detachment, Winthrop College

March 25, 1943 to August 7, 1943

In the early morning of March 25, 1943, the troop train we were traveling on pulled into the railroad station at Rock Hill, South Carolina. We had not been told, when leaving the Air Force Basic Training Base at Miami Beach, Florida, where we were being shipped to and when we arrived at the destination. But we were still somewhat in the dark as to where we were. Most of the cadets had never been to South Carolina before, let alone Rock Hill. After traveling all night in the railroad coaches, the cadets

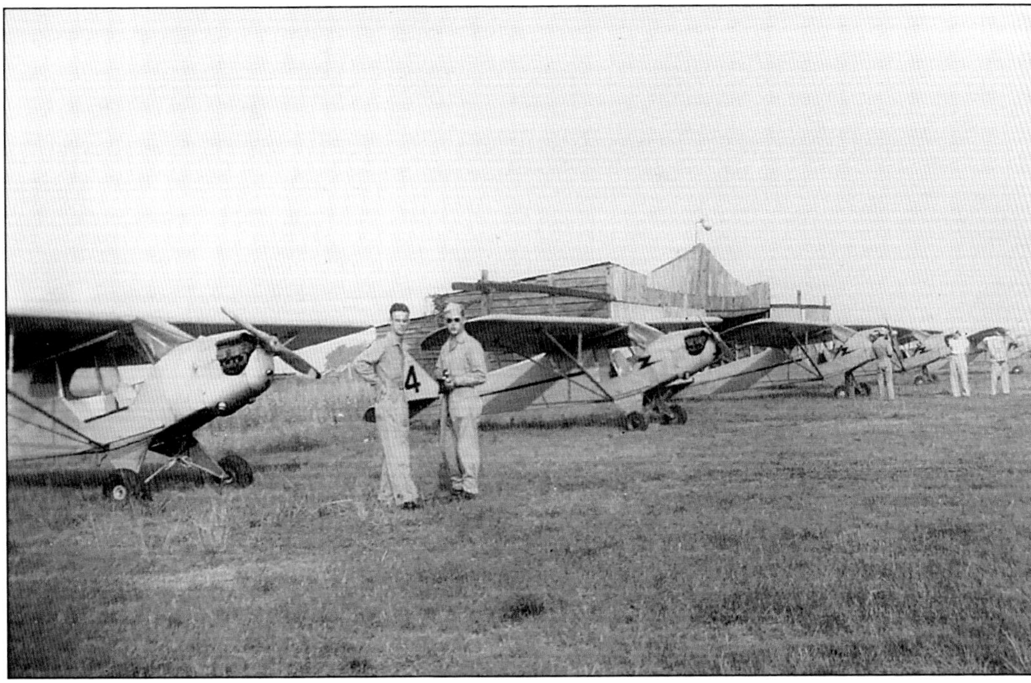

Roddey Field, Rock Hill, SC, July 1943 *These men were members of the Army Air Forces 41st College Training Detatchment.*

were anxious to disembark from the train. We fell into formation at the station and marched up Oakland Avenue to what we were to learn was Winthrop College, a South Carolina School for Girls.

The Army Air Force had invaded Winthrop College only a short time before (I understand it was March 1, 1943) the Army Air Force, 41st College Training Detachment, had been established at and became a part of the college—a school of 1,400 girls we were told.

The primary purpose of the Air Force College Training Detachment was to give college training to aviation cadets. This rule would prevent any association; however, we began our communication and association at twenty paces. The girls would walk to-and-fro on the campus street in front of Bancroft and stop to talk to us. We would keep our distance and stay on the porch. Sometimes we would stand on the edge of the campus street and they on the other side. It was strange standing among a group of cadets trying to carry on a conversation with a girl at the required distance. The conversation could not be too intimate.

The school imposed strict regulations on the students. We did not know whether or not our presence dictated or influenced the same. The girls were not allowed off campus and on back campus, except at specified times and for approved purposes and events. The girls complained about their dress code—their uniforms of blue and white. But, they were all nice looking and the standard of dress did not detract from this fact.

Our first few days we received instructions in close order drill, judo, had calisthenics and received orientation lectures. Classes in the college courses did not begin until our twelfth day, Monday, April 5th. At this time we became Class 43C.

We were to be known as "Student Cadets" and the cadet system was in force. This

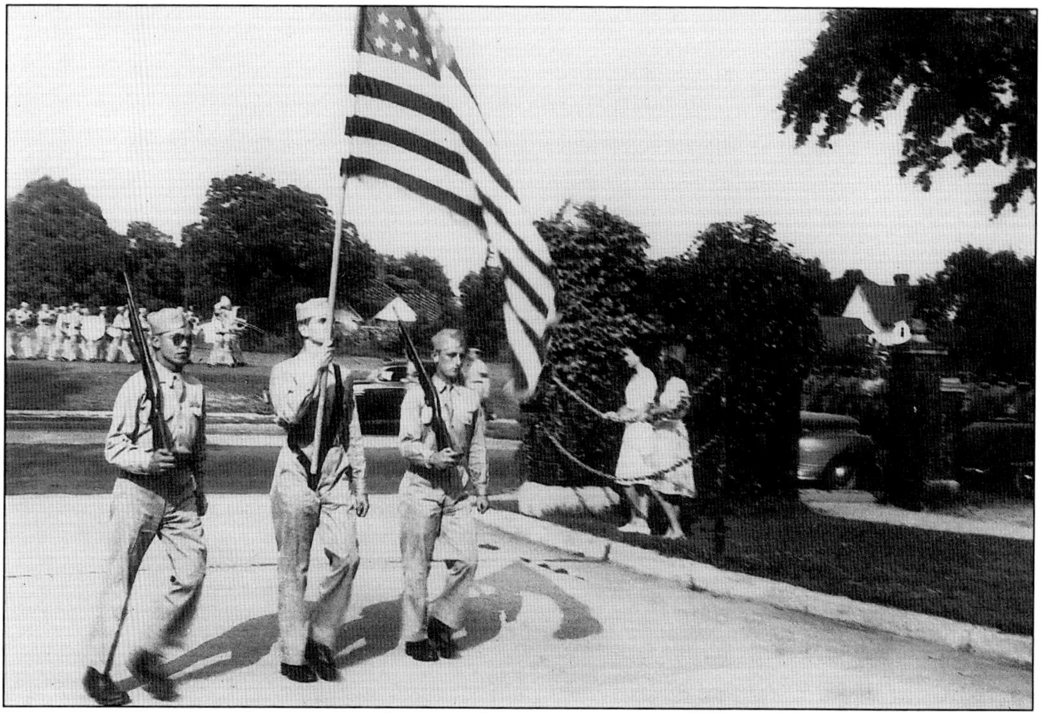

The 41st College Training Detatchment returning to campus from marching in review, July 1943 *From left to right are Carrol F. Dillon, Jim Daniels, and E.C. Detmer. (Photo taken by Bee White.)*

meant strict rules and regulations as to one's appearance and the care of the rooms. Any violations resulted in "gigs". A specified number of "gigs" meant the offender would walk "tours" on the triangular walk in front of Bancroft.

The school and the girls of Winthrop College were good to the cadets—they seemed to go out of their way to make the cadets welcome and their stay a pleasant one. When the Junior Class Play "Take It Off" was presented in the auditorium we were invited to attend. We were yet under restriction and went in a body, but we did go and enjoyed it. After our restriction was lifted, dances were routinely held in the gym. The Home Economics majors held afternoon dances for us in the Home Economics Building. The Home Economics dances were "girl break" which was a new experience for most of us. When the formal school dances came around, such as the Freshman Dance on May 1st and the Senior Dance at the time of graduation, we went as dates with the girls. We had usurped the domain of the Clemson students.

Other activities sponsored by the school for the cadets and the students included picnics at "the shack" and on back campus, and the regular free movie in the auditorium. After the movie we and the girls were permitted to leave campus to the extent of crossing Oakland Avenue to go to the Goodie Shoppe for cokes and confections.

The cadets attended classes in the regular classrooms of the college, but separate from the girls, taking courses in math, physics, geography and history, for which they obtained college credit. I received twelve hours of college credit for the courses which I took during my stay there. Our instructors were Winthrop professors. The only one I recall by name was Miss Ruth Roettinger, who taught history and was quite popular among the cadets and the Winthrop girls. As a matter of fact, she gave a party for her classes which we appreciated.

The cadets and Winthrop girls received their meals in the same dining room. We entered the dining from back campus across from the gymnasium. Although the girls and cadets were served at the same time, they were kept separated and the girls were seated on one side of the dining room and the cadets on the other. The food was well prepared and served on white table cloths, which men in the military service were not accustomed to. The cadets constantly praised the quality of the food. The girls on the other hand, complained about the food. They argued that because of the ration system in force at the time that the cadets were served a different menu. Whether this was true or not I do not know. The cadets, after leaving Winthrop, often remember how good the food was during their stay and compared to the normal military menu.

Although the cadets were at Winthrop College primarily to take college courses, they were still in the military service and had to follow the military tradition of close order drill. Why close order drill was essential to flying an airplane, or operating a radio compass, or Nordan bomb site was always questioned by the cadets. The cadets marched up and down the campus streets and on drill fields, one of which was located on back campus behind the building known as the nursery school and the other in the field directly across Oakland Avenue from front campus where Dickens Student Building is now located. The campus streets were not cluttered with automobiles in those days and platoons of cadets marched briskly along the campus buildings passing in review for the watching coeds. Men on campus at Winthrop College were quite a novelty at that time and the Winthrop girls were both amazed and curious to see the cadets moving amongst them. We were equally as amazed and curios for none of us

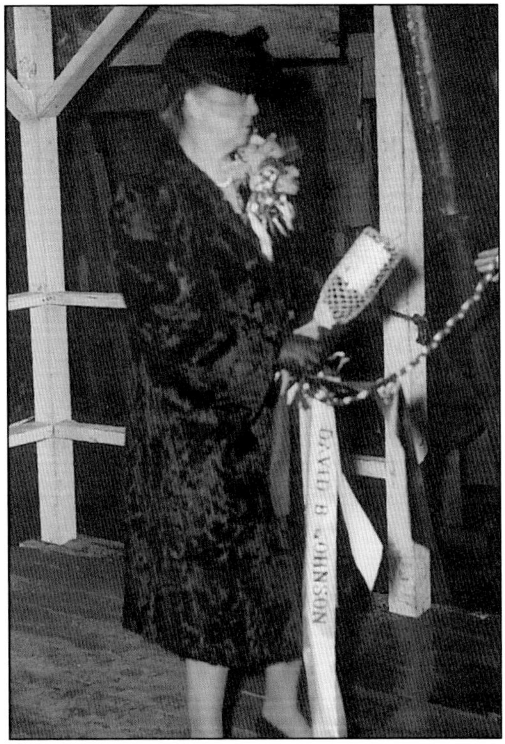

Mrs. D.B. Johnson christening the Liberty ship the S.S. *David B. Johnson* in Brunswick, GA, 1944. *Liberty ships were special cargo ships named for noted Americans, and they delivered badly needed supplies to the allies.*

expected, when we enlisted in the Air Force, to end up on a campus of a girls' school.

From time to time, the cadets would hold formal retreat and march in review in the field across Oakland Avenue from front campus and opposite the Winthrop Training School. Our only audience consisted of a few of the girls.

From time to time, small groups of cadets were shipped to the Classification Center for Aviation Cadets in Nashville, Tennessee so that the time one spent at the C.T.D. varied. Fifteen men shipped on May 16th, nine of June 20th, sixty-four on July 3rd, etc.; however, the majority stayed for the scheduled time. Some of us hoped to learn the criteria being used to determine who

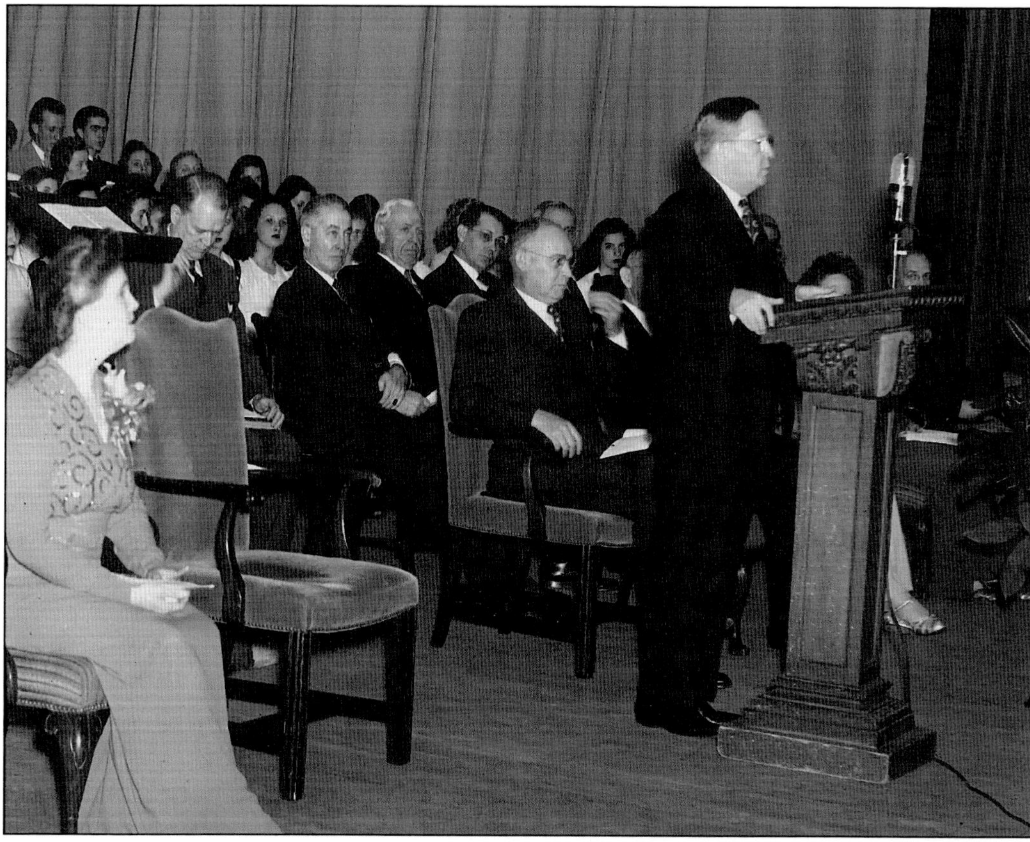

HENRY R. SIMS GIVING AN ADDRESS ON NOVEMBER 16, 1945, THE NIGHT BEFORE HE WAS INAUGURATED PRESIDENT *It was also the 50th anniversary of Winthrop College's move from Columbia to Rock Hill—a fitting moment for such an outstanding college tradition..*

was to be shipped, in order to stay at Winthrop for the duration.

Part of the training for the cadets consisted of pilot training at Roddey Field, Rock Hill, South Carolina. Flight training for Class 43C was given from July 6, 1943, to July 12, 1943, and consisted of twelve lessons, a total of ten hours in Piper Cubs, Model J. 3F. 65HP. The instructors were civilian instructors, two of which were Fay Daughtery and James R. Williams. There was also a W.T. Bert Jr. and a James H. Woods.

On our last night at Winthrop College, a graduation dance was held in the gymnasium for the cadets and their dates, most of whom were Winthrop girls. Although everyone had a wonderful time, there was some sadness in the air because the cadets knew their stay at Winthrop had come to an end. The next morning, August 7th, the departing "student cadets" were formed into platoons in the front of Bancroft Hall, after which they marched down Oakland Avenue towards the center of town and the railroad station in Rock Hill where they were to board a troop train for Nashville, Tennessee. It was a Saturday morning and the Winthrop girls were allowed to leave campus. As the cadets marched down Oakland Avenue, the girls ran along the sidewalk opposite the platoons abreast of their favorite cadet. As the train pulled out of the Rock Hill Station, some of the cadets looked back at the Winthrop girls who were waving goodbye and vowed to return.

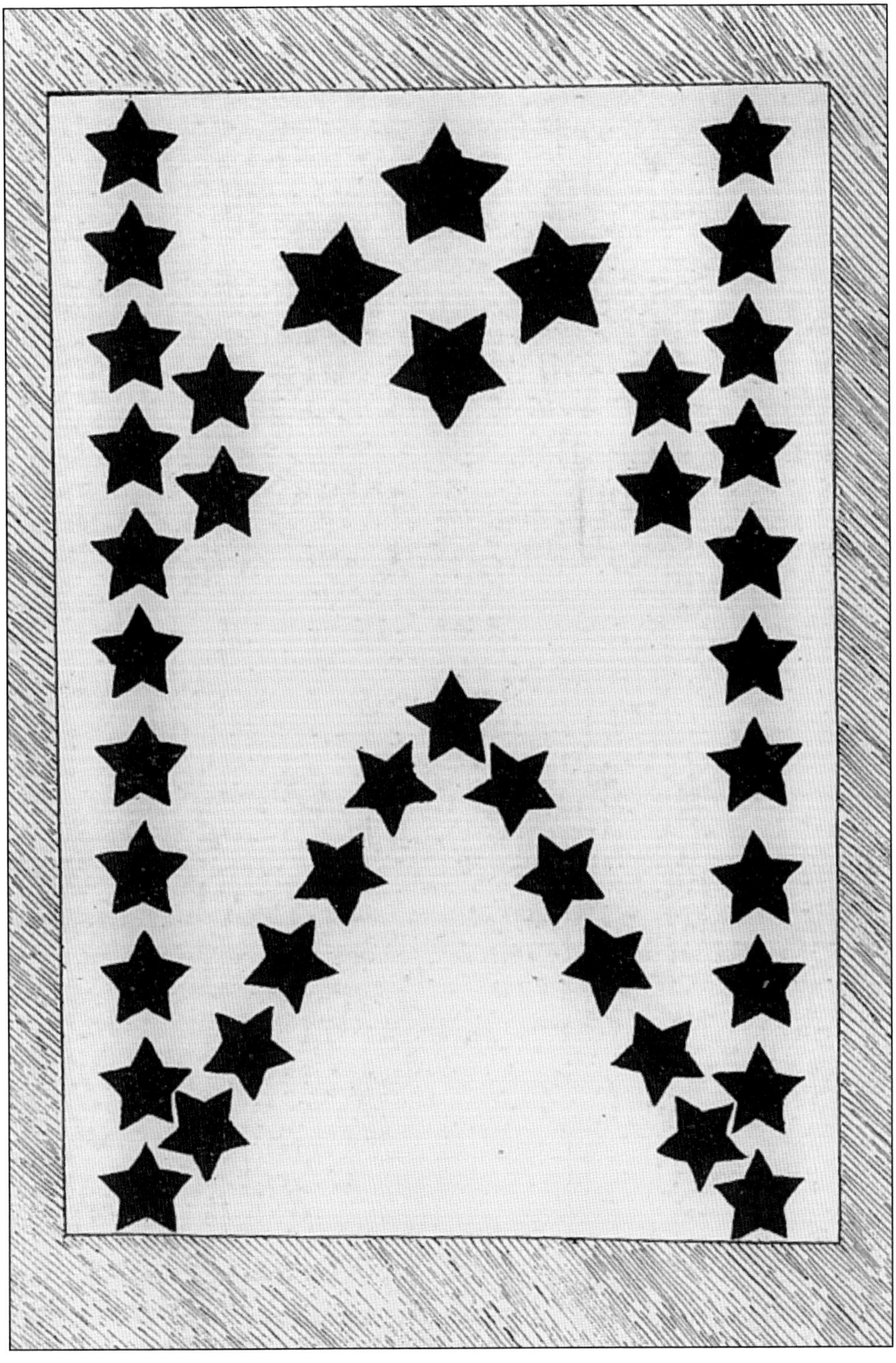

WINTHROP'S SERVICE FLAG, 1919

College Song

FAIREST flower of the Southland,
Alma Mater of our youth,
Guide our minds in search of wisdom,
And our souls in search of truth.

CHORUS

Winthrop College! Winthrop College!
How our hearts beat high with pride!
Ever shall we stand together,
Winthrop daughters, side by side.

Fond memories that cluster
'Round our campus and our halls,
Naught can never dim the luster
Which thy hallowed name recalls.

Page One Hundred Sixty-five

WINTHROP COLLEGE SONG, FROM THE 1929 *TATLER*